Human–Computer Interaction Series

Editors-in-Chief

Desney Tan
Microsoft Research, Redmond, WA, USA

Jean Vanderdonckt
Louvain School of Management, Université catholique de Louvain,
Louvain-La-Neuve, Belgium

The Human–Computer Interaction Series, launched in 2004, publishes books that advance the science and technology of developing systems which are effective and satisfying for people in a wide variety of contexts. Titles focus on theoretical perspectives (such as formal approaches drawn from a variety of behavioural sciences), practical approaches (such as techniques for effectively integrating user needs in system development), and social issues (such as the determinants of utility, usability and acceptability).

HCI is a multidisciplinary field and focuses on the human aspects in the development of computer technology. As technology becomes increasingly more pervasive the need to take a human-centred approach in the design and development of computer-based systems becomes ever more important.

Titles published within the Human–Computer Interaction Series are included in Thomson Reuters' Book Citation Index, The DBLP Computer Science Bibliography and The HCI Bibliography.

More information about this series at http://www.springer.com/series/6033

Evangelos Karapanos · Jens Gerken ·
Jesper Kjeldskov · Mikael B. Skov

Editors

Advances in Longitudinal HCI Research

 Springer

Editors
Evangelos Karapanos (iD)
Cyprus University of Technology
Limassol, Cyprus

Jesper Kjeldskov
Aalborg University
Aalborg East, Denmark

Jens Gerken
Westphalian University of Applied Sciences
Gelsenkirchen, Nordrhein-Westfalen
Germany

Mikael B. Skov
Aalborg University
Aalborg East, Denmark

ISSN 1571-5035   ISSN 2524-4477 (electronic)
Human–Computer Interaction Series
ISBN 978-3-030-67324-6   ISBN 978-3-030-67322-2 (eBook)
https://doi.org/10.1007/978-3-030-67322-2

This Springer imprint is published by the registered company Springer Nature Switzerland AG
The registered company address is: Gewerbestrasse 11, 6330 Cham, Switzerland

Contents

Reviews of, and Case Studies On Longitudinal HCI Research

Introduction to "Advances in Longitudinal HCI Research"

Evangelos Karapanos, Jens Gerken, Jesper Kjeldskov, and Mikael B. Skov

Abstract Aimed as an educational resource for graduate students and researchers in HCI, this book brings together a collection of chapters, addressing theoretical and methodological considerations, and presenting case studies of longitudinal HCI research. In this short introduction to the book, we reflect on the need for longitudinal studies in human–computer interaction research, we define what is and what is not longitudinal research and outline the selected contributions.

Keywords Longitudinal research · Empirical studies

1   Why Do We Need Longitudinal Research?

One could argue that most of our knowledge in HCI research is about the short term. A recent survey of empirical studies of nudging in HCI [1] found only 35% of the reviewed studies to have a duration longer than a day, and 19% of them to have a duration longer than a month. This echoes Hornbæk's [2] finding back in 2006 that out of 180 studies of usability being reviewed, only 13 (7%) had a duration longer than five hours. What does this mean for our knowledge on the usability and effectiveness of interactive technology? In an early longitudinal study of usability, Mendoza and Novick [3] logged users' reports of frustration over a period of eight weeks. They found that the types and causes of errors changed over time, along with users' responses to frustration episodes, and suggested that "we may know more about the problems of novice users than we know of the problems of experienced users." In the same way, one could think that our knowledge about the effectiveness of the nudging mechanisms reviewed in Caraban et al.'s survey [1] is mostly limited

E. Karapanos (✉)
Cyprus University of Technology, Limassol, Cyprus
e-mail: evangelos.karapanos@cut.ac.cy

J. Gerken
Westphalian University of Applied Sciences, Gelsenkirchen, Germany

J. Kjeldskov · M. B. Skov
Aalborg University, Aalborg, Denmark

© Springer Nature Switzerland AG 2021   1
E. Karapanos et al. (eds.), *Advances in Longitudinal HCI Research*,
Human–Computer Interaction Series, https://doi.org/10.1007/978-3-030-67322-2_1

to their initial effects. As the authors suggest, nudges can backfire or lead to weaker than anticipated effects, for a number of reasons such as habituation, reactance, or lack of educational gains [1].

Recent technological, policy, and market trends further highlight the importance of studying prolonged use. Already fifteen years ago, den Ouden and Brombacher [4] noted a change in the consumer electronics industry. The time and coverage of product warranty had increased due to legislation and competition. This resulted in an increasing number of user complaints that covered aspects beyond the out-of-the-box experience. Today, products are increasingly becoming service-centered, and their revenue models and the emphasis of the tech industry are shifting from initial adoption to sustained engagement. Think of the wearable health market as an example. While the initial hype was generated by a technology push paradigm, leveraging users' fascination with tracking their behaviors, a successful product today needs to prove effective behavior change and users are increasingly willing to engage in paid behavior change programs. Similarly, Facebook, Uber, and Spotify (and the list goes on), all depend on sustaining user engagement. Moreover, as Odom explains in Chap. "Tensions and Techniques in Investigating Longitudinal Experiences with Slow Technology Research Products" of this book, these digital services and products collect vast amounts of data from us, such as photos, music listening behaviors, and other forms of behavioral data. How do we know their long-term side effects on our privacy, safety, and well-being? Our knowledge on the long-term impact of these technologies, and how to design for lasting positive effects, is often limited.

2 Defining Longitudinal Research

One could wonder: Should all research about the short versus long-term effects of interactive technology be longitudinal? For a research study to be characterized as longitudinal, it needs to take at least two measurements of the same variable at different points in time [5]. This allows us to look at changes within the same individual. Did their perception of the usability of the product change over time? Did the relative importance of different product qualities, such as usability, usefulness or novelty, change over time? The appropriate duration between measurements and the number of measurements mostly depends on the phenomena and their dynamics one aims to capture in such research. For example, the learning effects of a new input device might be studied over the course of 20 sessions, scheduled across 20–25 days [6]. The impact of a new electronic patient recording system and studying how novice users become experts over time might require much longer time frames, such as 15 months as in Kjeldskov et al. [7].

However, a longitudinal design also entails a number of challenges, such as participant dropouts (panel attrition) or constructs becoming invalid over time as participants' perceptions of them change (panel conditioning and construct validity), but also the high costs longitudinal studies imply (c.f. [5, 9]). Some of the alter-native approaches to studying change over time have been previously discussed in HCI research [8, 9]. At the top level, one may distinguish between repeated cross-sectional, longitudinal, and retrospective designs.

Repeated cross-sectional designs differ from longitudinal, in that they recruit different participants in each data-gathering wave. For large surveys in social sciences, this is a typical procedure, for example when assessing the changes in opinion polls in politics over time. However, this approach can also be adapted to compare user groups, based on the assumption that the differences between groups resemble differences over time. For instance, one could measure user performance with users of different levels of expertise (e.g., novice versus expert users), or different lengths of ownership of a product. Given that one cannot study intra-individual change, such designs imply a risk of failing to control for external variation, and falsely attributing variation across the different user groups to the manipulated variable. Prümper et al. [10] for instance highlighted this problem, by showing that different definitions of novice and expert users lead to varying results.

Longitudinal designs can be further classified into within subjects repeated sampling designs, prospective panel designs, and revolving panel designs. The first two differ only in terms of the number of data-gathering waves. *Repeated sampling designs* entail only two waves of data gathering. As an example, Kjeldskov et al. [7] studied the same seven nurses, using a healthcare system, right after the system was introduced in a hospital and 15 months later, while Karapanos et al. [11] studied how ten individuals formed overall evaluative judgments of a novel pointing device, during the first week of use as well as after four weeks of using the product. *Prospective panel designs*, on the other hand, incorporate at least three data-gathering waves, thus enabling an inquiry into the exact form and process of change. However, with more data-gathering waves being added, the challenges of longitudinal research are attenuated, as participants may drop out of the study or become accustomed to the measurement, thus raising issues of construct validity. *Revolving panel designs* attempt to address these problems by adding a smaller number of new participants at each data-gathering wave.

Finally, in *retrospective designs,* data are gathered only at a single point in time and participants are asked to retrospect on two or more periods in the past. While retrospective designs provide a lightweight approach to studying change over time and remove the risk of panel attrition as there is only one data-gathering wave, they suffer from retrospection bias, as participants are asked to report on events that took place weeks, months, or years in the past [5]. A number of methods that aim at reducing retrospection bias have been presented in HCI research over the past decade (e.g., [12, 13]).

3 What This Book Covers

This book brings together a collection of chapters, addressing theoretical and methodological considerations and presenting case studies of longitudinal HCI research. We outline below the contributions from the ten selected chapters.

Theoretical Perspectives

The first two chapters discuss theoretical concepts around the design and execution of longitudinal studies.

In Chap. "Longitudinal Studies in HCI Research: A Review of CHI Publications from 1982–2019" Kjærup, Skov, Kjeldskov, Gerken, and Reiterer explore existing longitudinal studies in HCI research through a review of CHI publications from 1982 to 2019. A key goal of the chapter is to understand how previous HCI research described through CHI papers have conducted longitudinal studies in order to inform and inspire future studies. Building on the literature review and analysis, this chapter offers a classification of studies and recommendations for future longitudinal HCI research.

In Chap. "Longitudinal Studies in Information Systems," Nielsen provides an account of how longitudinal research in the field of information systems has evolved and what HCI can learn from this. After mapping the past 20 years of longitudinal research in the field of information systems, the author presents five exemplar longitudinal studies, uses them to illustrate the difference between variance and process studies, and elaborates on the implications this distinction has on decisions regarding the design and execution of longitudinal studies in HCI.

Methodological Considerations in Longitudinal HCI Research

The next four chapters in the book discuss methodological issues related to longitudinal studies.

In Chap. "Recommendations for Conducting Longitudinal Experience Sampling Studies," van Berkel and Kostakos discuss a number of concerns that surface when employing the experience sampling method (ESM) in longitudinal studies, given the high degree of participant engagement that the method necessitates, and propose practical recommendations that can assist researchers in mitigating those concerns. Among others, they discuss issues of participant motivation, study adherence, response reliability, and response bias introduced by the longitudinal nature of such studies.

In Chap. "Longitudinal First-Person HCI Research Methods," Lucero, Desjardins, and Neustaedter reflect on the use of first-person research methods, such as autoethnography and autobiographical design, which by their very own nature, typically span extended periods of time, such as several months, or even (many) years. Staying true to the values of first-person research methods, the authors present three case studies through personal, reflective accounts of what went on during the studies, the strengths of their approach, and the challenges they faced, providing fruitful insights for researchers wishing to engage with first-person methods. Drawing on the differences and the commonalities across their three experiences, the authors discuss a number of critical factors of the study design and execution, such as the degree of engagement of the researcher, issues relating to data collection fatigue and data safety, the role of reflection as the primary mode of inquiry, and the question of how to decide when to conclude the study.

In Chap. "Imagining the Future of Longitudinal HCI Studies: Sensor-Embedded Everyday Objects as Subjective Data Collection Tools," Karahanoğlu and Ludden, drawing inspiration from quantified self and the ubiquity of mobile and wearable sensors, explore the potential of sensor-embedded everyday objects as tools, or probes, for subjective data collection in longitudinal studies. To explore their design space, their opportunities, and barriers, they conduct three online focus groups with HCI experts. The authors present a number of concepts that came out of this process and propose on issues that we should pay attention to when creating such tools, such as reducing participant effort, collecting one type of data at a time, and finding friendly ways to embed these objects in daily life.

Lastly, in Chap. "Experiments, longitudinal studies, and sequential experimentation: how using "intermediate" results can help design experiments," Kaptein introduces us to an underused, yet highly valuable experimental design for HCI, that of sequential experimentation, where "intermediate results are used to make changes to the experimental design as the experiment is still running." This, Kaptein argues, provides a number of benefits to traditional experiments, such as randomized clinical trials (RCTs), where all decisions, such as the number of participants, are made beforehand. To name one, sequential experiments enable researchers to stop a study early, when sufficient evidence has been collected, thus saving resources in tedious and costly longitudinal studies. Kaptein discusses a model for sequential experimentation, the multi-armed bandit problem, and introduces software that enables HCI researchers to conduct sequential experiments.

Reviews of, and Case Studies on Longitudinal HCI Research

The remaining four chapters present different examples of longitudinal research across different strands of HCI research.

In Chap. "Tensions and Techniques in Investigating Longitudinal Experiences with Slow Technology Research Products," Odom argues that the ease with which we can accumulate personal digital data, from photo albums, to music, and other types of digital data, raise new questions about how we should interact with those digital platforms over the long term, and how to study those through a longer time frame. The author presents and reflects on two case studies of long-term deployment of "slow" technology: One that aims to "motivate users to interact in reflective, contemplative and curious ways […] and to operate slowly, in the background of everyday life." Odom provides a very interesting account of the type of inquiry needed and the tensions that exist in the long-term study of slow technology, such as "providing a space for ongoing discussions with participants while being mindful not to draw too much attention to the design artifact itself."

In Chap. "Opportunities and Challenges for Long-Term Tracking," Epstein, Eslambolchilar, Kay, Meyer, and Munson review the challenges involved in the long-term tracking of one's own behaviors. They present two case studies of long-term tracking and reflect on ways to mitigate the challenges, such how to design personal informatics tools that maintain adherence, and how to treat lapses in tracking as opportunities for self-reflection. They conclude with a number of recommendations for conducting studies that involve long-term tracking of personal data, such as how to treat missing data, how to leverage secondary sources of data, and regarding the ethical, legal, and social implications of long-term tracking.

In Chap. "Augmenting Gestural Interactions with Mid-air Haptic Feedback: A Case Study of Mixed-method Longitudinal UX-testing in the Lab," van den Bogaert, Rutten, and Geerts present a longitudinal study of a novel output technology, ultra-sound mid-air haptic feedback. The authors tackle a common problem when working with novel technologies—they often cannot be deployed in the field. The authors present here a longitudinal study conducted in a laboratory environment, where participants go through eight repeated exposures to the mid-air haptic feedback mechanism over five weeks. The authors present a number of interesting insights around the dynamics of users' experience with the technology over the course of the eight repeated exposures and reflect on the methodological takeaways from this study, including questions around the optimal duration of each laboratory session, recruitment, and the role of the fun factor and remuneration in ensuring participant's adherence.

Finally, in Chap. "A Six-Month, Multi-Platform Investigation of Creative Crowd-sourcing," Khan, Lykourentzou, and Metaxas present a longitudinal study of seven crowdsourcing communities focusing on macro-tasks: complex, longer tasks, which are difficult to break down and usually involve creativity, as opposed to micro-tasks, ones that are simple, short, and involve unskilled work. The authors present the analysis of publicly available data that they collected over the course of six months, involving more than thirteen thousand tasks, and provide a number of interesting recommendations for the design of crowdsourcing communities.

References

1. Caraban A, Karapanos E, Gonçalves D, Campos P (2019) 23 ways to nudge: a review of technology-mediated nudging in human-computer interaction. In: Proceedings of the 2019 CHI conference on human factors in computing systems pp 1–15
2. Hornbæk K (2006) Current practice in measuring usability: challenges to usability studies and research. Int J Hum Comput Stud 64(2):79–102
3. Mendoza V, Novick DG (2005) Usability over time. In: Proceedings of the 23rd annual international conference on design of communication: documenting & designing for pervasive information. pp 151–158
4. Den Ouden E, Yuan L, Sonnemans PJ, Brombacher AC (2006) Quality and reliability problems from a consumer's perspective: an increasing problem overlooked by businesses? Qual Reliab Eng Int 22(7):821–838
5. Menard S (2002) Longitudinal research, vol 76. Sage, Chicago
6. MacKenzie IS, Zhang SX (1999) The design and evaluation of a high-performance soft keyboard. In: Proceedings of the SIGCHI conference on human factors in computing systems. pp 25–31
7. Kjeldskov J, Skov MB, Stage J (2005) Does time heal?: a longitudinal study of usability. In: Proceedings of the Australian computer-human interaction conference 2005 (OzCHI'05). Association for Computing Machinery
8. Karapanos E, Martens JB, Hassenzahl M (2010) On the retrospective assessment of users' experiences over time: memory or actuality?. In: CHI'10 extended abstracts on human factors in computing systems. pp 4075–4080

9. Gerken J (2011) Longitudinal research in human-computer interaction [Dissertation]. University of Konstanz, Konstanz
10. Prümper JOCHEN, Zapf D, Brodbeck FC, Frese M (1992) Some surprising differences between novice and expert errors in computerized office work. Behav Inf Technol 11(6):319–328
11. Karapanos E, Hassenzahl M, Martens JB (2008) User experience over time. In: CHI'08 extended abstracts on Human factors in computing systems. pp 3561–3566
12. Karapanos E, Martens JB, Hassenzahl M (2012) Reconstructing experiences with iScale. Int J Hum Comput Stud 70(11):849–865
13. von Wilamowitz Moellendorff M, Hassenzahl M, Platz A (2006) Dynamics of user experience: how the perceived quality of mobile phones changes over time. In: User experience—towards a unified view, Workshop at the 4th Nordic conference on human-computer in-teraction

Theoretical Perspectives

Longitudinal Studies in HCI Research: A Review of CHI Publications From 1982–2019

Maria Kjærup, Mikael B. Skov, Peter Axel Nielsen, Jesper Kjeldskov, Jens Gerken, and Harald Reiterer

Abstract Longitudinal studies in HCI research have the potential to increase our understanding of how human–technology interactions evolve over time. Potentially, longitudinal studies eliminate learning or novelty effects by considering change through repeated measurements of interaction and use. However, there seems to exist no agreement of how longitudinal HCI study designs are characterized. We conducted an analysis of 106 HCI papers published at the CHI conference from 1982 to 2019 where longitudinal studies were explicitly reported. We analysed these papers using classical longitudinal study metrics, e.g. duration, metrics, methods, change or stability. We illustrate that longitudinal studies in HCI research are highly diverse in terms of duration lasting from few days to several years and different metrics are applied. It appears that the paper contribution type highly influences study design, while only a little more than half of the papers discuss or illustrate change/stability during their studies. We further underline considerations of durations versus saturation, identifying points of measurements and matching contribution types with research questions. Finally, we urge researchers to extend implications presented on perceiving duration as a singular attribute, as well as longitudinal systematic approaches to 'in situ' studies and ethnography in HCI.

M. Kjærup (✉) · M. B. Skov · P. A. Nielsen · J. Kjeldskov
Aalborg University, Aalborg, Denmark
e-mail: mariak@cs.aau.dk

M. B. Skov
e-mail: dubois@cs.aau.dk

P. A. Nielsen
e-mail: pan@cs.aau.dk

J. Kjeldskov
e-mail: jesper@cs.aau.dk

J. Gerken
Westphalian University of Applied Sciences, Gelsenkirchen, Germany
e-mail: jens.gerken@w-hs.de

H. Reiterer
University of Konstanz, Konstanz, Germany
e-mail: harald.Reiterer@uni-konstanz.de

© Springer Nature Switzerland AG 2021   11
E. Karapanos et al. (eds.), *Advances in Longitudinal HCI Research*,
Human–Computer Interaction Series, https://doi.org/10.1007/978-3-030-67322-2_2

Keywords Longitudinal · Literature review · Study design · Duration · Change

1   Introduction

Longitudinal studies in human–computer interaction (HCI) research have been applied and discussed for several years, and the potential of conducting studies that are longitudinal by nature is almost quite evident, e.g. the opportunity to measure or observe changes over time [6].

Longitudinal studies or longitudinal research are commonly applied and used in other research disciplines. For example, in social science, it has been used to focus on studying phenomena over an extended period of time and to study changes within these phenomena. Pettigrew [16] defines longitudinal research in social science as lengthwise and thereby as research studies that span a period of time. For this chapter, we adopt a definition on longitudinal data in HCI research from Gerken [6], who states '*longitudinal data present information about what happened to a set of research units [in our case, the participants of a study] during a series of time points*'. Thus, duration of time and change is highly important for longitudinal studies. But various challenges and obstacles have been identified for longitudinal studies, e.g. that they can be very cumbersome or labour-intensive (high demand on resources) and also risks of panel attrition.

Several conference events have been organized at the annual premier international HCI conference The ACM CHI Conference on Human Factors in Computing Systems (CHI) over the past years, e.g. workshops [4], with these subgoals '*in-depth discussion of key issues both appropriate methodology and research questions that lend themselves to longitudinal study*' and '*generation and dissemination of best practices for longitudinal research to the CHI community*', resonating a need for consensus on longitudinal HCI. Also, previous user experience (UX) research has started to shift their focus from initial UX to more prolonged sustained use, thereby requiring longitudinal studies [10].

In this chapter, we will give an overview of how previous CHI contributions have conducted longitudinal studies, for inspiration. Additionally, we will present recommendations for future longitudinal HCI research.

It is important to note that longitudinal research should be seen as a specific tool and not the silver bullet to empirical research in any field. So, while it is important to promote the application of longitudinal research, it is also necessary to understand the pitfalls and difficulties that come with it. By providing this analysis, we aim to shed some light on these aspects as well.

2   The Challenge of Identifying Longitudinal HCI

There is already much HCI research that is longitudinal, but it is also fair to state that much less research is explicitly longitudinal. Various forums at the CHI conference have addressed a need for stronger focus on longitudinal research within HCI, e.g. workshops [3, 4, 8], panels [23], SIGs [7, 22] and courses [2]. However, we still have little empirical evidence about how we as an HCI community understand what longitudinal research is for HCI studies, how we should think about it, which methods apply, and how it should be evaluated. Only two small sections are dedicated to this broad topic in a newly updated version of one of the common textbooks on HCI research methods [12]. Ethnographic studies are often longitudinal—at least implicitly—but not always. Case studies often provide a snapshot and hence not longitudinal, but not always. The timespan of experiments is traditionally short, but several are longitudinal. There seem to exist a genuine lack of clarity as to what longitudinal is and should be in HCI research. In our reading of the 106 CHI papers, we found that only one paper referenced a source text for longitudinal data analysis (appendix reference [41]). Instead, others would reference other HCI publications on HCI longitudinal studies, while most of them included no references on longitudinal studies or research at all. There seem to be no common, unified definition for longitudinal research in HCI, only emerging definitions formed in panels and discussions in the context of CHI, and not even these are referenced that often.

3   Studying Change

In the social sciences, longitudinal research has been more common, with periodic censuses which aim to understand societal developments being one of the popular and oldest examples [13]. So as a starting point we can state that longitudinal research has been used to focus on studying phenomena over an extended period of *time* and to study *changes* within the phenomena. But how so? From a more technical perspective, we can follow Taris who contrasts longitudinal research with cross-sectional research [21]. In cross-sectional research, there is only one single measurement for each individual or case in the study—ideally at the same point in time. Typically, such research is applied in HCI, e.g. when running a survey or to compare different interaction techniques in a controlled experiment. Longitudinal studies however are '*running lengthwise*' as Pettigrew puts it [16]. This means that there need to be at least two measurements for each case and for the same variable at different points in time. This then allows for comparison of data among the time variable and thereby the study of changes.

Change is the primary variable of most interest in longitudinal research, and the appropriate conceptualization of change is central [18]. The emphasis is also here on change and from the point of measurement of variance they claim that longitudinal research must contain three or more repeated measurements. In Pettigrew's longitudinal process research, the empirical analysis is directed at understanding the process of change (over time), the contents of the change, and the context in which it happens. Guidelines have been established to inform how to develop and evaluate longitudinal research on change. The necessary conceptualizing of change, they state, requires an explication of a theory of change, duration of change as well as predictors of change. Different aspects should be clarified including the level of change of interest, group average change, intraunit change, or interunit differences in intraunit change. It is often the relationship between variables that is the most interesting and this can be examined only by a longitudinal study.

Elements of comparison are vital for longitudinal studies, and quantitative approaches are implemented for comparison and significant relationships between set variables. Ployhart and Vandenberg [18] address statistical analysis in their guidelines and urge to be aware of potential violations in statistical assumptions inherent in longitudinal designs (e.g. correlated residuals, non-independence). The potential errors have to do with the nature of longitudinal research where variables change; they become more or less heterogeneous, over time. Being precise about which variables are expected to change, why they are changing and (when relevant) the nature of dynamic relationships over time. Time is not the only valid variable, as they emphasize; most constructs do not change, evolve or develop because of time, rather they do so over time. An example is that time does not make children grow into adults; genetics and environment are the causes. Pettigrew [16, 17] argues that pragmatically judgements in longitudinal research will be made based on the themes and research questions being pursued, the empirical setting of the research, researcher–subject relationships and funding and other resource constraints. What researchers can say something about will be dependent on the variables, which are measured.

4   Method

The primary goal of our study is to explore previous CHI papers where longitudinal studies have been applied and reported. Particularly, we are interested in analysing how CHI papers have studied change or stability over time, what time or duration is in CHI studies, and finally what kind of research methods that longitudinal studies apply. For this analysis, we ground our work in the definition stating *'longitudinal data present information about what happened to a set of research units [in our case, the participants of a study] during a series of time points'* [6].

In our paper selection, we were inspired by the four phase analysis on empirical studies illustrated in Bargas-Avila and Hornbæk [1], but since our analysis focuses on only one outlet (CHI proceeding series), most of the exclusion steps are not applicable for our study. Thus, we conducted three phases when selecting publications for our study namely identification, retrieval, and analysis. For readability, when referencing appendix references outside of findings, we will clearly mark it.

4.1 Phase 1: Identification of Publications

We used the exact query or search term 'longitudinal' in the ACM Digital Library (DL) database and further limited our search to only include publications from the proceeding series Human Factors in Computing Systems conference (CHI). We searched for the query in all ACM DL fields including title, abstract, keywords and full text. The CHI conference has been held annually since 1982 and the ACM DL include all conference proceedings from 1982 (the first CHI) until 2019 (the latest CHI). We found that the query term 'longitudinal' is significantly unique to capture the type of publications that we would like to include.

We have only included published CHI papers in this analysis. We certainly acknowledge that longitudinal studies are also published at other HCI venues. We address this in discussion, referencing a previous analysis that adds interesting and complementary perspective on longitudinal studies in HCI research.

4.2 Phase 2: Retrieval of Selected Publications

We retrieved 137 publication entries out of the 138 entries from phase 1. One entry in the ACM DL included no PDF and referred to a CHI 2008 workshop call on information visualization. This entry was excluded from our set. The 137 publication entries (PDFs) were archived, and we then printed and numbered all entries in alphabetical order after first author's last name. For our study, this phase involved only the above exclusion of publications as we only had one data source (the ACM DL) and therefore, no duplicates were included in our set of publications. We have included the entire list with all 137 CHI publications in the reference appendix in this chapter.

4.3 Phase 3: Publications for Analysis

During this third phase, we wanted to exclude papers that did not, e.g. report from an empirical study as our goal was to analyse how CHI research conduct longitudinal studies and not only how they talk about these studies. A total of 31 publications was excluded from the analysis, all listed here as appendix references. First, we removed twelve entries where the publication did not report from an empirical study [5, 6, 7, 17, 21, 25, 26, 61, 65, 66, 86, 123]. Secondly, we excluded eleven publications where the term longitudinal referred to something different than the study or research method [35, 50, 52, 56, 67, 69, 76, 102, 129, 130, 137]. Thirdly, we excluded seven publications where the study had not yet been done, but where the authors suggest a longitudinal study should be done [22, 23, 31, 101, 103, 108, 135]. Finally, we removed one publication where the paper did not have sufficient details on how or whether an empirical longitudinal study actually had been conducted [91]. A resulting list of 106 CHI papers was used for our analysis and can be found in the reference appendix of this chapter (they are marked with an '*').

We initially described the 106 publications using themes and characteristics of longitudinal research from related disciplines (as introduced in the background). Here, we used the definition from Gerken [7] on longitudinal data on what happens to a set of research units (participants) over a series of time points. Based on this, we constructed a framework for analysis that consisted of entries for duration, variables and metrics, data types, research methods, study context, how the term longitudinal is used and applied and finally a short summary of the paper. Additionally, the 106 CHI papers were re-read with a focus on argumentation for or against longitudinal aspects, how it was implemented in methods and how findings were impacted by the longitudinal aspects of the study. Following, papers were sorted and analysed through emergent themes, reflected in the findings. We also analysed and categorized all 106 papers, regarding their specific type of contribution they present, taking inspiration from the CHI contribution types as illustrated in the CHI 2017 website where it is stated that '… *a single paper may often fall between contribution types, or offer its own unique contribution…*' While we certainly acknowledge that CHI papers often make several contributions, we have attempted to determine a primary contribution of each paper for us to discuss different kinds of studies in relation to contribution type.

5   Overview of Longitudinal HCI Research

In the following overview, we present key characteristics for the 106 CHI contributions, namely duration, metrics and change. We would like to stress that when we reference papers in this section, the number refers to the numbers in the Appendix References.

First, our analysis showed that two contribution types amounted for almost 70% of the papers namely 'understanding users' with 43 papers (40.5%), while 'development and refinement of interface artefacts or techniques' has 29 papers (27%). This is perhaps not surprising as CHI papers deal with developing or creating new user interfaces and interaction techniques, but also studying user interaction with systems. Looking at the other contribution categories we see that 'systems, tools, architecture, and infrastructure' have 15 papers, while 'methodology' and 'theory' have 11 and, respectively, five papers. Finally, we were unable to categorize three papers towards primary contribution [1, 121, 133]. In the following, we will for practical reasons refer to the contribution types as interfaces, understanding, systems, methodology or theory.

5.1 Study Duration: Plateauing and Evolution

Our findings illustrate that the duration reported in the included CHI papers varies greatly for longitudinal studies. This is shown in Table 1. Also, we identified two different but related tendencies in our analysis related to study duration that we refer to as plateauing and evolution. In the following, we will illustrate duration, and we will illustrate plateauing and evolution.

Our analysis showed that duration ranges from only a few days, e.g. [115], up to several years, e.g. [112], and it can be argued that CHI longitudinal studies are measured over days, weeks, months or years. We identified 22 studies where the duration is not reported or unclear—these are listed as 'Not specified' in the first column of Table 1. Instead, these papers focus on describing, e.g. the number of sessions carried out, the duration of the individual sessions, interval between sessions

Table 1 Categorization of the 106 included CHI papers from the period 1982–2019

		Duration (Longitudinal study)				
		Not specified (N = 22)	14 days or shorter (N = 16)	2 to 4 weeks (N = 12)	1 to 11 months (N = 31)	1 year or longer (N = 25)
Paper primary contribution	**Interface artefacts or techniques (N = 29)**	20, 40, 47, 73, 79, 80, 93, 134	46, 51, 72, 82, 87, 104, 113, 114, 115, 126, 131, 132	44, 48, 59, 94, 106, 116	15, 18, 94	
	Understanding users (N = 43)	24, 30, 38, 49, 90	58, 122	36, 53, 64, 128	12, 13, 19, 27, 28, 29, 45, 77, 81, 83, 84, 95, 98, 99, 100	3, 4, 10, 16, 32, 55, 78, 92, 96, 107, 109, 110, 111, 112, 120, 127, 136
	Systems, tools, architecture and infrastructure (N = 15)	60, 62	70, 85	34, 37	8, 9, 68, 89, 117, 119, 125	33, 71
	Methodology (N = 11)	11, 118			41, 42, 43, 54, 57, 63,	75, 88, 105
	Theory (N = 5)	2, 14, 74				39, 124
	Uncertain (N = 3)	1, 133				121

The x-axis illustrates the duration of the study described in each paper (four types+ non-specified), whereas the y-axis describes primary contribution type. Numbers in the table refer to the appendix reference list or tasks within this session [20, 47, 49, 72, 73, 79, 80, 93, 134]. In the following, we primarily consider and discuss the papers with a reported duration (N = 84), and in the following we will unfold observations regarding CHI paper study durations.

Interestingly, it appears that the contribution type affects the study duration. Interface papers employ relatively short studies (less than a month), whereas papers on understanding have rather long studies (often a year or longer). For the 21 interface papers that do report the study duration, 18 of them (85%) integrate longitudinal studies with duration less than a month. Whereas for understanding papers, 30 of the 43 papers (71%) report from longitudinal studies that are at least one month long; and 17 of the 42 papers (41%) conduct studies that are one year or longer. As the most 'extreme' example, Sillence et al. [112] conducted a study over five years. However, a few understanding papers employ short study durations (less than two weeks), e.g. Jain [58].

While interaction papers mostly have short study durations, we found it interesting to observe that systems papers have rather long study periods where 9 papers out of 15 (60%) have study duration of at least one month, for example the study in [71] with a two-year study. But systems papers also employ short study periods like [34] with three weeks of study. Furthermore, we only found one study, [34], among the systems papers conducted in a laboratory. Here, the participants played a game for approximately one hour in an attempt to learn mandarin as a second language. Language education and self-study took place outside the scope of the study.

Some of the CHI papers report from retrospective studies, where the duration refers to the time the collected data covers. The data collection is done electronically and is already produced, stamped or tagged, and available on servers. For example, [4, 110, 127, 136]) are all understanding papers where the data cover over one year. As an illustrative example, Yuruten [136] conducts statistical analysis on a well-known public data set, previously collected for another purpose and used in other studies. More of these studies explore data from anonymous users of social networks (Twitter, discussion forums, collaborative music making site). This has some disadvantages according to Wang and Kraut [127] who argue that due to the snapshot quality of their included measurements, they are not able to make strong causal claims. But Settles and Dow [110] use this kind of data collection as a supplement to their own surveys.

5.1.1 Plateauing in Performance

We identified a focus in several studies on what we refer to as plateauing in performance (i.e. plateauing defines reaching a state of little or no change after a period of activity or progress). While only six of the included papers directly use the term [3, 46, 79, 81, 114, 115], we found that 20 papers discussed issues related to plateauing, and it played a significant role in defining longitudinal characteristics of the studies.

Plateauing in performance was particularly in focus for more papers on interface artefacts and techniques, which were typically carried out in laboratory environments, e.g. with a relatively modest duration of few days [115] and up to 6 weeks [15].

While [3, 81] are both understanding papers, with a duration of months to years, the plateauing described refers to behaviour and habits, not performance. For some duration was not even specified, rather there was a focus on number of sessions. For example, the number of sessions wherein learning a new mapping would still be feasible [47], where the amount of time elapsed for performance with a new input method would settle compared to a familiar one [73] and where the difference becomes negligible [79], sessions required to mathematically project when users would reach expert levels [80]. It is however worth noting that the description of what constitutes a session, at what interval sessions should be carried out and the number of sessions varies wildly. A session might be timeboxed (e.g. [59, 82, 87, 114]) or might consist of a certain task e.g. typing an amount of phrases [44, 46, 72, 94, 113, 131]. Sessions can be carried out within an interval—as an example [59] held laboratory sessions at an interval of at least 12 h and not more than two days, whereas [115] stated the importance of carrying out sessions at the same time on consecutive days. Conducting laboratory sessions, there might be practical constraints that dictate session duration, interval and number of sessions, although it is not explicitly argued.

In relation to plateauing, a number of interface artefacts and techniques papers argue that stability in performance can often be reached within days or weeks (e.g. [15, 44, 46, 48, 59, 72, 82, 94, 115]). Of course, different aims necessitate different duration, for [115] the aim was to explore a new input modality in a target acquisition task as well as participants initial attitude towards this modality, thus they planned for five daily sessions, whereas for [15] the aim was to determine the fastest and most consistently stable input of one new and one known condition, after participants passed the label of novice user, thus they planned for 20 sessions. Castellucci and Mackenzie [15] found that while two interaction techniques (graffiti and unistroke) had equally high error correction rates, the new technique was considerably more consistent than the other *'Investing the same time learning unistroke can result in significantly faster stroke time and higher text entry speed'*, whereas Sporka et al. [115] argued the need for a longer study duration for stronger evidence on performance plateauing.

A key plateauing concern is to understand when do users move from being novices to being experts during the conduction of an experiment? Thus, several experiments here involve prospective users where they use a new interface or a new interaction technique over a period of time. As an exemplary study of accounting for longitudinal aspects in plateauing in performance, MacKenzie and Zhang [80] (although not specifying a duration) applied a 2×20 within-subject factorial design to see the development from novice to expert with a new developed text-entry technique. They found that expert levels (theoretical upper-bound) were not reached within 20 sessions, but mathematically projected it would take around 30 sessions. They relate to the longitudinal aspects arguing learning time is a usability issue, therefore longitudinal empirical evaluation is important; *'We want to establish not only a layout's potential for experts, but also the learning time for typical users to meet and exceed entry rates with a QWERTY layout'*. MacKenzie and Shawn further describe a so-called crossover point, where performance with a new technique would exceed current practice. However, they point out that this *'elusive crossover point'* may not

always be reached if the new technique is simply not good enough or needs refinement. For example, Son et al. argue that in their case for two-thumb typing in VR that
although one condition implemented showed improvements, further work is needed
to reach an adequate performance level in comparison to non-VR typing [113]. Additionally, MacKenzie and Zhang argue that the number of users for these evaluations
are typically lower than usual, however the vital part is that they are evaluated over
a prolonged period of time [80].

Majaranta et al. [82] challenged previous evidence that gaze typing is slow by
changing the gaze time from constant to adjustable and evaluated on this in a series
of ten laboratory sessions. They concluded that after four 15-min sessions, equal
to one hour of practice, learning decelerated prominently. They reached a plateau
in learning. However, Jain [59] argues that a concern is to actually pinpoint the
exact moment when subjects cross a threshold from novice to expert and through a
longitudinal study, they were able to demonstrate that after an hour of practise, their
users were able to transition to expert users within their particular system. Reporting
on the point where performance plateaued was found in other studies expressed as
either minutes/hours of practice or the specific day/session [15, 46, 48, 82].

5.1.2 Evolution

Our analysis showed that 12 studies explicitly concern evolution—something
evolving over time. These studies are concerned with how, e.g., personal information management behaviour evolves over time [10] or how evolutionary patterns of
communication strategies emerge over a project life cycle and how these might affect
delivery performance and quality of new product development [16]. The studies had
common traits: They were carried out in the field, in low-control situations, or 'in
the wild' [98], as well as they had a duration equal to or above one month and
up to several years. As an example, Chattopadhyay et al. [18] explicitly emphasize
the choice of longitudinal methods to explore how use cases of their collaborative
presentation plug-in would evolve naturally. In a one-month long deployment, data
was collected through observation, interviews, one focus group, supported by system
interaction logs and video recordings. This enabled authors to observe and report on
'*emerging practices and shifting dynamics*' for evolving presenter and attendee practices. However, the authors qualify this as initial insights and argue for larger-scale
studies to validate, elaborate and qualify these findings. Likewise, a study from last
year by Niemantsverdriet et al. [95] is concerned with social interaction, exemplified
by a longitudinal study of shared use of a lighting control system and how social
dynamics evolved around coordination.

Many of the evolution studies are concerned with understanding users. A recent
exemplary study is Erete and Burrell [32], who explore citizen participation in local
government. The study ran for three years and it reports on how online tools were
organically adapted by citizens in order to engage in local governance in three
communities. One result showed, that they were able to capture change in uses:
'*During this study, we observed residents in Community 2 use an open discussion*

board initially and change to a private email list'. Through a triangulated approach involving observation, interviews and qualitative content analysis, authors gathered extensive empirical data on a regular basis and subjected these to inductive analysis. Whereas Erete and Burrell's study is mostly descriptive, Parkes et al. [98] address evolution and clear temporal aspects for introducing technological interventions in their research question on how children's use and interpretation of the tangible system Topobo will evolve over time. Here, several case studies of monthly use without an explicit study protocol or researcher involvement allow teachers to unfold the possibilities and constraints for Topobo together with children of various ages and in various contexts.

5.2   Use of Metrics, Variables and Methods

A considerable amount of the 106 CHI papers report from studies that apply mixed methods in their research design. We found that 62% of the papers employ both quantitative and qualitative research methods, while 31% employ quantitative research methods and just 7% employ qualitative research methods.

5.2.1   Metrics and Variables

Several quantitative papers deal with interface artefacts or techniques (48%), and they often apply metrics or variables that make results easily comparable to previously reported results, e.g. [44, 73, 113], or to previous models, e.g. [20]. Several of these papers deal with text entry via text input interfaces, and they are often concerned with measuring typed-in words per minute—a common quantitative metric in the quantitative-only papers (e.g. [44, 46, 59, 79, 80, 93, 113, 131, 134]), but also in the mixed-method papers (e.g. [20, 72, 82, 114]). Other metrics or variables used in these papers are number of errors/corrections, error/correction rates, time elapsed between one action/keystroke to the next, stroke duration, etc. varying on the study technology and focus.

Interestingly, twelve out of 33 quantitative research papers (36%) are understanding papers. Here, we found a focus on stringent variables and a vocabulary to match, as illustrated in these papers [4, 12, 13, 111, 127, 128]. Although varying in duration (weeks to years), all have an emphasis on variables for statistical analysis on a large data set from a large sample size. For [4, 13, 111, 127] they outline one to two dependent and several independent variables. White and Richardson [128] set up two primary parameters on which to measure: community size and contact rate. Some studies, e.g. [4, 111, 127] relied exclusively on data retrieved from servers, while other studies, e.g. [12, 13], supplement such data with survey data. Some of the understanding papers are concerned with more abstract constructs; motivation, bias and user experience (e.g. [36, 64, 100]). For example, Fiore et al. [36] compared four conditions which differed in elements of intrinsic or extrinsic motivation. Karapanos

[64] uses the AttrakDiff 2 questionnaire to evaluate deployment of a new technology as the author argues: '*For evaluative, high level summary judgments single item measurements are appropriate and commonly used (e.g., to measure subjective wellbeing)*'.

Few CHI papers report from a qualitative-only study (7%). As an example, Pasquetto et al. [99] conduct two qualitative case studies, primarily relying on firstly a literature review and secondly ethnographic long-term observations, with a focus on open data policy and practice in major scientific collaborations. Their research questions regard rationales, definitions and infrastructure of open data, as well as their relationship. Categorizing this as an understanding paper, they conclude on how definitions change and how the relationships are more complex than before assumed and how this affects policy and practices.

Some important limitations of longitudinal data analysis are explicitly emphasized in [12, 55], e.g. Burke and Kraut [12] state that it is impossible to rule out every possible 'third factor' that might account for a portion of an association between an independent variable and its effect on the dependent variable. Hutto et al. [55] argue that longitudinal study research inherently has great power as correlational research due to the fact that time-dependent, repeated observations are considered as they state: '*When input A is consistently and reliably observed preceding outcome B for the exact same group of individual's time after time, we have greater confidence in suggesting a causal relationship between A and B*'. Burke and Kraut [12] nuance this for their particular study saying that '*like many large-scale observational social science studies, we cannot draw definitive causal conclusions, even with longitudinal data*' as unmeasured variables unavoidably existed that they were not aware of in their study design. They further speculate that even though they found only few quantitative differences, if qualitative differences had been taken into account, they might have reached a different conclusion.

5.2.2 Research Methods and Study Design

The level of control of studies varies, depending on the context it was carried out in, as well as the objective of the study. Studies in the context of the laboratory had inherently relatively high control. In a relatively high control field experiment of text input techniques, Ghosh and Joshi [44] presented participants with a guideline for how many sessions that could be carried out when, how often, and what constituted a session. However, some more low control field settings introduced new interface techniques and instructed participants to use it freely over a specified duration while logging their interactions, e.g. [51, 104, 132]. The study design of Garzonis et al. [40] is somewhat different. They divided their study into four stages with one week of field study with daily prompted but randomly scheduled interactions, followed by laboratory studies and web-based surveys, thus triangulating research methods. With five hypotheses, they aimed both at investigating the intuitiveness of two conditions (auditory icons and earcons) as well as hypothesized on the order of laboratory and field-based activities. In line with this, Jain and Boyce [57] in a case study introduced a four-staged model of longitudinal data elicitation, as well as assessed the model with empirical evidence from a case of comparing two mobile applications. Firstly, a usability study was carried out, following three weeks of interacting and diary keeping, thirdly a retrospective reconstruction interview, completed with a follow-up survey after four months of use. With this study design, they were able to conclude on how user preferences for the two applications shifted and stabilized, providing a completely different picture than the one from the start of the study.

Mchlachlan et al. [89] reference a concept, as inspiration for their study design, Multi-dimensional In-depth Long-term Case studies (MILCs). They employ this study design for evaluating adoption of a large data set visualization system. In line with this, Gerken et al. [42, 43] employed concept maps, in their case used to evaluate the usability of Application Programming Interfaces. Concept maps, they argue, are particularly good at addressing concerns of qualitative data gathering in longitudinal studies, as they visualize data and make it easier to identify changes over time.

Four studies concern social media and being social online [3, 110, 111, 127], e.g. Wang and Kraut [127] studied the link between social media participation and work performance. They analysed logged activity on social media and compared these with internal performance ratings. They collected data once every year from the same participants to study baseline performance and year-to-year variability and concluded that employers should encourage adoption of social media among their employees. Armchambault and Grudin [3] investigated the usefulness of social media for organizational communication over a study period of three years. Here, they annually invited 1000 randomly selected employees to answer a survey, upon answering they were subsequently excluded from participating again. By having representable samples, authors reported on growth in use and acceptance over the years, as well as changes in behaviour and concerns. Additionally, recently, Saha et al. [105] propose in a case study to view social media as passive sensing for longitudinal studies of behaviour and well-being, as one aspect of sensing in a larger project named Tesserae project. Passive sensing as an unobtrusive data collection method, specifically through radio reflections, is proposed by Hsu et al. in response to '*Studies (that) rely on diaries and questionnaires, which are subjective, erroneous and hard to sustain in longitudinal studies*' [54].

5.3 Measuring or Discussing Change

As introduced in the background section, measuring change (or stability) is a primary concern for longitudinal studies. Our analysis revealed that 66% of the CHI papers explicitly report on change (or stability). We have included papers that illustrate, analyse or discuss aspects of change in their paper. We assessed the studies' points of measurement (PoM) and distinguish between studies with less than three PoMs and studies with three or more PoMs.

For measuring change or stability, 20 papers directly address that issues exist with what they refer to as 'snapshot' and cross-sectional studies [3, 10, 12, 34, 41, 48,

53, 55, 58, 81, 85, 89, 97, 100, 109, 117, 122, 125, 127, 134]. However, they do not dismiss these studies, rather they see longitudinal as supplementary for exploring different, temporal aims. As an example, Fan et al. [34] supplemented previous laboratory studies focusing on short-term recall, with a longitudinal study to focus on measurable improvement in learning outcomes. As well, Gerken et al. argue '*In a purely cross-sectional design, one might come to the conclusion that a much higher difference between mouse and laser-pointer does exist compared to a more realistic test setting including practice*' [41]. For Oviatt et al. [97] the extended study duration over three sessions revealed a stability over time, which they claimed as valuable to inform future design guidelines on 'adaptive temporal thresholds' on multimodal integration patterns.

A little more than half of the included papers (54%) report from studies with three or more PoMs, while they also focus on measuring change or stability. Karapanos et al. [64], for example, argue that longitudinal studies should integrate three or more POMs to enable greater insight into the exact form of change.

Mott et al. [93] found that mastery comes with repetition and they based their study on several POMs of varying length and interval to regularly measure progress. They stress that the longitudinal nature of their study over eight POMs allowed them to observe user performance with changes over time of two techniques where they expected the learning curves of the two techniques to be different. However, sometimes the change is not captured within the original duration, in which case some studies turn to prediction models in favour of extending the duration, e.g. [80].

The changes and stability of use of technologies are also in focus in studies through observations intended to predict which factors influence sustained use e.g. [68, 81]. Also, change is not always easy to pinpoint, but can happen over long periods of time (e.g. [10, 16, 19]). Several studies point out that conceptual change or stability is inherently time dependent, e.g. motivation, relationships, integration and habituation [27, 28, 36, 81, 100]. For example, Fiore et al. [36] studied motivation to initiate participation in longitudinal studies through four conditions of incentives, and although they saw effects on recruitment for some conditions, these did not extend to continued participation. This seems to be a particular problem for longitudinal studies, particularly visible in [128] and also addressed in [88, 105]. Longitudinal studies like [81, 100] focus on motivation for exercise, and Macvean and Robertson [81] stress that new products inherently have the problem of novelty wearing off. They found that their prototype iFitQuest successfully facilitated light exercise over a seven-week period. It initially encouraged moderate to vigorous intensity exercise in many participants, but this tended to level out in the last few weeks of the study. Although the novelty of the product or service in itself can wear off, it might inform long-term changes in behaviour (e.g. [68, 84, 119]) or the longitudinal study might reveal unintentional consequences of design [77]. Kim and Mankoff [68] and Teevan et al. [119] both found that making the invisible visible, in the form of, respectively, indoor air quality and changes in web content, saw users reflecting on and changing their behaviour. For Lee et al. [77] their field work on employing a social robot in a workplace resulted in a so-called ripple effect where non-participants would become part of the social interaction as observers or directly involved in the interaction. The extend of the ripple effect was perceived to be unanticipated.

We found that 26 papers report from studies with 1–2 POMs (26%), and 12 of these papers address change or stability. Interestingly, a large number of studies (34%) did not describe, report or discussed change or stability explicitly [1, 4, 8, 9, 11, 18, 29, 30, 37, 38, 39, 40, 45, 53, 57, 58, 62, 63, 70, 71, 75, 83, 84, 98, 104, 106, 110, 116, 117, 120, 126, 128, 132, 136]. These papers typically focus on, e.g. describing, testing or recommending without mentioning, illustrating or reporting on change over time.

Some studies have pre- and post-measurements [8, 9, 19, 64, 119], Karapanos et al. [64] stress the limitation of having only two PoMs, arguing they are only measuring current states and not the changes that happened in between. Two studies [112, 120] have a particularly long duration, where the duration in these cases could be expressed more appropriately as an interval between two points of measurements. For [112] Sillence et al. studied changes in online health from surveys spaced five years apart and Tullis [21] re-attempted a study, where participants were asked to point out the pictures they chose six years ago to represent a pictorial password. In the cases where studies primarily rely on automated data logs or highly frequent sensor data, it is not easy to determine PoMs. As an example, Voida et al. [125] used a continuous data log of user interactions, as well as a post-study interview. Although the authors argue they provide initial evidence of shifts in activities with the introduction of their intervention, they also argue for future work to focus on the whole life cycle of these shifts, which would require more PoMs. Additionally, when data collection is carried out retrospectively, it is not easy to determine PoMs, this was seen for [4, 30, 110, 127, 136].

6 Considerations for Longitudinal HCI Study Design

While the three themes under findings constitute a primary contribution of this chapter, we will in the following unfold some of the interesting characteristics of longitudinal HCI research. This discussion unfolds themes from our findings and relates them to longitudinal research (questions).

6.1 Duration Against Saturation

Rogers [19] argued in a feature for interactions magazine that the burning question in HCI research used to be *'How many participants do I need?'* but that the hotly debated question now was *'How long should my study run for?'* This certainly also characterizes longitudinal studies in HCI research, and our findings show that the publications in our study had very different durations. Rogers and Marshall has echoed the importance of running long-term studies 'in the wild' [20]. Stacked up against running such long duration studies, however, is the cost and tenure of researchers involved as *'papers must be written, and research budgets are tight'*.

Our findings suggest that the paper contribution seemed to play a role in determining the duration of a study and it seemed somewhat evident that you need to study over extended periods of time if your aim is to understand how people adapt or use technology in real life contexts, often referred to as in situ or field studies. But on the other hand, new interaction techniques were often tested in terms of learning, as techniques were compared against baselines. We argue that *plateauing in performance* for new interfaces and interaction techniques, often with a short duration, has a stronger focus on data saturation rather than duration, where sessions and interval between sessions are more important, rather than the length of the study. Another trend we found was *evolution* studies focusing on patterns of change or stability, ultimately with the aim of predicting natural and evolving interactions with technologies or in order to infer design decisions, usually manifest over a longer duration. A goal for longitudinal studies is to run for as long as it takes for changes or stability to emerge [18]. When novelty bias wears off, the integration into routines and habits begin and will reveal stability. How long this takes depends on the cycles inherent in the object and context of the study.

6.2 Point of Measurement: An HCI Perspective

Points of measurements receive much attention in related disciplines stating multiple points of measurements as a common definition. In HCI research, Kjeldskov et al. [11] conducted a longitudinal study involving two usability tests on an electronic patient record system with an interval of one year between measurements. This enabled them to conclude that many usability problems endure, despite interacting with the system regularly in between measurements. They concluded that poor design did not disappear over time even with learning and increased familiarity. We saw such study design in five of our included papers, but Karapanos et al. (appendix reference [64]), emphasize a limitation to this design '... *one may not readily infer time effects as these might be random contextual variation, given that we have only two measurements'*.

According to Karapanos et al. [9], longitudinal studies with more than two measurements points are *'the gold standard'* for measuring change. They do argue that it is increasingly laborious when generalizing over large populations of users and products. However, we argue that this 'gold standard' of more than two points of measurements is something to pay attention to in longitudinal study design as underlining certainty of change and stability. Karapanos et al. [9] present retrospective evaluation as an alternative to longitudinal studies. The retrospective evaluation relies on the elicitation of user's experience from memory, but our study suggests that study design employs data logging to aid recall or to altogether replace recalling of events. In the event of relying on or supplementing with data logs, continuous measurements were often used. While retrospective or continuous data logging might obscure the distinct points of measurements, here lies possibilities for future research for a negotiation on how this will adapt.

6.3   Contribution Type and Research Questions

Besides this comprehensive analysis of CHI papers, we are only aware of one other similar analysis, although less extensive, that has been presented by [6] as part of a proposed taxonomy for research questions in longitudinal research in HCI. In the following, we will show how the main findings of our study relate to this taxonomy. The taxonomy encompasses two main branches: the research interest in average or cumulative data over time and the research interest in changes over time.

Average or cumulative over time is not considered 'true' longitudinal research in several other disciplines. But Gerken argues that it is common practice in HCI research to call these longitudinal as they share the characteristic of having multiple points of measurements [6]. This does not mean that this type of contribution is not valuable or appropriate; however, in terms of analysis, it is comparable to a cross-sectional problem. Without proper framing of research questions and data gathering, you will not get the full benefit of the longitudinal design and cannot conclude on change over time. Examples of these studies can be seen in some studies not concerned with change (appendix reference [70, 104, 106, 126, 132]).

Interest in change (over time) is additionally branched into two different contributions namely effect of change and process of change. The effect of change is concerned with the outcome of change or pre- and post-measurements, whereas process of change is concerned with the shape of a change process, what events occur and answering in-depth how and why questions. Interest in the effect of change can be seen in research questions regarding the outcome of change and for pre-post measurements. As an example of the first, Gerken et al. (Appendix reference [41]) were concerned with the performance of novel pointing techniques. They compared a laser pointer to mouse pointing and were interested to see how long it takes participants to learn to use the laser pointer. So while they applied multiple PoM they were actually focusing on the outcome of a learning process. In line with this are several of the studies concerned with plateauing in performance, where they are interested in learning, comparison or the 'crossover point'. For examples in pre-post measurements see (Appendix reference [8, 9, 19, 64, 119, 128]).

For interest in the process of change, we also recognize plateauing in performance papers as addressing the shape of change. One example is input device experiments which try to fit learning data to the power law of practice, which in itself is a description of the shape of change. Also, what we termed evolution papers are often concerned with the shape of change. An example can be seen in (Appendix reference [16]) as authors were interested in hierarchical communication patterns and strategies of these and how these strategic patterns change during a project life cycle. According to Gerken's taxonomy, the interest in process of change can also be expressed as interest in occurrences of events or more specifically whether or when events occur. An example of a research question is: '*Whether and when do people adopt a specific new technology in their daily routine?*' [6]. Although not explicitly formulated as a research question, rather formed from inductive analysis, (Appendix reference [32]) saw how one community changed from using one technology to another during the study. However, they do not argue why this happened.

Meanwhile, we also recognize that studies not included in this review concern the shape of change over time (e.g. for field deployments of design artefacts). For example, Odom et al. designing intentionally for slowness (stating regular points of measurements) [14, 15] and Gaver et al. who present empirical understandings on how to overcome the often short-lived effects of most environmental HCI interventions [5]. Often these studies, while not explicitly longitudinal, concern introducing change in the form of new (to the user) technologies and reporting in what ways attitudes, behaviour and practice changes.

7 Implications for Longitudinal HCI Research

Summarizing our overview of common characteristics and three points of consideration above, we will now outline three implications for longitudinal HCI studies, that we perceive as important to consider. These relate to studies that involve measuring longitudinal data on what happens to a set of participants during a series of time points as articulated and pointed out by Gerken [7].

Firstly, time duration should not be considered a singular attribute in longitudinal studies. Our analysis found that it is important for HCI researchers to consider duration not as a singular attribute, but in relation to points of measurements or even expected change rate. Therefore, just conducting a long-term study does not make the study longitudinal, and in fact, sometimes it is not even necessary to run for a long period of time, if the observed variable changes quickly and can be measured with multiple points of measurements in a short duration.

Secondly, longitudinal data measures should be considered when conducting studies in the wild, or sometimes known as field or in situ studies. Our analysis further showed that field studies sometimes already have the necessary duration to actually conduct longitudinal measures using multiple and systematic points of measurements to measure changes (or stability) over time. But our study also showed, that despite having the duration for longitudinal collection, many of them lack a systematic study design to express change over time for mainly qualitative approaches.

Thirdly, subject progression is important when conducting laboratory studies. While our analysis found that laboratory studies involving longitudinal aspects have rather different characteristics, e.g. duration or session lengths, we observed that for several of these studies, it was important to track subject progression throughout the study, for example when subjects go from being novices to experts (e.g. when learning a new interaction technique or a new type of interface or prototype). This relates closely to plateauing and evolution in longitudinal studies and involves selecting and defining meaningful measure metrics and variables. Thus, researchers should be careful when designing such studies and decide how progression can be determined.

8 Conclusion

We have conducted an analysis of 106 publications at the CHI conferences published in the period 1982–2019 in which longitudinal studies are reported. Our motivation for this study was the lack of empirical understanding on how previous HCI studies have conducted longitudinal studies and we hope that such an understanding can bring forward discussions of longitudinal HCI, with the ultimate aim to reach common consensus and a shared definition. Our findings illustrated that HCI longitudinal studies are highly diverse in terms of duration lasting from studies conducted over a few days to studies conducted over several years. In our findings, we explained two longitudinal trends, namely plateauing in performance and evolution studies. These do not cover the entire pool of included papers, but they do describe important characteristics of several longitudinal HCI studies.

Studies considered in our analysis integrate different metrics, and we found that the paper contribution type highly influences the longitudinal study design. We further found that more than half of the papers discuss or illustrate change or stability during their studies. We analysed previous longitudinal research published on CHI for researchers wishing to conduct longitudinal studies to take inspiration and advice, as well as learn from past challenges and successes.

References

1. Bargas-Avila JA, Hornbæk K (2011) Old wine in new bottles or novel challenges. In: Proceedings of the 2011 annual conference on Human factors in computing systems—CHI'11. ACM Press: New York, USA, p 2689
2. Baxter KK, Avrekh A, Evans B (2015) Using experience sampling methodology to collect deep data about your users. In: Proceedings of the 33rd annual ACM conference extended abstracts on human factors in computing systems—CHI EA '15. ACM Press: New York, USA, pp 2489–2490
3. Bickmore TW, Consolvo S, Intille SS (2009) Engagement by design. In: Proceedings of the 27th international conference extended abstracts on human factors in computing systems—CHI EA '09. ACM Press: New York, USA, p 4807
4. Courage C, Jain J, Rosenbaum S (2009) Best practices in longitudinal research. In: Proceedings of the 27th international conference extended abstracts on human factors in computing systems—CHI EA '09. ACM Press: New York, USA, p 4791
5. Gaver W, Michael M, Kerridge T, Wilkie A, Boucher A, Ovalle L, Plummer-Fernandez M (2015) Energy babble: mixing environmentally-oriented internet content to engage community groups. In: Conference on human factors in computing systems—proceedings. pp 1115–1124
6. Gerken J (2011) Longitudinal research in human—computer interaction. Universität Konstanz

7. Jain J, Rosenbaum S, Courage C (2010) Best practices in longitudinal research. In: Proceedings of the 28th of the international conference extended abstracts on human factors in computing systems—CHI EA '10. ACM Press: New York, USA, p 3167

8. Karapanos E, Jain J, Hassenzahl M (2012) Theories, methods and case studies of longitudinal HCI research. In: Proceedings of the 2012 ACM annual conference extended abstracts on human factors in computing systems extended abstracts—CHI EA '12. ACM Press: New York, USA, p 2727

9. Karapanos E, Martens J, Hassenzahl M (2010) On the retrospective assessment of users' experiences over time. In: Proceedings of the 28th of the international conference extended abstracts on human factors in computing systems—CHI EA '10. ACM Press: New York, USA, p 4075

10. Karapanos E, Zimmerman J, Forlizzi J (2009) User experience over time: an initial framework. Chi2009 Proceedings of the 27Th annual CHI conference hum factors computer system vol 1–4. pp 729–738

11. Kjeldskov J, Skov MB, Stage J (2010) A longitudinal study of usability in health care: does time heal? Int J Med Inform 79:e135–e143. https://doi.org/10.1016/j.ijmedinf.2008.07.008

12. Lazar J, Feng J, Hochheiser H (2017) Research methods in human-computer interaction, 2nd ed. Morgan Kaufmann

13. Menard S (2002) Longitudinal research, 2nd ed. SAGE Publications

14. Odom W, Wakkary R, Hol J, Naus B, Verburg P, Amram T, Chen AYS (2019) Investigating slowness as a frame to design longer-term experiences with personal data. In: Proceedings of the 2019 CHI conference on human factors in computing systems—CHI'19. ACM Press: New York, USA, pp 1–16

15. Odom WT, Sellen AJ, Banks R, Kirk DS, Regan T, Selby M, Forlizzi JL, Zimmerman J (2014) Designing for slowness, anticipation and re-visitation. In: Proceedings of the 32nd annual ACM conference on human factors in computing systems—CHI'14. ACM Press: New York, USA, pp 1961–1970

16. Pettigrew AM (1990) Longitudinal field research on change: theory and practice. Organ Sci 1:267–292. https://doi.org/10.1287/orsc.1.3.267

17. Pettigrew AM (1997) What is a processual analysis? Scand J Manag 13:337–348. https://doi.org/10.1016/S0956-5221(97)00020-1

18. Ployhart RE, Vandenberg RJ (2010) Longitudinal research: the theory, design, and analysis of change. J Manage 36:94–120. https://doi.org/10.1177/0149206309352110

19. Rogers Y (2011) Interaction design gone wild. Interactions 18:58

20. Rogers Y, Paul M (2017) Research in the wild. Morgan & Claypool, London

21. Taris T (2000) A primer in longitudinal data analysis. SAGE Publications

22. Vaughan M, Courage C (2007) SIG: capturing longitudinal usability. In: CHI'07 extended abstracts on human factors in computing systems—CHI'07. ACM Press: New York, USA, p 2149

23. Vaughan M, Courage C, Rosenbaum S, Jain J, Hammontree M, Beale R, Welsh D (2008) Longitudinal usability data collection. In: Proceeding of the twenty-sixth annual CHI conference extended abstracts on human factors in computing systems—CHI'08. ACM Press: New York, USA, p 2261

Appendix References CHI 1982–2019

1* Alcaidinho J (2016) Canine behavior and working dog suitability from quantimetric data. In: Proceedings of the 2016 CHI conference extended abstracts on human factors in computing systems—CHI EA '16. ACM Press: New York, USA, pp 193–197

2* Aragon CR, Williams A (2011) Collaborative creativity. In: Proceedings of the 2011 annual conference on Human factors in computing systems—CHI'11. ACM Press: New York, USA, p 1875

3* Archambault A, Grudin J (2012) A longitudinal study of facebook, linkedin, & twitter use. In: Proceedings of the 2012 ACM annual conference on human factors in computing systems—CHI'12. ACM Press: New York, USA, p 2741

4* Arguello J, Butler BS, Joyce L, Kraut R, Ling KS, Wang X (2006) Talk to me: foundations for successful individual-group interactions in online communities. In: Proceedings of the 2006 SIGCHI conference on human factors in computing systems—CHI'06. ACM Press: New York, USA, p 959

5 Baxter KK, Avrekh A, Evans B (2015) Using experience sampling methodology to collect deep data about your users. In: Proceedings of the 33rd annual ACM conference extended abstracts on human factors in computing systems—CHI EA '15. ACM Press: New York, USA, pp 2489–2490

6 Beale R, Vaughan M, Courage C, Rosenbaum S, Jain J, Hammontree M, Welsh D (2008) Longitudinal usability data collection. In: Proceeding of the twenty-sixth annual CHI conference extended abstracts on human factors in computing systems—CHI'08. ACM Press: New York, USA, p 2261

7 Bickmore TW, Caruso L, Clough-Gorr K (2005) Acceptance and usability of a relational agent interface by urban older adults. In: CHI'05 extended abstracts on human factors in computing systems—CHI'05. ACM Press: New York, USA, p 1212

8* Bickmore TW, Picard RW (2004) Towards caring machines. In: Extended abstracts of the 2004 conference on Human factors and computing systems—CHI'04. ACM Press: New York, USA, p 1489

9* Bickmore TW, Consolvo S, Intille SS (2009) Engagement by design. In: Proceedings of the 27th international conference extended abstracts on human factors in computing systems—CHI EA '09. ACM Press: New York, USA, p 4807

10* Boardman R, Sasse MA (2004) "Stuff goes into the computer and doesn't come out": a cross-tool study of peronal information management. In: Proceedings of the 2004 conference on human factors in computing systems—CHI'04. ACM Press: New York, USA, pp 583–590

11* Bruun A, Gull P, Hofmeister L, Stage J (2009) Let your users do the testing: a comparison of three remote asynchronous usability testing methods. In: Proceedings of the 27th international conference on human factors in computing systems—CHI 09. ACM Press: New York, USA, p 1619

12* Burke M, Kraut RE (2014) Growing closer on facebook: changes in tie strength through social network site use. In: Proceedings of the 32nd annual ACM conference on human factors in computing systems—CHI'14. ACM Press: New York, USA, pp 4187–4196

13* Burke M, Kraut R, Marlow C (2011) Social capital on facebook: differentiating uses and users. In: Proceedings of the 2011 annual conference on human factors in computing systems—CHI'11. ACM Press: New York, USA, p 571

14* Campbell RL (1990) Developmental scenario analysis of smalltalk programming. In: Proceedings of the 1990 SIGCHI conference on human factors in computing systems empowering people—CHI'90. ACM Press: New York, USA, pp 269–276

15* Castellucci SJ, MacKenzie IS (2008) Graffiti versus unistrokes: an empirical comparison. In: Proceeding of the twenty-sixth annual CHI conference on human factors in computing systems—CHI'08. ACM Press: New York, USA, p 305

16* Cataldo M, Ehrlich K (2012) The impact of communication structure on new product development outcomes. In: Proceedings of the 2012 ACM annual conference on human factors in computing systems—CHI'12. ACM Press: New York, USA, p 3081

17 Chang JS, Doucette AF, Yeboah G, Welsh T, Nitsche M, Mazalek A (2018) A tangible VR game designed for spatial penetrative thinking ability. Extended abstracts of the 2018 CHI conference on human factors in computing systems. ACM, New York, USA, pp 1–4

18* Chattopadhyay D, O'Hara K, Rintel S, Rädle R (2016) Office social: presentation interactivity for nearby devices. In: Proceedings of the 2016 CHI conference on human factors in computing systems. ACM: New York, USA, pp 2487–2491

19* Chu SL, Schlegel R, Quek F, Christy A, Chen K (2017) "I make, therefore i am": The effects of curriculum-aligned making on children's self-identity. In: Proceedings of the 2017 CHI conference on human factors in computing systems. ACM: New York, USA, pp 109–120

20* Clarkson E, Clawson J, Lyons K, Starner T (2005) An empirical study of typing rates on mini-QWERTY keyboards. In: CHI'05 extended abstracts on human factors in computing systems—CHI'05. ACM Press: New York, USA, p 1288

21 Clarkson E, Lyons K, Clawson J, Starner T (2007) Revisiting and validating a model of two-thumb text entry. In: Proceedings of the SIGCHI conference on human factors in computing systems—CHI'07. ACM Press: New York, USA, pp 163–166

22 Clawson J, Lyons K, Rudnick A, Iannucci RA, Starner T (2008) Automatic whiteout++: correcting mini-QWERTY typing errors using keypress timing. In: Proceeding of the twenty-sixth annual CHI conference on human factors in computing systems—CHI'08. ACM Press: New York, USA, p 573

23 Constantinides M (2015) Apps with habits: adaptive interfaces for news apps. In: Proceedings of the 33rd annual ACM conference extended abstracts on human factors in computing systems—CHI EA '15. ACM Press: New York, USA, pp 191–194

24* Cook GJ, Grabski SV (1992) An empirical examination of software-mediated information exchange and communication richness. In: Posters and short talks of the 1992 SIGCHI conference on human factors in computing systems—CHI'92. ACM Press: New York, USA, p 46

25 Courage C, Jain J, Rosenbaum S (2010) Best practices in longitudinal research. In: Proceedings of the 28th of the international conference extended abstracts on human factors in computing systems—CHI EA '10. ACM Press: New York, USA, p 3167

26 Courage C, Jain J, Rosenbaum S (2009) Best practices in longitudinal research. In: Proceedings of the 27th international conference extended abstracts on human factors in computing systems—CHI EA '09. ACM Press: New York, USA, p 4791

27* Dantec CA Le, Farrell RG, Christensen JE, Bailey M, Ellis JB, Kellogg WA, Edwards WK (2011) Publics in practice: ubiquitous computing at a shelter for homeless mothers. In: Proceedings of the 2011 annual conference on human factors in computing systems—CHI'11. ACM Press: New York, USA, p 1687

28* Dantec C Le (2012) Participation and publics: supporting community engagement. In: Proceedings of the 2012 ACM annual conference on human factors in computing systems—CHI'12. ACM Press: New York, USA, p 1351

29* Day J, Foley J (2006) Evaluating web lectures: a case study from HCI. In: CHI'06 extended abstracts on human factors in computing systems—CHI EA '06. ACM Press: New York, USA, p 195

30* Ducheneaut N, Yee N, Nickell E, Moore RJ (2006) "Alone together?": exploring the social dynamics of massively multiplayer online games. In: Proceedings of the 2006 SIGCHI conference on human factors in computing systems—CHI'06. ACM Press: New York, USA, p 407

31 Dudley C, Jones SL (2018) Fitbit for the mind?: An exploratory study of "cognitive personal informatics." Extended abstracts of the 2018 CHI conference on human factors in computing systems. ACM, New York, USA, pp 1–6

32* Erete S, Burrell JO (2017) Empowered participation: how citizens use technology in local governance. In: Proceedings of the 2017 CHI conference on human factors in computing systems. ACM: New York, USA, pp 2307–2319

33* Erickson T (1996) The design and long-term use of a personal electronic notebook: a reflective analysis. In: Proceedings of the 1996 SIGCHI conference on human factors in computing systems common ground—CHI'96. ACM Press: New York, USA, pp 11–18

34* Fan X, Luo W, Wang J (2017) Mastery learning of second language through asynchronous modeling of native speakers in a collaborative mobile game. In: Proceedings of the 2017 CHI conference on human factors in computing systems. ACM: New York, USA, pp 4887–4898

35 Fiorani M, Mariani M, Minin L, Montanari R (2008) Monitoring time-headway in car-following task. In: Proceeding of the twenty-sixth annual CHI conference extended abstracts on human factors in computing systems—CHI'08. ACM Press: New York, USA, p 2143

36* Fiore AT, Cheshire C, Shaw Taylor L, Mendelsohn GA (2014) Incentives to participate in online research: an experimental examination of "surprise" incentives. In: Proceedings of the 32nd annual ACM conference on human factors in computing systems—CHI'14. ACM Press: New York, USA, pp 3433–3442

37* Fitchett S, Cockburn A, Gutwin C (2014) Finder highlights: field evaluation and design of an augmented file browser. In: Proceedings of the 32nd annual ACM conference on human factors in computing systems—CHI'14. ACM Press: New York, USA, pp 3685–3694

38* Flounders C (2001) "Are you there Margaret? It's me, Margaret": speech recognition as a mirror. In: CHI'01 extended abstracts on Human factors in computing systems—CHI'01. ACM Press: New York, USA, p 459

 39 Friess E (2008) Defending design decisions with usability evidence: a case study. In: Proceeding of the twenty-sixth annual CHI conference extended abstracts on human factors in computing systems—CHI'08. ACM Press: New York, USA, p 2009

40* Garzonis S, Jones S, Jay T, O'Neill E (2009) Auditory icon and earcon mobile service notifications: intuitiveness, learnability, memorability and preference. In: Proceedings of the 27th international conference on human factors in computing systems—CHI 09. ACM Press: New York, USA, p 1513

41* Gerken J, Bieg H-J, Dierdorf S, Reiterer H (2009) Enhancing input device evaluation: longitudinal approaches. In: Proceedings of the 27th international conference extended abstracts on human factors in computing systems—CHI EA '09. ACM Press: New York, USA, p 4351

42* Gerken J, Jetter H, Reiterer H (2010) Using concept maps to evaluate the usability of APIs. In: Proceedings of the 28th of the international conference extended abstracts on human factors in computing systems—CHI EA '10. ACM Press: New York, USA, p 3937

43* Gerken J, Jetter H, Zöllner M, Mader M, Reiterer H (2011) The concept maps method as a tool to evaluate the usability of APIs. In: Proceedings of the 2011 annual conference on human factors in computing systems—CHI'11. ACM Press: New York, USA, p 3373

44* Ghosh S, Joshi A, Joshi M, Emmadi N, Dalvi G, Ahire S, Rangale S (2017) Shift+Tap or Tap+LongPress?: The upper bound of typing speed on InScript. In: Proceedings of the 2017 CHI conference on human factors in computing systems. ACM: New York, USA, pp 2059–2063

45* Gray CM (2014) Evolution of design competence in UX practice. In: Proceedings of the 32nd annual ACM conference on human factors in computing systems—CHI'14. ACM Press: New York, USA, pp 1645–1654

46* Gupta A, Balakrishnan R (2016) DualKey: miniature screen text entry via finger identification. In: Proceedings of the 2016 CHI conference on human factors in computing systems. ACM: New York, USA, pp 59–70

47* Harada S, Takagi H, Asakawa C (2011) On the audio representation of radial direction. In: Proceedings of the 2011 annual conference on human factors in computing systems—CHI'11. ACM Press: New York, USA, p 2779

48* Harada S, Wobbrock JO, Malkin J, Bilmes JA, Landay JA (2009) Longitudinal study of people learning to use continuous voice-based cursor control. In: Proceedings of the 27th international conference on human factors in computing systems—CHI 09. ACM Press: New York, USA, p 347

49* Harrison J, Chamberlain A, McPherson AP (2019) Accessible instruments in the wild: engaging with a community of learning-disabled musicians. Extended abstracts of the 2019 CHI conference on human factors in computing systems. ACM, New York USA, pp 1–6

 50 Hass C, Rosenzweig E (2017) Rivet counting and ocean crossing: case examples illuminating the fracticality of the theory-practice cycle and the importance of horizon expansion. In: Proceedings of the 2017 CHI conference extended abstracts on human factors in computing systems. ACM: New York, USA, pp 1012–1017

51* Hoggan E, Brewster SA (2010) Crosstrainer: testing the use of multimodal interfaces in situ. In: Proceedings of the 28th international conference on human factors in computing systems—CHI'10. ACM Press: New York, USA, p 333

 52 Houben S, Weichel C (2013) Overcoming interaction blindness through curiosity objects. In: CHI'13 extended abstracts on human factors in computing systems on—CHI EA '13. ACM Press: New York, USA, p 1539

53* Howard S, Kjeldskov J, Skov MB, Garnæs K, Grünberger O (2006) Negotiating presence-in-absence: contact, content and context. In: Proceedings of the 2006 SIGCHI conference on human factors in computing systems—CHI'06. ACM Press: New York, USA, p 909

54* Hsu C-Y, Hristov R, Lee G-H, Zhao M, Katabi D (2019) Enabling identification and behavioral sensing in homes using radio reflections. In: Proceedings of the 2019 CHI conference on human factors in computing systems—CHI'19. ACM Press: New York, USA, pp 1–13

55* Hutto CJ, Yardi S, Gilbert E (2013) A longitudinal study of follow predictors on twitter. In: Proceedings of the 2013 CHI conference on human factors in computing systems. ACM: New York, USA, pp 821–830

56* Irons DM (1982) Cognitive correlates of programming tasks in novice programmers. In: Proceedings of the 1982 conference on human factors in computing systems—CHI'82. ACM Press: New York, USA, pp 219–222

57* Jain J, Boyce S (2012) Case study: longitudinal comparative analysis for analyzing user behavior. In: Proceedings of the 2012 ACM annual conference extended abstracts on human factors in computing systems extended abstracts—CHI EA '12. ACM Press: New York, USA, p 793

58* Jain J, Ghosh R, Dekhil M (2008) Multimodal capture of consumer intent in retail. In: Proceeding of the twenty-sixth annual CHI conference extended abstracts on human factors in computing systems—CHI'08. ACM Press: New York, USA, p 3207

59* Jain M, Balakrishnan R (2012) User learning and performance with bezel menus. In: Proceedings of the 2012 ACM annual conference on human factors in computing systems—CHI'12. ACM Press: New York, USA, p 2221

60* Jensen C, Lonsdale H, Wynn E, Cao J, Slater M, Dietterich TG (2010) The life and times of files and information: a study of desktop provenance. In: Proceedings of the 28th international conference on human factors in computing systems—CHI'10. ACM Press: New York, USA, p 767

61 Jones W, Bellotti V, Capra R, Dinneen JD, Mark G, Marshall C, Moffatt K, Teevan J, Van Kleek M (2016) For richer, for poorer, in sickness or in health...: the long-term management of personal information. In: Proceedings of the 2016 CHI conference extended abstracts on human factors in computing systems—CHI EA '16. ACM Press: New York, USA, pp 3508–3515

62* Ju WG, Lee BA, Klemmer SR (2007) Range: exploring proxemics in collaborative whiteboard interaction. In: CHI'07 extended abstracts on human factors in computing systems—CHI'07. ACM Press: New York, USA, p 2483

63* Kantner L, Goold SD, Danis M, Nowak M, Monroe-Gatrell L (2006) Web tool for ealth insurance design by small groups: usability study. In: CHI'06 extended abstracts on human factors in computing systems—CHI EA '06. ACM Press: New York, USA, p 141

64* Karapanos E, Hassenzahl M, Martens J-B (2008) User experience over time. In: Proceeding of the twenty-sixth annual CHI conference extended abstracts on human factors in computing systems—CHI'08. ACM Press: New York, USA, p 3561

65 Karapanos E, Jain J, Hassenzahl M (2012) Theories, methods and case studies of longitudinal HCI research. In: Proceedings of the 2012 ACM annual conference extended abstracts on human factors in computing systems extended abstracts—CHI EA '12. ACM Press: New York, USA, p 2727

66 Karapanos E, Martens J, Hassenzahl M (2010) On the retrospective assessment of users' experiences over time. In: Proceedings of the 28th of the international conference extended abstracts on human factors in computing systems—CHI EA '10. ACM Press: New York, USA, p 4075

67 Khan MT, Hyun M, Kanich C, Ur B (2018) Forgotten but not gone: identifying the need for longitudinal data management in cloud storage. In: Proceedings of the 2018 CHI conference on human factors in computing systems—CHI'18. ACM Press: New York, USA, pp 1–12

68* Kim S, Paulos E, Mankoff J (2013) inAir: a longitudinal study of indoor air quality measurements and visualizations. In: Proceedings of the 2013 CHI conference on human factors in computing systems. ACM: New York, USA, pp 2745–2754

69 Kirman B, Linehan C, Lawson S (2012) Get lost: facilitating serendipitous exploration in location-sharing services. In: Proceedings of the 2012 ACM annual conference extended abstracts on human factors in computing systems extended abstracts—CHI EA '12. ACM Press: New York, USA, p 2303

70* Kleek MG Van, Bernstein M, Panovich K, Vargas GG, Karger DR, Schraefel M (2009) Note to self: examining personal information keeping in a lightweight note-taking tool. In: Proceedings of the 27th international conference on human factors in computing systems—CHI 09. ACM Press: New York, USA, p 1477

71* Kleek MG Van, Styke W, Schraefel M c., Karger D (2011) Finders/keepers: a longitudinal study of people managing information scraps in a micro-note tool. In: Proceedings of the 2011 annual conference on human factors in computing systems—CHI'11. ACM Press: New York, USA, p 2907

72* Költringer T, Van MN, Grechenig T (2007) Game controller text entry with alphabetic and multi-tap selection keyboards. In: CHI'07 extended abstracts on human factors in computing systems—CHI'07. ACM Press: New York, USA, p 2513

73* Kristensson PO, Denby LC (2009) Text entry performance of state of the art unconstrained handwriting recognition: a longitudinal user study. In: Proceedings of the 27th international conference on human factors in computing systems—CHI 09. ACM Press: New York, USA, p 567

74* Larsen SB, Bardram JE (2008) Competence articulation: alignment of competences and responsibilities in synchronous telemedical collaboration. In: Proceeding of the twenty-sixth annual CHI conference on human factors in computing systems—CHI'08. ACM Press: New York, USA, p 553

75* Latulipe C, Carroll EA, Lottridge D (2011) Evaluating longitudinal projects combining technology with temporal arts. In: Proceedings of the 2011 annual conference on human factors in computing systems—CHI'11. ACM Press: New York, USA, p 1835

76 Lee K, Kim S, Myaeng S-H (2013) Measuring touch bias of one thumb posture on direct touch-based mobile devices. In: CHI'13 extended abstracts on human factors in computing systems on—CHI EA '13. ACM Press: New York, USA, p 241

77* Lee MK, Kiesler S, Forlizzi J, Rybski P (2012) Ripple effects of an embedded social agent: a field study of a social robot in the workplace. In: Proceedings of the 2012 ACM annual conference on human factors in computing systems—CHI'12. ACM Press: New York, USA, p 695

78* Lee U, Kim J, Yi E, Sung J, Gerla M (2013) Analyzing crowd workers in mobile pay-for-answer q&a. In: Proceedings of the 2013 CHI conference on human factors in computing systems. ACM: New York, USA, pp 533–542

79* Lyons K, Starner T, Plaisted D, Fusia J, Lyons A, Drew A, Looney EW (2004) Twiddler typing: one-hand chording text entry for mobile phones. In: Proceedings of the 2004 conference on human factors in computing systems—CHI'04. ACM Press: New York, USA, pp 671–678

80* MacKenzie IS, Zhang SX (1999) The design and evaluation of a high-performance soft keyboard. In: Proceedings of the 1999 SIGCHI conference on human factors in computing systems the CHI is the limit—CHI'99. ACM Press: New York, USA, pp 25–31

81* Macvean A, Robertson J (2013) Understanding exergame users' physical activity, motivation and behavior over time. In: Proceedings of the 2013 CHI conference on human factors in computing systems. ACM: New York, USA, pp 1251–1260

82* Majaranta P, Ahola U, Špakov O (2009) Fast gaze typing with an adjustable dwell time. In: Proceedings of the 27th international conference on human factors in computing systems—CHI 09. ACM Press: New York, USA, p 357

83* Maldonado H, Lee B, Klemmer S (2006) Technology for design education: a case study. In: CHI'06 extended abstracts on human factors in computing systems—CHI EA '06. ACM Press: New York, USA, p 1067

84* Mann A-M, Hinrichs U, Read JC, Quigley A (2016) Facilitator, functionary, friend or foe?: Studying the role of iPads within learning activities across a school year. In: Proceedings of the 2016 CHI conference on human factors in computing systems—CHI'16. pp 1833–1845

85* Mariakakis A, Parsi S, Patel SN, Wobbrock JO (2018) Drunk user interfaces: determining blood alcohol level through everyday smartphone tasks. Proc 2018 CHI conference human factors computing system—CHI'18, 1–13 April 2018. https://doi.org/10.1145/3173574.317 3808

86 Marquardt N, Greenberg S (2015) Sketching user experiences: the hands-on course. In: Proceedings of the 33rd annual ACM conference extended abstracts on human factors in computing systems—CHI EA '15. ACM Press: New York, USA, pp 2479–2480

87* Masliah MR, Milgram P (2000) Measuring the allocation of control in a 6 degree-of-freedom docking experiment. In: Proceedings of the 2000 SIGCHI conference on human factors in computing systems—CHI'00. ACM Press: New York, USA, pp 25–32

88* Mattingly SM, Gregg JM, Audia P, Bayraktaroglu AE, Campbell AT, Chawla N V., Das Swain V, De Choudhury M, D'Mello SK, Dey AK, Gao G, Jagannath K, Jiang K, Lin S, Liu Q, Mark G, Martinez GJ, Masaba K, Mirjafari S, Moskal E, Mulukutla R, Nies K, Reddy MD, Robles-Granda P, Saha K, Sirigiri A, Striegel A (2019) The tesserae project: large-scale. longitudinal, in situ, multimodal sensing of information workers. In: Extended abstracts of the 2019 CHI conference on human factors in computing systems. ACM: New York, USA, pp 1–8

89* McLachlan P, Munzner T, Koutsofios E, North S (2008) LiveRAC: interactive visual exploration of system management time-series data. In: Proceeding of the twenty-sixth annual CHI conference on human factors in computing systems—CHI'08. ACM Press: New York, USA, p 1483

90* Meyer J, Wasmann M, Heuten W, El Ali A, Boll SCJ (2017) Identification and classification of usage patterns in long-term activity tracking. In: Proceedings of the 2017 CHI conference on human factors in computing systems. ACM: New York, USA, pp 667–678

91 Millen DR, Yang M, Warner M (2013) Best practices for enterprise social software adoption. In: CHI'13 extended abstracts on human factors in computing systems on—CHI EA '13. ACM Press: New York, USA, p 2349

92* Molapo M, Densmore M, DeRenzi B (2017) Video consumption patterns for first time smartphone users: community health workers in Lesotho. In: Proceedings of the 2017 CHI conference on human factors in computing systems. ACM: New York, USA, pp 6159–6170

93* Mott ME, Williams S, Wobbrock JO, Morris MR (2017) Improving dwell-based gaze typing with dynamic, cascading dwell times. In: Proceedings of the 2017 CHI conference on human factors in computing systems. ACM: New York, USA, pp 2558–2570

94* Ni T, Bowman D, North C (2011) AirStroke: bringing unistroke text entry to freehand gesture interfaces. In: Proceedings of the 2011 annual conference on human factors in computing systems—CHI'11. ACM Press: New York, USA, p 2473

95* Niemantsverdriet K, van de Werff T, van Essen H, Eggen B (2018) Share and share alike? Social information and interaction style in coordination of shared use. In: Proceedings of the 2018 CHI conference on human factors in computing systems—CHI'18. ACM Press: New York, USA, pp 1–14

96* Nilsen E, Jong H, Olson JS, Biolsi K, Rueter H, Mutter S (1993) The growth of software skill: a longitudinal look at learning & performance. In: Proceedings of the 1993 SIGCHI conference on human factors in computing systems—CHI'93. ACM Press: New York, USA, pp 149–156

97* Oviatt S, Lunsford R, Coulston R (2005) Individual differences in multimodal integration patterns: what are they and why do they exist? In: Proceedings of the 2005 SIGCHI conference on human factors in computing systems—CHI'05. ACM Press New York, USA, p 241

98* Parkes AJ, Raffle HS, Ishii H (2008) Topobo in the wild: longitudinal evaluations of educators appropriating a tangible interface. In: Proceeding of the twenty-sixth annual CHI conference on human factors in computing systems—CHI'08. ACM Press: New York, USA, p 1129

99* Pasquetto I V, Sands AE, Darch PT, Borgman CL (2016) Open data in scientific settings: from policy to practice. In: Proceedings of the 2016 CHI conference on human factors in computing systems. ACM: New York, USA, pp 1585–1596

100* Pfeifer LM, Bickmore T (2011) Is the media equation a flash in the pan?: the durability and longevity of social responses to computers. In: Proceedings of the 2011 annual conference on human factors in computing systems—CHI'11. ACM Press: New York, USA, p 777

101 Rector K (2014) The development of novel eyes-free exercise technologies using participatory design. In: Proceedings of the extended abstracts of the 32nd annual ACM conference on human factors in computing systems—CHI EA '14. ACM Press: New York, USA, pp 327–330

102 Ren J, Schulman D, Jack B, Bickmore TW (2014) Supporting longitudinal change in many health behaviors. In: Proceedings of the extended abstracts of the 32nd annual ACM conference on human factors in computing systems—CHI EA '14. ACM Press: New York, USA, pp 1657–1662

103 Richter H (2002) Understanding meeting capture and access. In: CHI'02 extended abstracts on human factors in computing systems—CHI'02. ACM Press: New York, USA, p 558

104* Robinson S, Rajput N, Jones M, Jain A, Sahay S, Nanavati A (2011) TapBack: towards richer mobile interfaces in impoverished contexts. In: Proceedings of the 2011 annual conference on human factors in computing systems—CHI'11. ACM Press: New York, USA, p 2733

105 Saha K, Bayraktaroglu AE, Campbell AT, Chawla NV, De Choudhury M, D'Mello SK, Dey AK, Gao G, Gregg JM, Jagannath K, Mark G, Martinez GJ, Mattingly SM, Moskal E, Sirigiri A, Striegel A, Yoo DW (2019) Social media as a passive sensor in longitudinal studies of human behavior and wellbeing. Extended abstracts of the 2019 chi conference on human factors in computing systems. ACM, New York, USA, pp 1–8

106* Sato M, Puri RS, Olwal A, Ushigome Y, Franciszkiewicz L, Chandra D, Poupyrev I, Raskar R (2017) Zensei: embedded, multi-electrode bioimpedance sensing for implicit, ubiquitous user recognition. In: Proceedings of the 2017 CHI conference on human factors in computing systems. ACM: New York, USA, pp 3972–3985

107* Schwartz T, Denef S, Stevens G, Ramirez L, Wulf V (2013) Cultivating energy literacy: results from a longitudinal living lab study of a home energy management system. In: Proceedings of the 2013 CHI conference on human factors in computing systems. ACM: New York, USA, pp 1193–1202

108 Seay AF, Jerome WJ, Lee KS, Kraut RE (2004) Project massive: a study of online gamin communities. In: Extended abstracts of the 2004 conference on human factors and computing systems—CHI'04. ACM Press: New York, USA, p 1421

109* Seay AF, Kraut RE (2007) Project massive: self-regulation and problematic use of online gaming. In: Proceedings of the SIGCHI conference on human factors in computing systems—CHI'07. ACM Press: New York, USA, pp 829–838

110* Settles B, Dow S (2013) Let's get together: the formation and success of online creative collaborations. In: Proceedings of the 2013 CHI conference on human factors in computing systems. ACM: New York, USA, pp 2009–2018

111* Shami NS, Nichols J, Chen J (2014) Social media participation and performance at work: a longitudinal study. In: Proceedings of the 32nd annual ACM conference on human factors in computing systems—CHI'14. ACM Press: New York, USA, pp 115–118

112* Sillence E, Briggs P, Harris P, Fishwick L (2006) Changes in online health usage over the last 5 years. In: CHI'06 extended abstracts on human factors in computing systems—CHI EA '06. ACM Press: New York, USA, p 1331

113 Son J, Ahn S, Kim S, Lee G (2019) Improving two-thumb touchpad typing in virtual reality. Extended abstracts of the 2019 CHI conference on human factors in computing systems. ACM, New York, USA, pp 1–6

114* Sporka AJ, Felzer T, Kurniawan SH, Poláček O, Haiduk P, MacKenzie IS (2011) CHANTI: predictive text entry using non-verbal vocal input. In: Proceedings of the 2011 annual conference on Human factors in computing systems—CHI'11. ACM Press: New York, USA, p 2463

115* Sporka AJ, Kurniawan SH, Mahmud M, Slavik P (2007) Longitudinal study of continuous non-speech operated mouse pointer. In: CHI'07 extended abstracts on human factors in computing systems—CHI'07. ACM Press: New York, USA, p 2669

116* Tak S, Cockburn A (2010) Improved window switching interfaces. In: Proceedings of the 28th of the international conference extended abstracts on human factors in computing systems—CHI EA '10. ACM Press: New York, USA, p 2915

117* Tan A, Kondoz AM (2008) Barriers to virtual collaboration. In: Proceeding of the twenty-sixth annual CHI conference extended abstracts on human factors in computing systems—CHI'08. ACM Press, New York, USA, p 2045

118* Taylor N, Cheverst K, Wright P, Olivier P (2013) Leaving the wild: lessons from community technology handovers. In: Proceedings of the 2013 CHI conference on human factors in computing systems. ACM: New York, USA, pp 1549–1558

119* Teevan J, Dumais ST, Liebling DJ (2010) A longitudinal study of how highlighting web content change affects people's web interactions. In: Proceedings of the 28th international conference on human factors in computing systems—CHI'10. ACM Press: New York, USA, p 1353

120* Tossell C, Kortum P, Rahmati A, Shepard C, Zhong L (2012) Characterizing web use on smartphones. In: Proceedings of the 2012 ACM annual conference on human factors in computing systems—CHI'12. ACM Press: New York, USA, p 2769

121* Tullis TS, Tedesco DP, McCaffrey KE (2011) Can users remember their pictorial passwords six years later. In: Proceedings of the 2011 annual conference extended abstracts on human factors in computing systems—CHI EA '11. ACM Press: New York, USA, p 1789

122* Vance A, Kirwan B, Bjornn D, Jenkins J, Anderson BB (2017) What do we really know about how habituation to warnings occurs over time?: A longitudinal fMRI study of habituation and polymorphic warnings. In: Proceedings of the 2017 CHI conference on human factors in computing systems. ACM: New York, USA, pp 2215–2227

123 Vaughan M, Courage C (2007) SIG: capturing longitudinal usability. In: CHI'07 extended abstracts on human factors in computing systems—CHI'07. ACM Press: New York, USA, p 2149

124 Vaughn LJ, Bortnick MJ, Carey J, Orgovan VR, Munko J (2018) Measuring response rate and increasing satisfaction in innovative environments: the impact of feedback. Extended abstracts of the 2018 CHI conference on human factors in computing systems. ACM, New York, USA, pp 1–7

125* Voida S, Mynatt ED (2009) It feels better than filing: everyday work experiences in an activity-based computing system. In: Proceedings of the 27th international conference on human factors in computing systems—CHI 09. ACM Press: New York, USA, p 259

126* Wang EJ, Zhu J, Jain M, Lee T-J, Saba E, Nachman L, Patel SN (2018) Seismo: blood pressure monitoring using built-in smartphone accelerometer and camera. In: Proceedings of the 2018 CHI conference on human factors in computing systems—CHI'18. ACM Press: New York, USA, pp 1–9

127* Wang Y, Kraut R (2012) Twitter and the development of an audience: those who stay on topic thrive! In: Proceedings of the 2012 ACM annual conference on human factors in computing systems—CHI'12. ACM Press: New York, USA, p 1515

128* White RW, Richardson M, Liu Y (2011) Effects of community size and contact rate in synchronous social q&a. In: Proceedings of the 2011 annual conference on human factors in computing systems—CHI'11. ACM Press: New York, USA, p 2837

129 Williamson JR, Williamson J, Kostakos V, Hamilton K, Green J (2016) Mobile phone usage cycles: a torus topology for spherical visualisation. In: Proceedings of the 2016 CHI conference extended abstracts on human factors in computing systems—CHI EA '16. ACM Press: New York, USA, pp 2751–2757

130 Wilson G, Carter T, Subramanian S, Brewster SA (2014) Perception of ultrasonic haptic feedback on the hand: localisation and apparent motion. In: Proceedings of the 32nd annual ACM conference on human factors in computing systems—CHI'14. ACM Press: New York, USA, pp 1133–1142

131* Wobbrock J, Myers B, Rothrock B (2006) Few-key text entry revisited: mnemonic gestures on four keys. In: Proceedings of the 2006 SIGCHI conference on human factors in computing systems—CHI'06. ACM Press: New York, USA, p 489

132* Xu Q, Casiez G (2010) Push-and-pull switching: window switching based on window over-lapping. In: Proceedings of the 28th international conference on human factors in computing systems—CHI'10. ACM Press: New York, USA, p 1335

133* Yee N, Ducheneaut N, Yao M, Nelson L (2011) Do men heal more when in drag?: conflicting identity cues between user and avatar. In: Proceedings of the 2011 annual conference on human factors in computing systems—CHI'11. ACM Press: New York, USA, p 773

134* Yeo H, Phang X, Castellucci SJ, Kristensson PO, Quigley A (2017) Investigating tilt-based gesture keyboard entry for single-handed text entry on large devices. In: Proceedings of the 2017 CHI conference on human factors in computing systems. ACM: New York, USA, pp 4194–4202

135 Yu B (2016) Adaptive biofeedback for mind-body practices. In: Proceedings of the 2016 CHI conference extended abstracts on human factors in computing systems—CHI EA '16. ACM Press: New York, USA, pp 260–264

136* Yürüten O, Zhang J, Pu PHZ (2014) Predictors of life satisfaction based on daily activities from mobile sensor data. In: Proceedings of the 32nd annual ACM conference on human factors in computing systems—CHI'14. ACM Press: New York, USA, pp 497–500

137 Zhang LH, Bucci P, Cang XL, MacLean K (2018) Infusing cuddlebits with emotion: build your own and tell us about it. Extended abstracts of the 2018 CHI conference on human factors in computing systems. ACM, New York, USA, pp 1–4

Longitudinal Studies in Information Systems

Peter Axel Nielsen⑩

Abstract Within the information systems research, there is a long tradition for longitudinal research, and it plays a significant role in the research literature. In this chapter, we will overview the reasons provided by researchers for when a longitudinal study is appropriate. Longitudinal studies have a particular focus on time and change. Time and change address a concern for understanding the details of human actors' behaviour and perceptions both as individuals and in social arrangements. This addresses 'how' to conduct a longitudinal study and why a deeper level of understanding is beneficial. In this chapter, we will map longitudinal research in information systems from the last two decades. This mapping shows critical distinctions that can be used in designing longitudinal research. The most important difference in longitudinal studies is between variance studies and process studies. Variance studies set the research design before the data collection, treat the change over time as a black box, favour a positivist stance and ask what-questions to see how the input causes the output over time. Process studies have a research design that emerges gradually as the data collection and analysis moves forward, favours an interpretive stance and asks what happens within the process.

Keywords Longitudinal research · Longitudinal case study · Information systems research · Literature review · Variance study · Process study

1 Introduction

Longitudinal research into information systems and research into human–computer interaction is related through what is studied yet less through the theories applied. Within the discipline of information systems, there is a long tradition for longitudinal studies. Information systems research is concerned with phenomena of development and use of information technologies aiming to support individuals, organisations, businesses and other social arrangements to benefit from the information being

P. A. Nielsen (✉)
Human-Centred Computing, Department of Computer Science, Aalborg University, Aalborg, Denmark
e-mail: pan@cs.aau.dk

© Springer Nature Switzerland AG 2021
E. Karapanos et al. (eds.), *Advances in Longitudinal HCI Research*,
Human–Computer Interaction Series, https://doi.org/10.1007/978-3-030-67322-2_3

collected, stored, computed and distributed. Theories of what information systems are and how their socio-technical nature should be understood exist in abundance [1]. It suffices here to state that it is both an academic research area and a professional practice area. It is a field that is multidisciplinary in seeking to bridge between engineering and the social sciences. We shall in this chapter see examples of information systems research.

The purpose of this chapter is to show what longitudinal research in information systems has evolved to and how we may learn from this. Longitudinal research is not at all new, but it has gained more momentum over the last two decades. Examples of longitudinal research will be presented and discussed. We shall, in particular, see how longitudinal studies contribute to depth in understanding and to understand the importance of change.

This chapter is a literature review and follows the research method explained by Paré et al. [2]. They distinguish between several types of literature review, and the type most appropriate here is a descriptive review as it reviews the extent of longitudinal studies within information systems research and seeks to elicit interpretable patterns in the underlying research methodologies.

The following sections start by outlining the landscape of longitudinal studies before showing exemplars of longitudinal research. By the end of the chapter, I shall summarise the principal elements and point at research design decisions to be made in any longitudinal study. This is relevant for longitudinal research in information systems and human–computer interaction alike.

2   The Landscape of Longitudinal Studies

The number of published articles within longitudinal information systems research is significant. A simple overview can be had from a literature search in Scopus. Scopus is a relevant search service as the highest-ranking research in information systems is published in journals of which Scopus catalogues a majority. In information systems journals, there are since 1999 published 378 articles where 'longitudinal' appears in the title, abstract or keywords. To reduce this to a more manageable level, we are here only looking at the eight journals that rank at the highest level among journals. These journals are referred to as the 'Basket-of-8' and are generally agreed to be outstanding. Of the 378 articles, there are 206 published in Basket-of-8 journals, that is 5.2% of the 3933 published articles in these journals.

The two old journals, Management Information Systems Quarterly and Information Systems Research, MISQ and ISR, commenced publishing in the late 1970s have published twice as many articles on longitudinal research as the others, see Table 1. These two journals are also reportedly oriented mostly towards a quantitative, positivist stance.

The distribution over the last two decades shows a steady increase in the number of articles on longitudinal research, see Fig. 1. The trendline suggests that five more articles are published per year for every six years passing.

Table 1 Frequency of longitudinal studies in 8 top journals

Journal	1999–2020
MISQ	54
ISR	47
EJIS	28
ISJ	23
JMIS	21
JAIS	19
JSIS	17
JIT	0

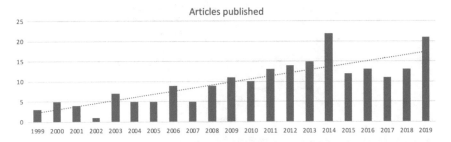

Fig. 1 Trends in longitudinal studies published in top journals in information systems. *Source* Scopus

The research impact is also increasing, see Fig. 2. The cumulative longitudinal research of 206 articles generates by now more than 2300 citations per year with an increase of almost 150 per year. 76 of 206 articles have by now more than 50 citations. It is reasonable to claim that the interest in conducting and publishing longitudinal research is increasing; and that the interest in reading and citing longitudinal research is increasing as well.

An analysis of frequencies of keywords, shown in Fig. 3 as the size of the node, and the edges link keywords that occur in the same article. The closer the keywords

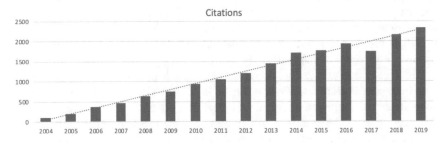

Fig. 2 Citations in all outlets to longitudinal studies published in top journals in information systems. *Source* Scopus

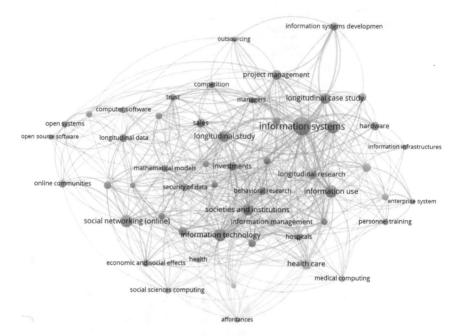

Fig. 3 Cluster analysis produced with VOSviewer based on data from Scopus

are in the graph, the more often they co-occur. The colouring of the graph shows six clusters. One cluster (red) is business-oriented with keywords like investment, sales, managers, information technology. Another cluster (purple) concerns social media with keywords like online communities and social networking. A cluster (blue) is directed at core information systems issues like information systems development, outsourcing and management information systems. An analysis on the same graph indicates that the older an article is, the more its keywords belong in the centre of the graph, and it thus suggests that the peripheral articles are more recently published longitudinal studies, e.g. social media studies and enterprise systems studies.

It is worth noticing that longitudinality appears in different forms. In the social media cluster, it gets referred to as 'longitudinal data'. In the business cluster, it is just 'longitudinal'. In contrast 'longitudinal study' is the preferred term in the cluster on economics and mathematical models, in another cluster it is 'longitudinal case study'. In the cluster with enterprise resource planning systems, it is 'longitudinal research' and 'longitudinal field study'.

The cluster analysis in Fig. 3 and the overview it provides also suggest that a broad range of research methods has been used. In trying to distinguish between qualitative or quantitative research, it is clear that no single search term describes this, see Table 2. The searching of terms used in the text body of the 206 articles is not entirely accurate, but it does provide an overview. As in most other fields of research, there is a tendency to be explicit in claiming a qualitative stance towards

Table 2 Search terms covering the text body of the 206 articles counting how many articles in which the search term occurred

Search term	1999–2020
Process	175
Change	148
Time OR temporal	144
Time	139
Qualitative	87
Quantitative	33
Measure OR variable OR hypothesis OR testing	113
Measure	73
Variable	68
Hypothesis	41
Test	95

empirical enquiry while a quantitative stance is often implicit and gets claimed less often than actually used.

It is reasonable to suggest that about half of the studies are quantitative, relying on measuring variables and testing the data against each other or sometimes against a hypothesis.

Table 2 also shows a common focus of many articles (85%) on 'process' and 'change' which we can take as part of the choice to do a longitudinal study. Almost at the same level, we see 'time' in a majority of articles.

3 Exemplars of Longitudinal Research

Of the 206 articles published during 1999–2020, five show some of the variety of longitudinal research and critical decisions of research design. The essential choices in particular concern the reasons for finding longitudinal study appropriate, how data were collected and analysed, as well as the type of research contribution.

3.1 Crowd Working and Community Participation

In the longitudinal study by Ma et al. [3], they have investigated crowd working turnovers in Amazon Mechanical Turk. Amazon Mechanical Turk, or MTurk for short, is a crowdsourcing marketplace widely used for surveys and other online tasks requiring many workers in a short time span. The turnover in crowd working is relatively high. Ma et al. wanted to study the potential positive influence of the online communities in which Turkers independently self-organise and discuss issues they have in common. They hypothesise effects of what they call the dual-context roles, i.e. active participation in MTurk and simultaneous active participation in an online community for Turkers. In particular, they are interested in whether the dual-context roles affect the Turkers desire to quit; if that is the case that has practical implications for crowd working organisations.

The study is longitudinal and quantitative, with two data collection points both performed through surveys among Turkers. At the first data collection point, 342 Turkers responded, and later 326 of these responded again at the second data collection point. The investigated model contains several hypotheses requiring two data collection points. For example, the sequential-update mechanism states that a factor measure at time T_1 influences the same factor at time T_2. The model's hypotheses also cover:

- Embeddedness (e.g. active community participation at T_1 negatively influences turnover intention at T_1).
- Cross-influence (e.g. affective community commitment at T_1 positively influences continuance in the community at T_2).
- Moderated heuristics (e.g. active community participation affects the relationship between affective commitment at T_1 and T_2).

A high response rate, pilot testing of the measurement instrument, and elaborate steps to ensure the identity of Turkers in the repeated survey all add to the validity of the study.

The analysis first compared two alternative models with the proposed model. One alternative model explained the data from a traditional perspective without the time dimension. Another alternative model then also included the sequential-update mechanism. In comparison, the proposed model had a better fit than the simpler alternative models. The analysis of the proposed hypotheses then showed that active community participation has a negative effect on turnover, i.e. the more community participation the better retention of Turkers. The supported hypotheses are shown in Fig. 4.

The longitudinality in the model and its integrated measures allow the researchers to conclude that their model has a better fit than previous models. The decision to utilise a longitudinal survey study with two data collection points is inherent in the proposed research model. Time plays a role in the research model, yet it is not mentioned what may happen between T_1 and T_2, what the process leading from T_1 to T_2 may be, or what could create a change.

3.2   Habituation of Security Warnings

The longitudinal study by Vance et al. [4] is quantitatively measured but in two different and supplementary ways. The study is reporting at the intersection of information systems research and human–computer interaction research about how habituation influences the perception of security warnings. Previous research suggests that habituation decreases the response to repeated stimulation, and the study investigates

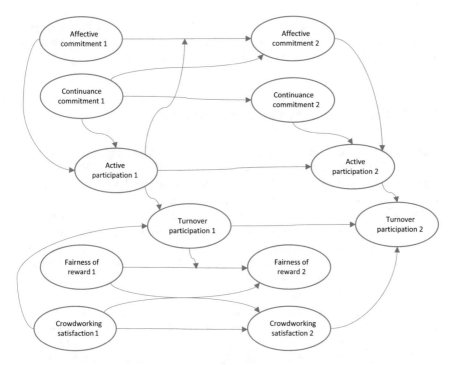

Fig. 4 Supported hypotheses in the longitudinal study by Ma et al. [3]

its influence on the effectiveness of security warnings. To this are added two modifying factors: (1) when habituation occurs, the repeated warnings are halted for a period; and (2) when habituation occurs, polymorphic signals are used.

In the first part of the study, data are collected from functional magnetic resonance imaging (fMRI) scanning and from eye tracking to measure habituation. The habituation measures were repeated over five days. With the fMRI scanning, they measured habituation by providing test subjects visual stimuli and observing repetition suppression in the brain. With the concurrent eye tracking, they measured eye-movement memory effect as a robust indicator of habituation.

The results from the five-day experiment are that subjects' attention to warnings declines over time, but also that the attention recovers partly between days. It further shows that changing the outlook of warning signals, i.e. polymorphic design, reduces the habituation.

The second part of the study is a three-week field experiment in which subjects are observed, and data are collected on actual responses to security warnings when installing apps. The results from the three-week field experiment are similar as habituation occurs over time. A difference is, however, that with polymorphic warning design, the attention remains high.

It is key to studying habituation that it must be considered over time. Along similar lines, it is necessary to study the attention to security warning outside of the laboratory as security warning is infrequent, and it is unrealistic to expose subjects to a high number of warnings in a short session. That is, time and realism are crucial and are also explicitly addressed in the research design.

3.3 ICT Implementation in an Indian Bank

Venkatesh et al. [5] have conducted a longitudinal study of how an Indian bank implemented ICT. The study ran for several years, covering more than 1000 employees and more than 1000 customers. The data collection and analyses were based on a mixed method utilising both quantitative and qualitative data.

The appropriateness of the mixed research method is argued based on the knowledge interest in creating a novel theory supported by two specific interests, namely (1) whether ICT implementation had a positive influence on the organisation in a developing country suits a confirmatory and quantitative research approach and (2) a question of how the implementation unfolded over time suits an exploratory and qualitative research approach.

The quantitative part was based on a survey yielding 2995 responses from employees before the implementation started and of these 1375 responded to the second and third survey after the implementation. For customers, the surveys were orchestrated as between-subjects with 892 (pre-implementation), 1208 (after one year) and 975 (after two years) responses. The longitudinal success of the ICT implementation was discouraging as the 'operational efficiency did not improve, and job satisfaction and customer satisfaction declined after the implementation' [5: 565].

Qualitative data were collected through semi-structured interviews during the same period. A final in-depth interview with 400 interviewees covered management, employees and customers. The purpose of the qualitative analysis was to seek explanations of why the ICT implementation had been ineffective. From this, they identified several reasons contributing to the implementation failure, and these can largely be attributed to the context being in a developing country, e.g. labour economics, Western isomorphism, parallel manual system and technology adaptation. For example, the parallel manual systems included issues like computer literacy and infrastructure uncertainty. The quantitative part and the qualitative part, in turn, led the researchers to propose a process model of ICT implementation in developing countries, see Fig. 5.

3.4 Organisational Influence Processes

Ngwenyama and Nielsen [6] studied a software company for more than three years. It is a longitudinal case study of implementation processes and how to overcome barriers to implementation. Barriers to implementation processes occur often. Existing research stating top management support and formal power is needed to

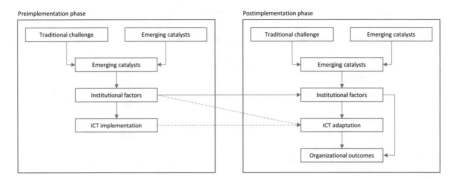

Fig. 5 Proposed process model for ICT implementation in developing countries showing how the relevant factors change over time, after Venkatesh et al. [5]

overcome these barriers. The study addresses how other tactics in organisational influence processes can complement top management's formal power.

The study is based on qualitative data collected by a participant-observer in 11 full-day meetings in the group responsible for the implementation process. The sessions were audio-recorded, and meeting minutes were written and approved by the participants. The group produced additional documentation in terms of plans, budgets and evaluations. The data analysis was abductive, and the driving question was how the implementation became successful in the absence of top management's formal power? To answer this, they analysed the qualitative data for evidence of tactics of organisational influence processes. These pieces of evidence were mapped to a framework of tactics encompassing rational persuasion, consultation, ingratiation, personal appeal, exchange/reciprocity, alliances/coalition, coercion/pressure and rewards/recognition.

The findings show that a major thrust is *lateral* influencing between peers primarily through reward and recognition. There are also elements of upward influencing to involve higher-level managers as mediators as well as downward influencing through mediators. The contribution to research comes in the form of propositions offered as an explanation of effective implementation processes and also as guides for practitioners. In particular, it explains how an implementation group that does not have formal authority can influence peers and their subordinates. Figure 6 shows this as a process model of organisational influence strategies.

It is argued why a longitudinal approach is necessary as influences processes are enacted over time. The understanding of dynamics requires an extended time span [7, 8]. The empirical data are qualitative stemming from participant observation as to gain insight into the experiences, behaviours and underlying reasons of the participants in the implementation process.

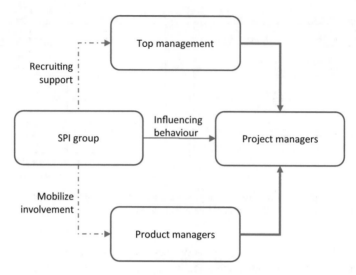

Fig. 6 Implementation process as organisational influence strategies, [6]

3.5 *Value of Online Communities*

Barrett et al. [9] have studied online communities and how they create value over time. The studied online community was within health care. The study ran for four years with data collected in an exploratory manner with an initial focus and later modified when important issues emerged as the community evolved over time. The online platform was owned by a start-up company to allow patients and their relatives to share knowledge and interests. The purpose of the study was to get to an understanding of how an online community can be valuable for the community members and the start-up. The study addressed this from a standpoint where values are multifaceted and encompass value systems such as financial, service, ethical, epistemic, reputational and platform values.

The empirical data were qualitative and collected through 38 semi-structured interviews, from strategy documents, from health authority policies, and through online observation in the community. The data analysis utilised a narrative strategy and temporal bracketing strategy [10]. The narrative told the story of how the online community evolved and the temporal analysis led to dividing the chronology into distinct phases to identify where strategies had changed, and events led to new stages.

They identify four value propositions: rating, connecting, tracking and profiling and the longitudinally study allows for explaining how the online community evolved from rating to profiling. For each value proposition, they can explain how it relates to the value systems (financial, service, ...) and how it involves community strategy, digital platform and stakeholder engagement. For example, the 'connecting' proposition extends the 'rating' proposition and the community strategy is 'building scale and enabling peer support', the digital platform is 'knowledge sharing', and stakeholder engagement involves 'charities & patients' [9: Fig. 2]. In this way, the contribution to research becomes a process model for creating value in online communities starting in 'rating' and ending in 'profiling' and at each stage explain what it entails.

It is indicative of this research that it explains the research design at length. It argues why a longitudinal approach is necessary for getting to understand how the use of the online platform evolves over time. It also contends why it needs to be explorative, and that it is based on qualitative data and an interpretive stance towards the data and the phenomena being studied.

3.6 Differences Between Longitudinal Studies

While all the above studies are longitudinal, they are also very different in how they are designed and conducted. They obviously vary in the topics being studied though both Ma et al. [3] and Barrett et al. [9] study online communities, and the studies of Venkatesh et al. [5] and Ngwenyama and Nielsen [6] concerns implementation processes. The most important differences are however found in the stance towards enquiry and how longitudinality has been addressed in the studies. Some studies are quantitative and based on a positivist stance, see Table 3. Others are clearly adhering to an interpretivist stance and based on interpreting qualitative data, and some even alludes to a stance more in line with a critical stance, e.g. [6] and [5].

Table 3 Differences between the exemplary studies

Exemplar	Topic	Type
Ma et al. [3]	Influence of online community on crowd working	Quantitative data, two data collection points, positivist stance
Vance et al. [4]	Habituation decreases the effectiveness of security warnings	Quantitative data, two series: (1) five days, (2) three weeks, positivist stance
Venkatesh et al. [5]	Socio-technical implementation processes in developing countries	Mixed quantitative and qualitative, positivist stance
Ngwenyama and Nielsen [6]	Organisational politics of implementation processes	Qualitative, interpretive stance, abductive analysis
Barrett et al. [9]	Values of online communities	Qualitative, interpretive stance, iteration between data and theory

4 Key Research Design Issues

It will be more evident how we can see the different issues of research design by basing it on a more general research methodology. Van de Ven's [11] methodology for engaged scholarship in the social sciences is appropriate for this. Van de Ven distinguishes between variance studies and process studies. He is not alone in making this distinction, and it is fundamental. Their incommensurability leads to a fork-decision for designing, conducting and evaluating social research.

A variance study starts with a what-questions. A variance study seeks to explain some input (independent) variables and statistically explain the output (dependent) variables. The explanation focusses on the output and whether the input causes the output. A variance study can be seen as a black box, of which only the inputs and outputs are visible. Many variance studies are not longitudinal though there is always an element of temporality as the input happens before the output. When they are longitudinal, it involves measuring the same variables two or several times where the time span depends on the causality being studied.

In the above exemplars:

- Exemplar 1 (Retention of crowd workers [3], cf. Sect. 3.1): Time is inherent in the research model, and the input–output variables are measured twice through surveys. Causality between the measurement at time T_1 and at time T_2 is key to the findings. It is key to the measuring of temporal order that respondents at T_1 are responding again at T_2.
- Exemplar 2 (Habituation of warnings [4], cf. Sect. 3.2): The research is divided in two supplementary parts. Part 1 is an experiment in a laboratory setting, with five repeated measures over five days. Input is time, and repeated exposure to warnings and output is habituation measured in the brain and in eye movements as less attention to warnings. Part 2 is a quasi-experiment in the field with the same variables measured in situ. The research design in part 2 adds realism to the experiment. The output variables were measured over a period of 15 weekdays by measuring participants' reactions to security warnings. In both parts, the causality is argued through statistical analysis.
- Exemplar 3, mixed-method part 1 (ICT implementation in a developing country [5], cf. Sect. 3.3): the input variable is the use of ICT, and the output variables measure job satisfaction, among others. This result came from repeated measuring (before, after one year, after two years) and showed a decline over time.

In all three variance studies, time plays a crucial role. It is easy to see that the input–output relationships are subjected to repeated measuring over time. For these studies, we may just as well think of time as being another input variable as time is part of what causes the output; that is, the output depends on time having passed.

A process study takes a starting point in how-questions. Process studies focus on the temporal order of events, dynamics and how social entities change and evolve over time. A process study seeks to explain 'how a sequence of events leads to some outcome' [11: 148]. The study can be seen as a study that opens the process to explain what is inside—to explain how the interior operates. In the above exemplars:

- Exemplar 3, mixed-method part 2 (ICT implementation in a developing country [5], cf. Sect. 3.3): From the variance study in part 1 it is already clear that the implementation process was unsuccessful. The continuation study, part 2, opens the black box to look inside the process. The variance study could not answer why the implementation process was not successful, but the process study can. The qualitative interviews reveal several important reasons behind the failure, e.g. Western isomorphism and parallel manual system. Time was important in explaining how and why the role of such institutional factors changed over time from the early chartering phase to the late shakedown phase—or why they did not change. In this way, the variance study and the process study complement each other well.
- Exemplar 4 (Organisational influence processes [6], cf. Sect. 3.4): The implementation process was studied through identifying events and how influence processes were designed and enacted. The study showed how organisational actors used different tactics to create results (events) and that in turn, led them to further actions and uses of tactics. There was a whole network of actors, events, uses of tactics, which led to the outcome. The events and actions played out over time, and most actions were enacted over a period of time before an effect could be seen.
- Exemplar 5 (Values of online communities [9], cf. Sect. 3.5): The study shows how values of online communities got created through strategies that shift over time. The strategies that were applied in the beginning were later not abandoned but focus moved to new strategies as the process progressed. We get to see all the moving parts within the process and time is part of progressing from one set of strategies to the next.

Again, the temporal aspects play a crucial role in these process studies. The temporal aspects come about in a different way than in the variance studies. In the process studies, time is part of actions, of dynamics, of sequences of events and time becomes part of not only explaining how events happen, but also part of why events happen.

It is also clear from Van de Ven that we should evaluate variance studies on their own merits, and we should assess process studies on their own merits. It is common in variance studies that all parts of the research design are complete before the data collection starts. The opposite is usually the case in process studies where there is often willingness to let the data influence the choice of theories and models, which in turn are part of how the data get interpreted. Table 4 summarises the above exemplars in terms of critical features of variance studies and process studies.

Table 4 Variance and process studies compared

	Variance study	Process study
General features [11]	Fixed entities Attributes have single meaning over time Causality as explanation Generality by statistics	Entities, attributes and events change over time Generality depends on the versatility Time ordering of events is critical
Longitudinal exemplars	Exemplar 1: Same measure at T_1 and T_2 Exemplar 2: Habituation measured consistently over time (first 5 days, then 15 days) Exemplar 3.1: Same measure repeated three time with one year in between	Exemplar 3.2: Attributes (institutional factors) emerges over time Exemplar 4: Events and actions (influence tactics) change over time, and their time ordering was key to the analysis Exemplar 5: Four distinct phases of strategising are explained by attributes and event changing over time

5 Implications

Based on longitudinal studies in the discipline of information systems, a few implications may be in place:

1. There is a fork-decision between longitudinal variance studies and longitudinal process studies depending on whether the research question is a What? or a How? The decision has implications for the research design, conduct and evaluation.
2. The reasons for conducting a longitudinal study and not a static study should be clear from the research. If a variance study has multiple data collection points that should be reflected in the applied theory, research model and hypotheses. Why is it not a static experiment? What is it that can change over time? If a process study extends over time, there should be a process- or change-oriented theory related to the explaining of phenomena. Why is it not a case study, a snapshot of a contemporary phenomenon? What are the underlying assumptions about change, process, events, actors, agency, etc.?
3. Data collection and analysis is the key to reflect the longitudinal structure of the research. Time should be considered in the data collection, and time is itself part of the data. The data analysis includes a time perspective and can be performed using concepts of time, events, changing attributes, etc.
4. The contribution to research is a model or theory (enhanced or novel) where time and change (of variables or events) are intrinsically relating the parts. That is, if time and change are removed from the model or theory, it falls apart.

These implications are to a large degree transferable to human–computer interaction research. The same distinction exists between variance and process studies though they are often packaged in different ways, and usually not called variance studies. Variance studies are often designed as laboratory experiments, field experiments or a surveys, cf., e.g. [12]. Process studies are often designed as case studies, ethnographic studies, cf. [12] and design and research in the wild [13].

Longitudinal research into human–computer interaction comes in many shades and forms [14], and not always with full explanations of how and why the research is longitudinal. From information systems research, we may learn as suggested here that we may benefit from explicating the reasons for why a study is deemed longitudinal rather than static, and the longitudinal nature of a study should be reflected in the applied theories. The suggestion is that there should be a primary concern for what is it that changes as time goes by. This extends well into how data will be collected and analysed, and how the research contribution gets explained.

6 Conclusion

In this chapter, we have seen an overview of longitudinal studies in information systems research. We have opened five exemplary articles to learn from these and to observe some of the significant differences. This led to more detailed explanation of the differences of how longitudinal research gets design as variance studies an as process studies. In turn, four implications were elicited, and it is suggested that these are relevant for human–computer interaction research.

There are differences between information systems research and human–computer interaction research, yet much can be learned and transferred in terms of how research gets designed and conducted. The differences are by large due to differences in applied theories.

References

1. Avgerou C (2000) Information systems: what sort of science is it? Omega 28:567–579. https://doi.org/10.1016/S0305-0483(99)00072-9
2. Paré G, Trudel MC, Jaana M, Kitsiou S (2015) Synthesizing information systems knowledge: a typology of literature reviews. Inf Manag 52:183–199. https://doi.org/10.1016/j.im.2014.08.008
3. Ma X, Khansa L, Kim SS (2018) Active community participation and crowdworking turnover: a longitudinal model and empirical test of three mechanisms. J Manag Inf Syst 35:1154–1187. https://doi.org/10.1080/07421222.2018.1523587
4. Vance A, Jenkins JL, Anderson BB, Bjornn DK, Kirwan CB (2018) Tuning out security warnings: a longitudinal examination of habituation through fMRI, eye tracking, and field experiments. MIS Q Manag Inf Syst 42:355–380. https://doi.org/10.25300/MISQ/2018/14124
5. Venkatesh V, Bala H, Sambamurthy V (2016) Implementation of an information and communication technology in a developing country: a multimethod longitudinal study in a bank in India. Inf Syst Res 27:558–579. https://doi.org/10.1287/isre.2016.0638
6. Ngwenyama O, Nielsen PA (2014) Using organizational influence processes to overcome IS implementation barriers: lessons from a longitudinal case study of SPI implementation. Eur J Inf Syst 23:205–222. https://doi.org/10.1057/ejis.2012.56

7. Pettigrew AM (1990) Longitudinal field research on change: theory and practice. Organ Sci 1:267–292. https://doi.org/10.1287/orsc.1.3.267
8. Pettigrew AM (1997) What is a processual analysis? Scand J Manag 13:337–348. https://doi.org/10.1016/S0956-5221(97)00020-1
9. Barrett M, Oborn E, Orlikowski WJ (2016) Creating value in online communities: the sociomaterial configuring of strategy, platform, and stakeholder engagement. Inf Syst Res 27:704–723
10. Langley A (1999) Strategies for theorizing from process data. Acad Manag Rev 24:691–710
11. Van de Ven AH (2007) Engaged scholarship: a guide for organizational and social research. Oxford University Press, Oxford
12. Lazar J, Feng JH, Hochheiser H (2017) Research methods in human-computer interaction, 2nd edn. Morgan Kaufmann, Cambridge, MA
13. Rogers Y, Marshall P (2017) Research in the wild. Synth Lect Human-Centered Inform https://doi.org/10.2200/s00764ed1v01y201703hci037
14. Kjærup M, Skov MB, Nielsen PA, Kjeldskov J, Gerken J, Reiterer H (2021) Longitudinal Studies in HCI research: a review of CHI publications from 1982–2019. In: Karapanos E, Gerken J, Kjeldskov J, Skov MB (eds) Advances in longitudinal HCI research. Springer

Methods for Longitudinal HCI Research

Recommendations for Conducting Longitudinal Experience Sampling Studies

Niels van Berkel and Vassilis Kostakos

Abstract The Experience Sampling Method is used to collect participant self-reports over extended observation periods. These self-reports offer a rich insight into the individual lives of study participants by intermittently asking participants a set of questions. However, the longitudinal and repetitive nature of this sampling approach introduces a variety of concerns regarding the data contributed by participants. A decrease in participant interest and motivation may negatively affect study adherence, as well as potentially affecting the reliability of participant data. In this chapter, we reflect on a number of studies that aim to understand better participant performance with Experience Sampling. We discuss the main issues relating to participant data for longitudinal studies and provide hands-on recommendations for researchers to remedy these concerns in their own studies.

Keywords Experience sampling method · Ecological momentary assessment · ESM · EMA · Self-report · Data quality · Reliability

1 Introduction

Responding to an increased interest in studying human life more systematically than traditional surveys—and in a more realistic and longitudinal setting than possible through observations—Larson and Csikszentmihalyi introduced the Experience Sampling Method in 1983 [1]. Researchers using the Experience Sampling Method (ESM) ask their participants to intermittently complete a short questionnaire assessing their current state, context, or experience over an extended period of time (typically a couple of weeks). Questionnaires are typically designed to ensure that participants focus on their current experience rather than to reflect over a longer

N. van Berkel (✉)
Aalborg University, Aalborg, Denmark
e-mail: nielsvanberkel@cs.aau.dk

V. Kostakos
The University of Melbourne, Melbourne, Australia
e-mail: vassilis.kostakos@unimelb.edu.au

© Springer Nature Switzerland AG 2021
E. Karapanos et al. (eds.), *Advances in Longitudinal HCI Research*,
Human–Computer Interaction Series, https://doi.org/10.1007/978-3-030-67322-2_4

period of time, thus minimising the effects of participants' (in)ability to accurately recollect past events [2].

Early ESM studies focused on capturing the daily activities and corresponding experiences of study participants [3]. In those studies, participants were asked to answer what they were currently doing repeatedly. Collecting self-reports at random slots throughout the day, as opposed to a one-off survey or interview, ensured that responses are collected during the participant's *"interaction with the material and social environment"* [3]. In other words, the idea to collect self-report data in situ and thereby increase the ecological validity of a study was motivated by a desire to increase the reliability of participant responses.

A recent survey indicated an increased adoption of the Experience Sampling Method, with a focus on (personal) mobile devices [4]. The use of mobile devices as opposed to paper-based questionnaires provides a number of advances in terms of control over participant entries (e.g. prevent 'parking lot compliance' [5]), interactive design opportunities [6, 7], and contextual sensing possibilities [8–10]. We discuss how these opportunities provided by mobile devices can be utilised in the assessment, improvement, and analysis of the reliability of participant data in longitudinal experience sampling studies.

1.1 Longitudinal Experience Sampling

The timescale of ESM studies varies significantly, with a recent literature review (analysing 461 papers) reporting studies ranging between 1 and 365 days [4]. The median duration of an ESM study was found to be 14 days, while a majority of 70.9% of studies reported a duration of less than one month [4]. The one-day studies in the sample are mostly trials to investigate the (technological) feasibility of a given study configuration (e.g. Westerink et al. [11]). The longest study, totalling a year, investigated long term patterns in location sharing among a large sample of Foursquare users [12]. The typical range of ESM studies is in the duration of weeks rather than months as researchers aim to find a *"balance between study duration and intervention frequency"* [13].

Longitudinal experience sampling is relatively short-term when compared to cross-sectional repeated surveys (also called periodic surveys or simply a survey using a longitudinal design), typically covering months or years [14]. These survey-type designs are often used to investigate changes in attitudes or behaviours over extended periods of time [14], for example in consumer research [15] or within professional organisations [16]. In addition to their usual shorter duration, there are a number of other key differences between repeated surveys and longitudinal experience sampling: the frequency of the questionnaires, the reflective nature of surveys vs. the in-the-moment perspective of ESM questionnaires, and the fact that ESM questionnaires are collected 'in the wild' aiming to cover a variety of contexts. The ESM shares many of the same challenges encountered in other methodologies employing human sensing [10, 17], such as citizen science or situated crowdsourcing.

1.2 Challenges

The sustained effort required of participants over an extended period of time introduces a number of challenges. First, the motivation of participants is likely to decrease over time as initial interest drops. Techniques to maintain a base level of motivation, whether through intrinsic or extrinsic motivation, are therefore key in enabling successful longitudinal use of the ESM. Participant motivation, or lack thereof, plays a key role in relation to data quality and quantity, the two remaining challenges. Second, adherence to study protocol—typically quantified as the number of questionnaires that have been answered—has been shown to decline over time due to study fatigue [18]. Another concern is the variance in the number of responses between participants, which could skew the analysis of ESM results—a critical type of bias introduced by such variance is 'selective non-responses', in which the responses of specific groups of the study's sample are over- or under-represented [19]. An analysis of four recent ESM studies reveals significant differences across participants in terms of their response rate [20]. Third, ensuring a sufficient level of response reliability is key in collecting participant responses, and critical in generating sound study inferences. Novel sampling techniques and filtering mechanisms can support the increase in reliability of participant responses.

Here, we discuss these three challenges in detail and provide concrete recommendations for researchers to address these challenges in their own studies (Sects. 2, 3, and 4). Following this, we discuss analysis techniques specific to the analysis of longitudinal response data (Sect. 5) as well a number of concrete guidelines for the design and subsequent reporting of ESM studies through a 'checklist for researchers' (Sect. 6). Finally, we present a number of future trends in the area of longitudinal experience sampling studies (Sect. 7) and conclude this chapter (Sect. 8).

2 Participant Motivation

Larson and Csikszentmihalyi classify the *"dependence on respondents' self-reports"* as the major limitation of the ESM, while simultaneously highlighting examples that show how these self-reports are *"a very useful source of data"* [2]. Regardless of whether we consider the quantity or quality of participant responses, participant motivation is key in ensuring a successful study outcome. Given the longitudinal and oftentimes burdensome nature of ESM studies, a number of research streams have explored how to increase and maintain participant motivation over time and its subsequent effects on participant responses. Here, we distinguish between intrinsic and extrinsic means of motivation.

2.1 Intrinsic Motivation

Intrinsic motivation has simply been defined as "*doing something for its own sake*" [21] rather than expecting a direct or indirect compensation. It is, however, incorrect to state that researchers can therefore not (positively) influence a participant's intrinsic motivation. As already stated by Larson and Csikszentmihalyi in their original publication on the Experience Sampling Method: "*Most participants find that the procedure is rewarding in some way, and most are willing to share their experience. However, cooperation depends on their trust and on their belief that the research is worthwhile*" [1]. Here, Larson and Csikszentmihalyi refer to what they later classify as 'establishing a research alliance'. This research alliance aims to establish a vested interest of the participant in the study and the research outcome.

However, identifying *how* to give concrete form to such a research alliance remains under-explored in the current ESM literature. Related methodologies such as citizen science face similar challenges and have investigated how to build and sustain engagement among participants. These results show that interest and curiosity, perceived self-competence, and enjoyment in the task all contribute to an individual's intrinsic motivation [22, 23]. Furthermore, Measham and Barnett found that fulfilling a participant's initial motivation for participation increases the duration of a participant's engagement [24]. Although direct empirical evaluations of these factors are scarce for the ESM, given the methodological overlap we can hypothesise that these factors have a similar positive effect on participation motivation in ESM studies. We note that the potential side effects of increasing participants' motivation have not yet been sufficiently explored, and could potentially influence study results.

Recommendation 1 Provide rich feedback regarding the study goals and the participants' contribution to those goals. Provide information throughout the study period.

Recommendation 2 Target participant recruitment to communities with a vested interest in the study outcomes.

2.2 Extrinsic Motivation

Extrinsic motivation, which Reiss defines as "*the pursuit of an instrumental goal*" [21], consists of various methods of motivation, including (financial) rewards or a competition between participants. Although earlier work in Psychology stated that extrinsic motivators would undermine an individual's intrinsic motivation (cf. the self-determination theory [25]), recent work largely refutes this claim [21].

A (financial) compensation of participants is common for ESM studies, with a fixed compensation at the end of the study period being the most widely used (45.7%) [4]. The effect of different financial compensation structures on participant motivation has not been extensively explored, in part due to incomplete reporting of study details [4]. These initial reports do highlight, however, that the use of micro-compensations (a small payment for each completed response) motivates participants in responding to ESM questionnaires. Although already applied by Consolvo and Walker in 2003 [26], this compensation structure has not been widely adopted in the HCI literature [4]. Mushtag et al. compare three different micro-compensation structures but do not contrast their results with, e.g. a fixed compensation [27]. Although the use of micro-compensation warrants further investigation, we note that this compensation structure may not be applicable to all studies due to potential negative effects on the study's ecological validity. As highlighted by Mushtag et al., participant reactivity to micro-compensation may confound self-reports in studies focusing on participant affect. Stone et al. warn of using excessive financial incentives, which could attract participants solely interested in the monetary reward rather than participating in the study [28].

Recommendation 3 Avoid excessive financial compensation and consider the use of micro-compensation when applicable.

The literature on the ESM has also explored a number of extrinsic motivation techniques besides financial compensation, with promising results. Hsieh et al. show that providing participants with visual information on their provided self-reports increased participant adherence by 23% over a 25 day period (study with desktop users) [6]. The visual feedback provided by Hsieh et al. allowed participants to explore their prior answers on questions related to interruption or mood. The authors state that such visualisations *"makes the information personally relevant and increases the value of the study to participants"* [6]. Van Berkel et al. studied the effect of gamification (e.g. points, leaderboard) on participant responses in a between-subject study. Their results show that participants in the gamified condition significantly increased both their response quality (quantified through crowd-evaluation) and their number of provided responses as compared to the participants in the non-gamified condition [7].

Recommendation 4 Include interactive feedback mechanisms in the study protocol to keep participants engaged and motivated.

3 Study Adherence

Participant adherence to protocol, i.e. the degree to which the questionnaire notifications are opened and answered, is critical in ensuring an informative study outcome. In Experience Sampling, study adherence is typically quantified as 'response rate' or 'compliance rate', defined as the *"number of fully completed questionnaires divided by the number of presented questionnaires"* [4]. Unsurprisingly, studies typically report a decrease in study adherence over time, see for example [29–31]. As researchers can expect a decrease in participant adherence over time, it is key to consider the trade-offs when designing a longitudinal study. Balancing the number of daily questionnaires, number of questionnaire items, questionnaire scheduling, and duration of the study, as well as other factors such as participant compensation and availability, in accordance with the research question is key. A number of studies have aimed to systematically study the effect of these variables, see, e.g., a recent study by Eisele et al. on the effect of notification frequency and questionnaire length on participant responses [32], or Van Berkel et al.'s investigation on the effect of notification schedules [31]. We argue that any researcher should consider these study parameters in relation to their research question and population sample. As such, there is not one study configuration that would be applicable to every study. Below, we outline some of the decisions that can motivate the balancing of these variables.

3.1 Questionnaire Scheduling

The literature describes three global techniques for questionnaire scheduling: signal contingent, interval contingent, and event contingent [33]. In a signal contingent schedule configuration, notification arrival is randomised over the course of a given timespan. In an interval contingent configuration, notification schedules follow a predefined interval, for example every other hour between 08:00 and 17:00. For event contingent configurations a predefined event is determined which triggers the notification (typically as recognised by the questionnaire system, but can also refer to a 'detection' by the participant) [4, 33–35]. The use of an event-based notification system enables more advanced study designs, and allows researchers to optimise the moment of data collection to contexts which are most relevant.

In a direct comparison between the three aforementioned scheduling techniques, results indicate that an interval-informed event contingent schedule, in which questionnaire notifications are presented upon smartphone unlock with a maximum number per given timespan, result in fewer total notifications sent but a higher overall number of completed responses as compared to a signal or interval contingent schedule [31]. Kapoor & Horvitz use contextual information to predict participant availability and find that using such a predictive model outperforms randomised scheduling in terms of identifying the availability of participants [36]. Church et al. recommend researchers to adjust the questionnaire schedule to match the participant's schedule [26]. Rather than imposing an identical start and end time on all participants, this approach would allow for custom start and end times, e.g. in the case of nightshift workers. Other work has explored more active-based scheduling techniques, where the presentation questionnaires are determined based on the participant's current contextual information. For example, Rosenthal et al. calculate individualised participant interruptibility costs [37], Mehrotra et al. expand on this through the notion of interruptibility prediction models [38], and Van Berkel et al. show that contextual information such as phone usage can be used to schedule questionnaires at opportune moments [39].

Regardless of the chosen scheduling approach, the timing of questionnaires can have a significant impact on participants' ability to respond to a questionnaire and therefore the respective data being collected. The aforementioned scheduling techniques all have their own strengths and weaknesses. Signal contingent scheduling (i.e. randomised) can be used to capture participants spontaneous (psychological) states but can be skewed towards commonly occurring events. An interval contingent configuration is useful to capture events which are expected to occur regularly and provides a consistent sampling strategy which allows for the modelling of time as a factor in relation to the answers provided by the participant. Due to the regular schedule with which notifications are presented, it increases the risk of (over)sampling the same event (e.g. start of a lecture). Finally, event contingent configurations are useful for capturing isolated or infrequently occurring events that can be detected either through sensor data or manually by the participant. Event-based schedules can result in an incomplete view of the participant's life if the event of interest only occurs in a limit variety of contexts [40].

Recommendation 5 Carefully consider the effect of the chosen questionnaire scheduling approach on the selection of participant responses.

3.2 Study Duration

The literature on ESM study design has recommended roughly similar maximum durations for ESM studies, e.g. a minimum duration of one week [1], two weeks [39], and two–four weeks [28]. Determining an appropriate study duration is a careful consideration that involves a variety of factors such as the frequency with which the phenomenon of interest occurs, the required effort to complete the questionnaire, and expected levels of motivation among the participant sample.

Researchers interested in longitudinal studies of extensive duration, e.g. months or years, will find that participants are likely unable or unwilling to repeatedly answer a set of questionnaires for the duration of the study. Given the extensive participant burden in ESM studies, we advise against the collection of self-reports across the entire duration of studies of this duration. Instead, researchers should consider the collection of manual responses for a (number of) period(s) within the duration of the entire longitudinal study—embedding the ESM within a larger study design. As such, researchers can combine the insights obtained through frequent ESM questionnaires with the information gained from repeated data collection over an extensive period of time. This approach, which has been called as 'wave-based' experience sampling, has been successfully employed in emotion research in a decade-long study consisting of three one-week sampling periods investigating the effect of age on emotion [41]. Similarly, already in 1983 Savin-Williams & Demo ran a one-week ESM study with a cohort of participants enrolled in a six-year longitudinal study [42].

The use of modern mobile devices allows researchers to passively collect an extensive amount of sensor data from study participants [9]. This data is collected unobtrusively and without additional burden to the participant, and can provide additional insights to the researcher. The unobtrusive nature of this data collection stands in stark contrast to the continuous effort required from participants in human contributions and can provide a continuous long-term data stream simply not feasible with manual data collection. As such, we recommend that researchers interested in extensive longitudinal studies combine both continuous passive sensing with intermittent periods of extensive questionnaire collection. Recent development work shows the possibility of changing ESM questionnaire schedules throughout the study period [43], enabling the possibility of intermittent periods of questionnaires.

From a participant perspective, being enrolled in a longitudinal study makes it easy to forget that sensor data is being collected. We stress that, given the potential sensitive nature of the unobtrusively (naturally following participant's informed consent) collected sensor data, researchers should aim to remind participants of any ongoing data collection. A practical approach for this in the context of smartphone-based studies is the continuous display of an icon in the smartphone's notification bar, reminding participants of their enrolment in the study and the active data collection [18]. Researchers have also allowed participants to temporarily halt data collection, see, e.g., Lathia et al. in which participants can (indefinitely) press a button to pause data collection for 30 min [40].

Recommendation 6 Combine longitudinal passive sensing with focused periods of ESM questionnaires to obtain both long-term and in-depth insights.

4 Response Reliability

A core idea behind the introduction of the ESM was to increase the reliability of self-report data by reducing the time between an event of interest and the moment when a participant provides data on this event, thus reducing reliance on a participant's ability to recall past events [1]. Although this approach has been widely embraced in a number of disciplines, recent work points out that the quality of participant data in ESM studies cannot be expected to be consistently of high reliability [18]. This is an important concern for longitudinal studies, as response quality reliability typically degrades over time. As such, recent work in the HCI community has explored techniques to infer and improve the reliability of participant responses. Here, we discuss the use of the crowd, quality-informed scheduling techniques, and the application of additional validation questions to infer response quality.

4.1 Use of the Crowd

Although the ESM traditionally collects data on observations or experiences as captured by participants individually, recent work has drawn out creative ways of combining the contributions of multiple individuals to increase the reliability of the collected data.

One strain of work has explored the use of 'peers' to obtain multiple datapoints on one individual. Using this approach, which has been labelled as 'Peer-MA' [44], a selected number of the participant's peers report what they believe to be the participant's current state with regard to the concept of interest. As described by Berrocal & Wac, this approach *"has the potential to enrich the self-assessment datasets with peers as pervasive data providers, whose observations could help researchers identify and manage data accuracy issues in human studies"* [44]. Chang et al. show how the use of peer-based data collection can also increase the quantity of the data collected [45]. By recruiting a sufficiently large (and motivated) network of participant peers, researchers may be able to distribute the burden of questionnaire notifications and thereby sustain data input for a more extensive period of time—increasing the prospective of longitudinal ESM studies. A critical open question with regard to this novel approach is the assessment and interpretation of the contributions of peers and the potential biases introduced through, e.g., different peer-relationships and the (absence of) peer physical presence.

In contrast to the aforementioned perspective in which the crowd contributions are focused on individuals, others have applied the crowd to increase the reliability of observations. For example, the aforementioned work by Van Berkel et al. not only asked participants to contribute a label regarding a given place, but also asked participants to judge the relevance of the contributions of others [7]. Based on these relevance labels, the quality of participant contributions can be quantified. Another example is the work by Solymosi et al., in which participants generated a map indicating a crowd's 'fear of crime' through repeated and localised experience sampling data collection [46]. A main advantage of this approach, in which the quality assessment is done by participants, is that the quality of contributions can be assessed without the need for a priori ground truth on the presented data. From a longitudinal study perspective, integrating crowd assessment into the study design may enable the study population to rotate, i.e. for participants to drop out and new participants to join, as study fatigue emerges.

Recommendation 7 Consider whether participant data can be validated or augment through the use of the crowd.

4.2 Quality-Informed Scheduling

Literature on questionnaire scheduling has primarily focused on participant availability following from a motivation to increase participant compliance. However, as pointed out by Mehrotra et al., an ill-timed questionnaire might lead participants to respond to a questionnaire without paying much attention, reducing the overall reliability of respondents' data [38]. In addition to increasing the quantity of responses, researchers have therefore also explored how the scheduling of questionnaires can affect the quality of participant responses. In the study by Van Berkel et al., participants completed a range of questions (working memory, recall, and arithmetic) while contextual data was being passively collected [39]. Their results show that participants were more accurate when they were not using their phone the moment a questionnaire arrived. Optimising the quality of responses by not collecting data when participants are actively using their phone may, however, negatively effect the quantity of answered questionnaires. Previous work shows participants are more likely to *respond* to questionnaires (i.e. focused on response quantity) when questionnaires are presented upon phone unlock (as compared to randomised or interval-based schedules) [31].

Recommendation 8 Introduce intelligent scheduling techniques to avoid interrupting participants when they do not have time to respond.

4.3 Validation Questions

Here, we discern two types of validation questions: explicitly verifiable questions (also known as ground truth questions) and reflective questions.

In order to assess the reliability and effort of online study participants, work on crowdsourcing has recommended the use of 'explicitly verifiable questions', also known as 'golden questions' [47]. These explicitly verifiable questions are often—but not always—quantitative in nature, relatively easy to answer, and the responses can be automatically assessed to be correct or incorrect. For example, Oleson et al. asked crowdworkers to verify whether a given URL matched with a given local business listing [48]. Kittur et al. describe two main benefits of using these questions. First, explicitly verifiable questions allow researchers to easily identify and subsequently exclude from data analysis those participants who do not provide serious input. Second, by including these questions participants are aware of the fact that their answers will be scrutinised, which Kittur et al. hypothesise may "*play a role in both reducing invalid responses and increasing time-on-task*" [47].

Although widely used in crowdsourcing, the uptake of explicitly verifiable questions in ESM studies is thus far limited. A challenging aspect for the uptake of explicitly verifiable questions in longitudinal ESM studies is the need to provide participants with varying question content. This would require the creation of a question database, use of an existing and labelled dataset, or automated generation of verifiable questions (see, e.g., Oleson et al. [48]). An earlier ESM study with 25 participants included a simple, and randomly generated, arithmetic task as means of verification [39]. In this task, participants were asked to add two numbers together, both numbers were randomly generated between 10 and 99 for each self-report questionnaire. Results showed a remarkably high accuracy of 96.6%, which could be indicative of differences in motivation and effort between online crowdsourcing markets and the participant population often encountered in ESM studies. However, whether the motivation of the respective study population indeed differs between online crowdsourcing and ESM studies requires further investigation across multiple studies as well as evaluation across a wider variety of explicitly verifiable questions.

Another approach which has seen recent uptake is the creation of verifiable questions based on participant sensor data [39]. This includes, for example, passive data collection on the participants' smartphone usage and subsequently asking participants to answer questions on, e.g., the duration of their phone use. The answer to this question is verifiable, is variable (changes throughout the day), and often challenging to answer correctly. Assessing the correctness of participant answers does, however, also raise questions. In particular, answer correctness should not be quantified as a binary state as it is unlikely that answers are completely correct.

Recent work has also explored the use of 'reflective questions' in increasing the reliability of participant contributions. In this approach, participants reflect on earlier events while supported by earlier data points—either collected actively by the participant or passively through, e.g., smartphone sensors. Rabbi et al. introduce 'ReVibe', introducing assisted recall by showing participants an overview of their location, activity, and ambience during the past day [49]. Their results show a 5.6% increase in the participants' recall accuracy. Intille et al. propose an image-based approach, in which participants take a photo or short video and use this material to reflect on past experiences [50]. This concept was further explored by Yue et al., who note that the images taken by participants can also provide additional information and insights to researchers [51].

Recommendation 9 Consider including additional questions (verifiable, ground truth, or reflective) to increase the reliability of participant answers.

5 Analysing Longitudinal ESM Data

Longitudinal research faces a unique set of challenges in the analysis of participant data not typically encountered in short-term or lab-based studies. The longitudinal nature of a study can alter a participant's perception or understanding of the variables of interest, and may result in an increasing inequality of the number of responses between participants and different contexts. Here, we discuss these three challenges—respectively known as response shift, compliance bias, and contextual bias—as faced in the analysis of longitudinal ESM studies.

5.1 Response Shift

Response shift can either refer to an individual's change in meaning of a given construct due to re-calibration (a change in internal standards), re-prioritisation (change in values or priorities), or re-conceptualisation (change in the definition) [52, 53]. As studies often focus on the same construct(s) for the entire study period, participants may experience a shift in their assessment of this construct. As an example by Ring et al. illustrates: *"a patient rates her pre-treatment level of pain as 7 on a*

10-point pain scale. She subsequently rates her post-treatment level of pain as 3.
This is taken to indicate that the treatment has caused an improvement of 4 points.
However, if she retrospectively rates her pre-treatment pain as having been a 5, the
actual treatment effect is 2. Likewise, if she retrospectively rates her pre-treatment
pain as having been 10, the actual treatment effect is 7." [54]. Similar to a change in
a participant's internal standards of a given construct, a participant may also evaluate
various constructs as carrying higher or lower importance as compared to the onset
of the study. By asking participants to rate the relative importance of individual constructs prior and following the study, the degree of re-prioritisation can be assessed.
Finally, re-conceptualisation can occur when participants re-evaluate the meaning
of a concept in relation to their personal circumstances. For example, a patient may
re-conceptualise their quality of life, either following their recovery or by adjusting
their perspective when confronted with a chronic disease.

A commonly used technique to identify the occurrence of response shift among
participants is the 'thentest', also known as the 'retrospective pretest-posttest design'.
At the end of the study, participants complete a posttest questionnaire immediately
followed-up with a retrospective questionnaire asking participants to think back to
their perception of a construct at the start of the study. By collecting these data points
at almost the same time, participants share the same internal standards during questionnaire completion. Therefore, the mean change between these two questionnaires
gives insight into the effect of time or treatment. For more details on the thentest, we
refer to Schwartz & Sprangers's guidelines [55].

Recommendation 10 Include a thentest in the design of your study when participant
perception of a given construct may change over the duration of the study.

5.2 Compliance Bias

Inevitable differences between participants' availability and motivation will result
in a difference in the number of collected responses between participants. As such,
the experience of response participants can skew the overall study results, a phenomenon known as compliance bias [20]. Participants with a higher than average
response rate may have a more vested interest in responding to notifications, for
example as they are personally affected by the phenomenon being investigated. Similarly, participants with a high or low response rate may have different psychological
characteristics or simply different smartphone usage behaviours. It is not unlikely
that these factors are a confounding factor in relation to the phenomenon being
studied—capturing responses primarily from a subset of the study population may
therefore decrease the reliability of the results. Although not widely reported, recent
work that re-analysed four independent ESM studies finds substantial differences
between study participants in the number of responses collected [20]. Researchers
can reduce compliance bias by balancing data quantity between participants during
the study through intelligent scheduling techniques—i.e. increasing the likelihood

that questionnaires will be answered by targeting notifications to arrive at a time and context suitable to the participant. Although this requires considerable infrastructure implementation and researcher ought to be careful not to introduce other biases, reducing compliance bias can increase the usefulness and reliability of a collected dataset.

Recommendation 11 Use intelligence scheduling techniques to improve response rates among low-respondents to balance response quantity between participants.

Recommendation 12 Analyse and report the differences between the number of participant responses post-data collection.

5.3 Contextual Bias

The schedule through which questionnaires are presented to participants, i.e. the chosen sampling technique, can significantly bias the responses of participants towards a limited number of contexts over time. As stated by Lathia et al., "*[...] time-based triggers will skew data collection towards those contexts that occur more frequently, while sensor-based triggers [...] generate a different view of behaviour than more a complete sampling would provide*" [40]. These concerns are amplified for longitudinal studies, in which researchers typically aim to cover a wide variety of contexts and identify longitudinal trends. If participants, however, only provide self-reports at contexts most convenient to them (e.g. by dismissing questionnaires arriving in the early morning or while at work), resulting data can be heavily skewed towards a limited number of contexts and therefore diminish the value of longitudinal data collection. The risk of contextual bias can be reduced by taking into account the context of completed self-reports in the scheduling of questionnaires. By considering to context in which individual participants have already answered questionnaires, researchers can diversity the context of collected responses.

Recommendation 13 Diversify the context of collected responses by scheduling questionnaires in contexts underrepresented in the existing responses of a participant.

6 Researcher Checklist

In order to increase a study's replicability and allow for a correct interpretation of presented results, it is critical that researchers report both the methodological choices and the outcomes of a presented study in detail. Current practice does not align with these standards, with prior work indicating that the majority of studies do not report on, e.g., the compensation of participants [4]. As compensation can affect participant motivation and compliance [28], it is important to report such metrics.

Building on previous work [4, 26, 56], we present a list of study design and result decisions which should be considered by researchers. We hope that this 'checklist' proves a useful starting point for researchers designing their ESM studies, as well as an overview of the variables we consider key in the reporting of the results of ESM studies.

Study design

1. Consider the target participant population and their potential interest in participation.
2. Determine the duration of the study, taking into account the study fatigue of prospective participants. Extensive longitudinal studies can combine longitudinal passive sensing with focused periods of self-report data collection.
3. Determine the most suitable questionnaire schedule in light of the respective trade-offs and benefits of scheduling techniques [31, 40].
4. Determine the length and frequency of questionnaire items, aiming for a short completion time of the questionnaire [18, 26].
5. Determine the timeout time for individual questionnaires, especially when sampling participant responses following a predetermined event as to reduce participant recall time.
6. Consider whether it is valuable to assess response shift in participant responses and consider including a thentest in the study design.
7. Consider the use of verifiable, ground truth, or reflective questionnaires to assess the quality of participant responses.
8. Consider whether it is important to achieve a balanced number of responses between participants. If desired, implement intelligent scheduling techniques to increase response rates among low-respondents.
9. Assess how participants can be best motivated to enrol and maintain compliance throughout the study period.
10. Assess the possibility of using the crowd to either assess or compare the contributions of participants.

Study results

1. Report both the number of participants who completed and dropped out of the study.
2. Report the (average) duration of participant enrolment.
3. Report the number of completed, dismissed, and timed-out responses.
4. Report the overall response rate.
5. Analyse and report the difference in response rate between participants [20].
6. Analyse and report any significant differences in the context of completed responses (e.g. time or location of completion) [40].
7. If relevant, analyse and report on the (differences in the) accuracy of participants on ground truth questions.
8. If relevant, analyse and report on any changes in the participants' perception of the study's construct, e.g. with the help of the thentest [55].

6.1 Overview of Recommendations

Finally, we present an overview of the recommendations introduced in this chapter in Table 1. The included references offer additional information on the motivation, methods, and guidelines with regard to the respective recommendation.

Table 1 Overview of recommendations with references for further reading

No.	Recommendation	References
1	Provide rich feedback regarding the study goals and the participants' contribution to those goals. Provide information throughout the study period	[1, 24]
2	Target participant recruitment to communities with a vested interest in the study outcomes	[21, 23]
3	Avoid excessive financial compensation and consider the use of micro-compensation when applicable	[27, 28]
4	Include interactive feedback mechanisms in the study protocol to keep participants engaged and motivated	[6]
5	Carefully consider the effect of the chosen questionnaire scheduling approach on the selection of participant responses	[31, 39, 40]
6	Combine longitudinal passive sensing with focused periods of ESM questionnaires to obtain both long-term and in-depth insights	[41, 42]
7	Consider whether participant data can be validated or augment through the use of the crowd	[7, 44, 45]
8	Introduce intelligent scheduling techniques to avoid interrupting participants when they do not have time to respond	[36–39]
9	Consider including additional questions (verifiable, ground truth, or reflective) to increase the reliability of participant answers	[49–51]
10	Include a thentest in the design of your study when participant perception of a given construct may change over the duration of the study	[55]
11	Use intelligence scheduling techniques to improve response rates among low-respondents to balance response quantity between participants	[20]
12	Analyse and report the differences between the number of participant responses post-data collection	[20]
13	Diversify the context of collected responses by scheduling questionnaires in contexts underrepresented in the existing responses of a participant	[40]

7 Future Trends

Since the introduction of the Experience Sampling Method in the late 1970s [1], its main use has been in the application of intensive but relatively short-term data collection (i.e. weeks rather than months). In this foundational work, Larson & Csikszentmihalyi describe a typical ESM study to have a duration of one week. Technological and methodological developments have had, and continue to have, a significant impact on how the ESM is used by researchers throughout their projects. For example, the introduction and widespread usage of smartphones has enabled researchers to collect rich contextual information [8, 9]. Similarly, researchers have come up with novel scheduling techniques to increase the sampling possibilities offered through the ESM. Following the impact of these developments on how the ESM is applied, we expect future innovations to increase the ability for researchers to apply the ESM in a longitudinal setting.

From a technological perspective, recent work has pointed to the further integration of self-report devices in the participants' daily life. This includes (stationary) devices physically located in a participant's home or work location [57], integration of questionnaires in mobile applications already frequently used by participants (e.g. messaging applications [58]), or through the use of (tangible) wearables [59, 60]. Although the effect of these alternative questionnaire delivery techniques on (sustained) response rate and input accuracy still needs to be explored in more detail, these alternative input methods can reduce participant strain as compared to a smartphone-based approach (retrieving phone, unlocking, opening a specific application, locking away the phone). Future studies can also consider the collection of questionnaires across multiple platforms, such as the use of a stationary device at home and work, combined with a mobile device or application for on-the-go.

Methodologically, a number of under-explored avenues may prove useful in enabling longitudinal ESM studies. In Sect. 3.2, we refer to 'wave-based' experience sampling, in which participants actively contribute only for a number of (discontinuous) periods within a larger duration consisting of passive sensing. Although already explored in the early days of the ESM [42], this approach has thus far not been extensively applied. Furthermore, although prior work shows the positive effect of including extrinsic motivators [6, 7], the studies were limited to weeks. Further works is required to study the impact of these incentives in longitudinal settings. Finally, we note that an extensive amount of work has explored ways to infer participant availability and willingness to answer a questionnaire, both within the scope of ESM research [38, 61] as well as the broader research on attention and availability [36, 62–64]. Translating these findings into practical and shareable implementations which can be readily used by other researchers remains a formidable challenge. Addressing this, e.g., by releasing the source code of these implementations, allows for experimentation with advanced scheduling techniques while simultaneously enabling research groups to validate, compare, and extend these scheduling algorithms.

Numerous open questions regarding the use of the ESM beyond a couple of weeks (e.g. covering months of active data collection) remain. In this chapter, we outlined both practical suggestions which are applicable to researchers *today* when designing their studies, as well as offer a number of potential areas for future work in the domain of longitudinal self-report studies.

8 Conclusion

The Experience Sampling Method has enabled researchers to collect frequent and rich responses from study participants. Enabled by the wide uptake of mobile devices, researchers can deliver a highly interactive and increasingly intelligent research tool straight into the hands of participants. Our overview shows that the introduction of smaller and more connected mobile hardware alone is not sufficient in enabling a push towards truly longitudinal studies. In order to extend the viable duration of ESM studies, further development of methodological practices is required. Investigating the effect of novel hardware solutions and study design configurations, both in the lab and in situ, will require a focused effort from the research community.

References

1. Larson R, Csikszentmihalyi M (1983) The experience sampling method. New Directions Methodol Soc Behav Sci
2. Csikszentmihalyi M, Larson R (1987) Validity and reliability of the Experience-Sampling method. J Nerv Ment Dis 175:526–536
3. Csikszentmihalyi M, Larson R, Prescott S (1977) The ecology of adolescent activity and experience. J Youth Adolescence 6:281–294
4. van Berkel N, Ferreira D, Kostakos V (2017) The experience sampling method on mobile devices. ACM Comput Surv 50(6):93:1–93:40
5. Smyth JM, Stone AA (2003) Ecological momentary assessment research in behavioral medicine. J Happiness Stud 4:35–52
6. Hsieh G, Li I, Dey A, Forlizzi J, Hudson SE (2008) Using visualizations to increase compliance in experience sampling. In: Proceedings of the 10th international conference on ubiquitous computing, UbiComp '08, (New York, NY, USA). ACM, pp 164–167
7. van Berkel N, Goncalves J, Hosio S, Kostakos V (2017) Gamification of mobile experience sampling improves data quality and quantity. In: Proceedings of the ACM on interactive, mobile, wearable and ubiquitous technologies (IMWUT), vol 1, no 3, pp 107:1–107:21
8. Raento M, Oulasvirta A, Eagle N (2009) Smartphones: an emerging tool for social scientists. Sociol Methods Res 37(3):426–454
9. Ferreira D, Kostakos V, Schweizer I (2017) Human sensors on the move. Springer International Publishing, pp 9–19
10. van Berkel N, Goncalves J, Wac K, Hosio S, Cox AL (2020) Human accuracy in mobile data collection. Int J Hum-Comput Stud, p 102396
11. Westerink J, Ouwerkerk M, de Vries G, de Waele S, van den Eerenbeemd J, van Boven M (2009) Emotion measurement platform for daily life situations. In: 3rd international conference on affective computing and intelligent interaction and workshops, pp 1–6

12. Guha S, Wicker SB (2015) Spatial subterfuge: an experience sampling study to predict deceptive location disclosures. In: Proceedings of the 2015 ACM international joint conference on pervasive and ubiquitous computing, UbiComp '15, (New York, NY, USA). Association for Computing Machinery, pp 1131–1135
13. Heron KE, Smyth JM (2010) Ecological momentary interventions: incorporating mobile technology into psychosocial and health behaviour treatments. Brit J Health Psychol 15(1):1–39
14. Shaughnessy JJ, Zechmeister EB, Zechmeister JS (2011) Research methods in psychology. McGraw-Hill, New York
15. Armantier O, Topa G, Van der Klaauw W, Zafar B (2017) An overview of the survey of consumer expectations. Econ Policy Rev 23–2:51–72
16. Stein RE, Horwitz SM, Storfer-Isser A, Heneghan A, Olson L, Hoagwood KE (2008) Do pediatricians think they are responsible for identification and management of child mental health problems? Results of the AAP periodic survey. Ambulatory Pediatr 8(1):11–17
17. van Berkel N, Budde M, Wijenayake S, Goncalves J (2018) Improving accuracy in mobile human contributions: an overview. In: Adjunct proceedings of the ACM international joint conference on pervasive and ubiquitous computing, pp 594–599
18. van Berkel N (2019) Data quality and quantity in mobile experience sampling. Phd thesis, The University of Melbourne
19. Hektner JM, Schmidt JA, Csikszentmihalyi M (2007) Experience sampling method: measuring the quality of everyday life. Sage
20. van Berkel N, Goncalves J, Hosio S, Sarsenbayeva Z, Velloso E, Kostakos V (2020) Overcoming compliance bias in self-report studies: a cross-study analysis. Int J Hum-Comput Stud 134:1–12
21. Reiss S (2012) Intrinsic and extrinsic motivation. Teach Psychol 39(2):152–156
22. Eveleigh A, Jennett C, Blandford A, Brohan P, Cox AL (2014) Designing for dabblers and deterring drop-outs in citizen science. In: Proceedings of the SIGCHI conference on human factors in computing systems, CHI '14, (New York, NY, USA). ACM, pp 2985–2994
23. Rotman D, Preece J, Hammock J, Procita K, Hansen D, Parr C, Lewis D, Jacobs D (2012) Dynamic changes in motivation in collaborative citizen-science projects. In: Proceedings of the ACM 2012 conference on computer supported cooperative work, CSCW '12, (New York, NY, USA). ACM, pp 217–226
24. Measham TG, Barnett GB (2008) Environmental volunteering: motivations, modes and outcomes. Australian Geographer 39(4):537–552
25. Deci E, Ryan RM (1985) Intrinsic motivation and self-determination in human behavior. Springer, Berlin
26. Consolvo S, Walker M (2003) Using the experience sampling method to evaluate ubicomp applications. IEEE Pervas Comput 2:24–31
27. Musthag M, Raij A, Ganesan D, Kumar S, Shiffman S (2011) Exploring micro-incentive strategies for participant compensation in high-burden studies. In: Proceedings of the 13th international conference on ubiquitous computing, UbiComp '11, (New York, NY, USA). ACM, pp 435–444
28. Stone AA, Kessler RC, Haythomthwatte JA (1991) Measuring daily events and experiences: decisions for the researcher. J Personal 59(3):575–607
29. Shih F, Liccardi I, Weitzner D (2015) Privacy tipping points in smartphones privacy preferences. In: Proceedings of the 33rd annual ACM conference on human factors in computing systems, CHI '15, (New York, NY, USA). Association for Computing Machinery, pp 807–816
30. Tollmar K, Huang C (2015) Boosting mobile experience sampling with social media. In: Proceedings of the 17th international conference on human-computer interaction with mobile devices and services, MobileHCI '15, (New York, NY, USA). Association for Computing Machinery, pp 525–530
31. van Berkel N, Goncalves J, Lovén L, Ferreira D, Hosio S, Kostakos V (2019) Effect of experience sampling schedules on response rate and recall accuracy of objective self-reports. Int J Hum-Comput Stud 125:118–128
32. Eisele G, Vachon H, Lafit G, Kuppens P, Houben M, Myin-Germeys I, Viechtbauer W (2020) The effects of sampling frequency and questionnaire length on perceived burden, compliance, and careless responding in experience sampling data in a student population

33. Wheeler L, Reis HT (1991) Self-recording of everyday life events: origins, types, and uses. J Personal 59(3):339–354
34. Barrett LF, Barrett DJ (2001) An introduction to computerized experience sampling in psychology. Soc Sci Comput Rev 19(2):175–185
35. Bolger N, Davis A, Rafaeli E (2003) Diary methods: capturing life as it is lived. Ann Rev Psychol 54(1):579–616
36. Kapoor A, Horvitz E (2008) Experience sampling for building predictive user models: a comparative study. In: Proceedings of the SIGCHI conference on human factors in computing systems, CHI '08, (New York, NY, USA). Association for Computing Machinery, pp 657–666
37. Rosenthal S, Dey AK, Veloso M (2011) Using decision-theoretic experience sampling to build personalized mobile phone interruption models. In: Lyons K, Hightower J, Huang EM (eds) Pervasive computing. Springer, Berlin, Heidelberg, pp 170–187
38. Mehrotra A, Vermeulen J, Pejovic V, Musolesi V (2015) Ask, but don't interrupt: the case for interruptibility-aware mobile experience sampling. In: Adjunct proceedings of the 2015 ACM international joint conference on pervasive and ubiquitous computing and proceedings of the 2015 ACM international symposium on wearable computers, UbiComp/ISWC'15 Adjunct, (New York, NY, USA). Association for Computing Machinery, pp 723–732
39. van Berkel N, Goncalves J, Koval P, Hosio S, Dingler T, Ferreira D, Kostakos V (2019) Context-informed scheduling and analysis: improving accuracy of mobile self-reports. In: Proceedings of ACM SIGCHI conference on human factors in computing systems, pp 51:1–51:12
40. Lathia N, Rachuri KK, Mascolo C, Rentfrow PJ (2013) Contextual dissonance: design bias in sensor-based experience sampling methods. In: Proceedings of the 2013 ACM international joint conference on pervasive and ubiquitous computing, UbiComp '13, (New York, NY, USA). Association for Computing Machinery, pp 183–192
41. Carstensen LL, Turan B, Scheibe S, Ram N, Ersner-Hershfield H, Samanez-Larkin GR, Brooks KP, Nesselroade JR (2011) Emotional experience improves with age: evidence based on over 10 years of experience sampling. Psychol Aging 26(1):21–33
42. Savin-Williams RC, Demo DH (1983) Situational and transituational determinants of adolescent self-feelings. J Personal Soc Psychol 44(4):824
43. Bailon C, Damas M, Pomares H, Sanabria D, Perakakis P, Goicoechea C, Banos O (2019) Smartphone-based platform for affect monitoring through flexibly managed experience sampling methods. Sensors 19(15):3430
44. Berrocal A, Wac K (2018) Peer-vasive computing: leveraging peers to enhance the accuracy of self-reports in mobile human studies. In: Proceedings of the 2018 ACM international joint conference and 2018 international symposium on pervasive and ubiquitous computing and wearable computers. ACM, pp 600–605
45. Chang Y-L, Chang Y-J, Shen C-Y (2019) She is in a bad mood now: leveraging peers to increase data quantity via a chatbot-based ESM. In: Proceedings of the 21st international conference on human-computer interaction with mobile devices and services, MobileHCI '19 (New York, NY, USA). Association for Computing Machinery
46. Solymosi R, Bowers K, Fujiyama T (2015) Mapping fear of crime as a context-dependent everyday experience that varies in space and time. Legal Criminol Psychol 20(2):193–211
47. Kittur A, Chi EH, Suh B (2008) Crowdsourcing user studies with mechanical turk. In: Proceedings of the SIGCHI conference on human factors in computing systems, CHI '08, (New York, NY, USA). Association for Computing Machinery, pp 453–456
48. Oleson D, Sorokin A, Laughlin G, Hester V, Le J, Biewald L (2011) Programmatic gold: targeted and scalable quality assurance in crowdsourcing. In: Workshops at the Twenty-Fifth AAAI conference on artificial intelligence
49. Rabbi M, Li K, Yan HY, Hall K, Klasnja P, Murphy S (2019) Revibe: a context-assisted evening recall approach to improve self-report adherence. In: Proceedings of the ACM Interaction Mobile Wearable Ubiquitous Technology, vol 3
50. Intille S, Kukla C, Ma X (2002) Eliciting user preferences using image-based experience sampling and reflection. In: CHI '02 extended abstracts on human factors in computing systems, CHI EA '02, (New York, NY, USA). Association for Computing Machinery, pp 738–739

51. Yue Z, Litt E, Cai CJ, Stern J, Baxter KK, Guan Z, Sharma N, Zhang GG (2014) Photographing information needs: the role of photos in experience sampling method-style research. In: Proceedings of the SIGCHI conference on human factors in computing systems, CHI '14, (New York, NY, USA). Association for Computing Machinery, pp 1545–1554

52. Sprangers MA, Schwartz CE (1999) Integrating response shift into health-related quality of life research: a theoretical model. Soc Sci Med 48(11):1507–1515

53. Schwartz CE, Sprangers MA, Carey A, Reed G (2004) Exploring response shift in longitudinal data. Psychol Health 19(1):51–69

54. Ring L, Höfer S, Heuston F, Harris D, O'Boyle CA (2005) Response shift masks the treatment impact on patient reported outcomes (PROs): the example of individual quality of life in edentulous patients. Health Qual Life Outcomes 3(1):55

55. Schwartz CE, Sprangers MA (2010) Guidelines for improving the stringency of response shift research using the thentest. Qual Life Res 19(4):455–464

56. Christensen TC, Barrett LF, Bliss-Moreau E, Lebo K, Kaschub C (2003) A practical guide to experience-sampling procedures. J Happiness Stud 4(1):53–78

57. Paruthi G, Raj S, Gupta A, Huang C-C, Chang Y-J, Newman MW (2017) Heed: situated and distributed interactive devices for self-reporting. In: Proceedings of the 2017 ACM international joint conference on pervasive and ubiquitous computing and proceedings of the 2017 ACM international symposium on wearable computers, UbiComp '17, (New York, NY, USA). Association for Computing Machinery, pp 181–184

58. Gong Q, He X, Xie Q, Lin S, She G, Fang R, Han R, Chen Y, Xiao Y, Fu X et al (2018) LBSLAB: a user data collection system in mobile environments. In: Proceedings of the 2018 ACM international joint conference and 2018 international symposium on pervasive and ubiquitous computing and wearable computers, UbiComp '18, (New York, NY, USA). Association for Computing Machinery, pp 624–629

59. Adams AT, Murnane EL, Adams P, Elfenbein M, Chang PF, Sannon S, Gay G, Choudhury T (2018) Keppi: a tangible user interface for self-reporting pain. In: Proceedings of the 2018 CHI conference on human factors in computing systems, CHI '18 (New York, NY, USA). Association for Computing Machinery

60. Hernandez J, McDuff D, Infante C, Maes P, Quigley K, Picard R (2016) Wearable ESM: differences in the experience sampling method across wearable devices. In: Proceedings of the 18th international conference on human-computer interaction with mobile devices and services, MobileHCI '16, (New York, NY, USA). Association for Computing Machinery, pp 195–205

61. Liono J, Salim FD, van Berkel N, Kostakos V, Qin AK (2019) Improving experience sampling with multi-view user-driven annotation prediction. In: IEEE international conference on pervasive computing and communications (PerCom, pp 1–11

62. Pielot M, Vradi A, Park S (2018) Dismissed! a detailed exploration of how mobile phone users handle push notifications. In: Proceedings of the 20th international conference on human-computer interaction with mobile devices and services, MobileHCI '18 (New York, NY, USA). Association for Computing Machinery

63. Visuri A, van Berkel N, Okoshi T, Goncalves J, Kostakos V (2019) Understanding smartphone notifications' user interactions and content importance. Int J Hum-Comput Stud 128:72–85

64. Weber D, Voit A, Auda J, Schneegass S, Henze N (2018) Snooze! investigating the user-defined deferral of mobile notifications. In: Proceedings of the 20th international conference on human-computer interaction with mobile devices and services, MobileHCI '18 (New York, NY, USA). Association for Computing Machinery

Longitudinal First-Person HCI Research Methods

Andrés Lucero, Audrey Desjardins, and Carman Neustaedter

Abstract In this chapter, we focus on longitudinal first-person research methods in HCI. First-person research involves data collection and experiences from the researcher themselves, as opposed to external users (or participants). We present three projects where longitudinal 'auto-approaches' to research and design in HCI were applied, namely one auto-ethnography and two autobiographical designs. These projects help illustrate the benefits and challenges of using these first-person research methods in longitudinal HCI and interaction design research. We conclude the chapter by reflecting on themes and lessons that resonate across the three projects (i.e., range of participation, data collection, time to reflect, concluding).

Keywords Auto-ethnography · Autobiographical design · Design research

1 Introduction

Within the fields of human–computer interaction (HCI) and interaction design, there has been a growing desire to more deeply understand the use of technology within real, everyday settings. The goal is to gain a deep and experiential understanding of the effect of technology on people, society, and everyday life. As a result, this goal has brought about methodological interrogations in the field over how one ought to study the increasing ubiquity of technology and the complex world in which it is used over long periods of time. As an addition to the array of HCI methodological tools, longitudinal first-person research methods offer a chance for researchers to not only investigate the mundane, ongoing, and ubiquitous presence of technology in everyday life, but also to acknowledge their own positionality in research and design, and to

A. Lucero (✉)
Aalto University, Po. Box. 11000, FI-00076 Aalto, Finland
e-mail: lucero@acm.org

A. Desjardins
University of Washington, Seattle, Washington 98195-3440, USA

C. Neustaedter
Simon Fraser University, Burnaby B.C. V5A 1S6, Canada

© Springer Nature Switzerland AG 2021   79
E. Karapanos et al. (eds.), *Advances in Longitudinal HCI Research*,
Human–Computer Interaction Series, https://doi.org/10.1007/978-3-030-67322-2_5

rely on first-hand experience as a mode of knowing. This shift in epistemological commitments has the potential of yielding rich, honest, and authentic reflections and insights about our ongoing lives with technology.

In this chapter, we refer to first-person research as research that involves data collection and experiences from the researcher themselves, as opposed to external users (or participants). While already informally part of long-standing design practices of making and testing technology, first-person design efforts and inquiries have recently become more visible through approaches such as the application of auto-ethnography [1–6] and autobiographical design [7–13].

In this chapter, we present three projects where longitudinal 'auto-approaches' to research and design in HCI were applied, namely one auto-ethnography and two autobiographical designs. These projects will help illustrate the benefits of using these first-person research methods in longitudinal HCI and interaction design research for the rich data and fruitful insights they can bring around topics that are often difficult to access, such as long-term use of personal technology (e.g., mobile phones), use of technology in the private sphere (e.g., the home), and over distance (e.g., long-distance relationships). The projects will also illustrate the challenges that one may need to overcome if using similar approaches, along with some possible solutions. First, we present reflections on an auto-ethnography of living without a mobile phone. Second, we explore the autobiographical design of a system for capturing and replaying family moments over time. Third, we describe the autobiographical design process of converting a cargo van into a livable space. Each of these projects is written from the first-person perspective of the project's main contributor. This reflects the very personal nature of first-person research and an individual's account of the project. We conclude the chapter by reflecting on themes and lessons that resonate across the three projects.

2 Three 'Auto-approaches' to Research and Design in HCI

2.1 Auto-ethnography: Living Without a Mobile Phone

Auto-ethnography [14, 15] is a qualitative research form, an approach to research and writing that aims to describe and systematically analyze (*graphō* in Ancient Greek, 'writing') personal experience (*autós* in Ancient Greek, 'self') to understand broader cultural meanings (*éthnos* in Ancient Greek, 'nation' or 'culture') of technology. Building on traditions in anthropology, this method relies on researchers observing, noting, and reporting on personal encounters, or engagement with technology. In HCI, researchers have often aimed at adapting this approach for an HCI audience, either by adopting a fully 'scientific' prose that avoids the use of evocative first-person narratives, and/or by concluding the auto-ethnography with specific design guidelines, or a concrete set of opportunities for design. There are a few notable exceptions to this, for example Sengers's [16] reflections on IT and pace of life,

[17] use of personal fitness and self-tracking technologies to lose weight, and [5] experiences living without a mobile phone for nine years, which we discuss as a first case.

2.1.1   Before Auto-ethnography

On brink of burnout in late 2002, I (Andrés Lucero) decided it was time to get rid of the very tool that for the previous three years had allowed me to juggle four simultaneous jobs as a web designer, a university lecturer, a professional soccer referee (Fig. 1), and a freelance designer: my mobile phone. The idea of living without a mobile phone addressed a personal need of improving my life by exploring ways to reduce stress. Getting rid of my phone was neither intended as a research project [17], nor motivated by *'getting research points for it'* [13]. What started as a personal experiment, resulted in two periods of time where I voluntarily stopped using a mobile phone (i.e., 2002–2008 and 2014–2017). Conducting this auto-ethnography was the means to assess if the lack of having a phone had had any real impact in my life.

It was only in 2014, after conversations with colleagues and inspired by the likes of PSY during his honest, unassuming, and frank closing plenary at the CHI 2015

Fig. 1 Professional soccer referee, one of four simultaneous jobs I was juggling with

conference[1] that I began considering the idea of writing an auto-ethnography of my experiences living without a mobile phone. Therefore, my first step was to develop a retrospective account [18] of my life without a mobile phone during the first period (i.e., 2002–2008). These retrospective accounts (or headnotes) consisted of events, experiences, and interpretations in relation to me not having a phone that were constructed from memory [19], using projects, notebooks, photographs, and emails to aid recall [15]. I was familiar with retrospective accounts from my time assessing first- and third-year Bachelor students' self-reflections in the Netherlands. In an at-the-time novel competency-based education system, students took the role of 'junior employees' and as such were responsible for their own competency development, choosing their own learning path. My role back then was to help them plan, read, and give feedback on their competency development. Switching roles to write my own retrospective accounts allowed me to identify important themes in my daily life that helped refine this study's focus, guide the ongoing literature review, and develop a language of description for my reflections.

2.1.2 During Auto-ethnography

Once I decided to write an auto-ethnography of my experiences living without a mobile phone, I had to more systematically collect data. During the second period (i.e., 2014–2017), I collected *reflections in action* [18] consisting of biweekly handwritten and digital notes taken on a notebook or iPad, respectively. These reflections in action were complemented by emails, photographs, and tweets. In addition, whenever traveling I recorded field notes [20], which I tried to write on the spot, or as soon as possible after the event.

As I was half way through the second period of the auto-ethnography, I began an ongoing and parallel process analyzing data. After a formative analysis based on *retrospective accounts, reflections-in-action*, and *field notes*, a summative analysis [18] was conducted where an overarching process of categorization and theming [20] took place. Recurring problems, changes in attitudes, and significant concerns emerged after deeper and more detailed reflections, which developed into meaningful units [18]. These units or themes form the foundation of this auto-ethnographic narrative.

In addition, I experimented with themes by drawing tables [20] and different types of visualizations to help clarify my thinking and keep an overview, similar to the one shown in Fig. 2. I also shared my experiences, my initial interpretations, and drafts at different stages of this auto-ethnography with colleagues and extended family members [15, 20]. Doing so allowed me to gather new perspectives and offer alternative interpretations. Finally, I compared and contrasted my experience against existing research [15].

As for the main insights of this study, these were connected to four meaningful main units or themes: *social relationships, everyday work, research career*, and

---

[1] https://twitter.com/emax/status/591149505170382848.

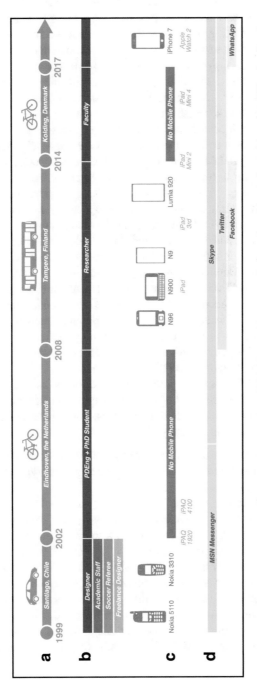

Fig. 2 Example of a timeline visualization that helped me clarify my thinking and keep an overview of: **a** cities and countries where I lived and main means of transportation used (cyan), **b** main occupations (gray), **c** 'no mobile phone' periods (2002–2008 and 2014–2017) plus mobile devices used at other times (magenta), and **d** main instant messaging, video chat, and social networking services used (yellow)

location and security. In *social relationships,* I discuss the wide range of people's reactions when they first hear about my lack of phone, the assumption that some people make in terms of being able to reach and be reached by others anytime, and the factors that allow me to make the choice of not having a mobile phone. Regarding *everyday work,* I reflect on life as an academic in a Nordic country where most of my social interactions with colleagues and students happen in a collocated fashion, and where people expect and respect delays in my responses to *urgent* emails, something that would be less acceptable in cultures where it is important to be busy. *Research career* deals with occasional feelings of peer pressure to own a mobile phone, a tendency to assume that having a mobile phone is a requirement to doing research in (mobile) HCI, and the potential benefits that being an outsider to a given field of research can bring in terms of allowing one to apply frames of reference from other domains. Finally, in location and security, I describe some of the extra planning needed when traveling to conferences due to a lack of Internet connection abroad, plus the increasing trend to require a mobile phone number as a security measure. Between the start and end of this study (i.e., 2002 and 2017), many things changed in my life. Together with my partner, we moved to different countries (i.e., the Netherlands, Finland, Denmark), became parents to two children, I went from being a post-Master and PhD student to researcher and faculty member, among other things. The longitudinal perspective of this work over such extended periods of time has also made me aware of what it means to be a privileged member of a hyper-connected and technology-saturated society, and of the importance of developing empathies into the lives of people unlike me, especially when considering difficult times such as those of the ongoing COVID-19 pandemic.

I was also trying to find ways to judge my auto-ethnography, but I could only find a series of key legitimacy and representation issues of auto-ethnographic accounts as delineated by [15, 18] and [20]. Based on these issues, I have identified seven main criteria for a successful auto-ethnography [5]:

1. **Study boundaries** [18]: requires auto-ethnographers to describe the limits of their study using the four facets of time, location, project type, and point of view.
2. **Authenticity** [20]: refers to establishing a study protocol that would allow someone else to follow the researcher's procedures [18]. [15] express authenticity as *reliability,* which refers to the narrator's credibility. In addition, authenticity is manifested as *(construct) validity* when the work evokes in readers a feeling that what has been represented could be true [15], and when correct operational measures for the concepts studied have been established [18].
3. **Plausibility** [20]: relates to structuring the narrative according to the academic article genre and finding gaps in the research literature. Plausibility is also expressed as *scholarship* by [18] when the work moves beyond emotional expression to deeper levels of reflection, highlighting connections to broader themes.

4. **Criticality** [20]: entails guiding readers through imagining ways of thinking and acting differently. Criticality is also referred to as *instrumental utility* by [18] when the work helps readers anticipate future possibilities and scenarios.
5. **Self-revealing writing** [20]: consists of revealing unflattering details about the auto-ethnographer.
6. **Interlacing actual ethnographic material and confessional content** [20]: suggests that personal material be limited to relevant information in relation to the research subject.
7. **Generalizability** [15]: focuses on the readers who determine if the story speaks to them about their life or that of others they know. Generalizability is also communicated as *external validity* by [18] when, thanks to the study's strength of themes and theories, its findings might apply to others.

2.1.3   After Auto-ethnography

Since the 2018 paper was published, I again voluntarily stopped using my phone during all of 2019, thus completing a decade living without a mobile phone. In addition, two students of mine, one PhD and one MA, have since started and completed their own research projects where they used auto-ethnography [21]. While I currently have no concrete plans to write about that tenth year living without a phone, here are some reflections if you are considering engaging in auto-ethnography.

Auto-ethnography will not make your research (life) easier. If you are considering engaging in auto-ethnography as a shortcut to avoid doing extensive user research, you might end up having to spend as much if not more work when conducting, analyzing, presenting, and publishing your work. While auto-ethnography may in most cases mean you do not need to recruit or engage with participants, you will end up spending significant time and effort systematically documenting, analyzing, and reflecting on your own experiences. It takes dedication, experience, and a degree of resilience to do auto-ethnography.

Then there is the issue of getting your research accepted and published at HCI venues. Most HCI researchers have neither been trained to write rich and evocative auto-ethnographies, nor to review them. I spent two years trying to get my auto-ethnography published. I was in part unlucky with some reviewers who wrote very personal and a couple of times even hurtful reviews—remember what I said about resilience? But I also had a hard time reaching the level of depth in my reflections that would grant acceptance—and here comes experience. But do not despair. There are ways to avoid the most obvious criticism aimed at auto-ethnography. For instance, you can apply a long-term perspective to your auto-ethnography by collecting data over weeks, months, years or even a decade as I did with my experiences living without a mobile phone. Alternatively, you can have several researchers concurrently working on the same project and applying auto-ethnography to the same topic [22]. As another example of this, you can complement the one-person small data perspective by taking a big data approach running for instance a pre- or post-auto-ethnography crowdsourced survey [21]. The big scale in data collection (i.e., in time or additional participant numbers) can help the one-person scale of the sample.

But above all, remember that the power and richness of auto-ethnography lie in that it shares voices that might not have been heard [23] and insights that might have been too subtle to elicit ([15, 18]).

2.2 Autobiographical Design: Capturing Memories of Family Life

Autobiographical design focuses on design research that draws on extensive, genuine usage by those creating or building a system. This enables designers/researchers to rapidly respond to real-life needs and frictions encountered when using the system, e.g., Desjardins' Living in a Prototype [8] and Neustaedter's Moments [11]. Through 11 interviews with established HCI researchers, [13] found that autobiographical design was a common practice in HCI; however, until recent times, it was rarely reported on. This is due to a perceived contradiction between the pervasiveness and usefulness of autobiographical design as a design practice and its incompatibility with widespread research practices. Further, [7] have discussed tensions that arise when conducting autobiographical design, such as the delicate balance between various roles including designer, researcher, observer, parent, and partner. This section describes how autobiographical design was used to explore the creation and use of a system for recording family moments.

2.2.1   Creating Moments

In 2014, as the father in a family of five with three young children (aged 1, 6, and 8 at the time), I (Carman Neustaedter) was interested in exploring ways that I might better capture my children's lives and our family as it grew together and experienced life. This could include special moments such as a child's first steps or family celebrations, as well as the more mundane stuff and the everyday moments we might share together. I could already use a camera to capture images or videos, but at times it was easy to miss important moments because I did not always know when they would occur before they happened. I also wanted to explore ways of capturing my family's life without having to be staring at a smartphone or camera screen to make sure I captured the moments 'just right.' I wanted to be part of the moments too and not just the photographer. I wanted something more automated.

For these reasons, I worked with an undergraduate student, Brendan DeBrincat, to create a system called *Moments* [24]. Moments was an always-on video recording system for families. It included a camera that was placed overlooking a space within my home along with a display to view and interact with the system. Figure 3 shows an iPad sitting on the kitchen counter. Atop the cupboard above it, a Kinect camera was

Fig. 3 A Moments display on the counter in the corner of kitchen and camera above

placed to capture video footage. The goal of Moments was to help families collect and reflect on past moments and experiences that took place in certain areas of the home. In the simplest description, the camera recorded and saved video all the time, and the iPad display allowed users to replay it (Figs. 4 and 5).

Fig. 4 Close-up of the Moments display

Fig. 5 Calendar selection interface

2.2.2 More Than just One with Autobiographical Design

Autobiographical design focuses on the study and design of technologies created for oneself and used by oneself [13]. It is this tight coupling of design and use that makes it a valuable method for exploring a design space. Yet often it is the case that more than just a single person is involved in a given research project. As a university professor, my role is to conduct research; however, in conjunction I also train and mentor students as researchers themselves. As mentioned, DeBrincat was an undergraduate researcher who worked very deeply on the Moments project by exploring the design space and iteratively implementing the system. This meant that our growing understanding of the design space had to be shared. Initially, I told DeBrincat about my vision for creating a system to record my family's everyday activities in the home. DeBrincat and I had several brainstorming sessions as part of weekly meetings where I would explain the needs I had for a system like Moments and what family life was like for me. DeBrincat used his own experiences growing up to understand the context for which he would be designing and my explanations of the needs for my family. As DeBrincat created the system, he had to make me aware of what was technologically feasible, what features were being created, and which were ready for my family to try it. As I used the system with my family, I had to share knowledge with DeBrincat about how the design was working and where it needed tweaks and additional work. Once the design solidified, DeBrincat completed his portion of the project.

My family and I continued to use the design for the remainder of two years. This allowed us to gain a very deep understanding of how the technology impacted family life, what worked well about it, and where challenges lay. Such long-term usage and deep experiential understanding are very difficult to achieve through other types of deployments that might include external families. It was for these reasons that I chose to use autobiographical design: I had a genuine need for the system and wanted to obtain a detail and nuanced understanding of the technology and its impact. Twenty months into our usage of Moments, I had my PhD Student, Yasamin Heshmat, join the project to help assess the overall experience that my family was having. As family members we all had a detailed understanding of how we used Moments and how it affected family life, but I wanted to have someone work with us to be able to articulate those experiences and 'tease them out of us', so to speak. Heshmat planned an interview-based study that involved talking with each family member about their experiences. I worked with her to plan out what questions would be most relevant to ask based on my background as an HCI researcher and my knowledge of the system. Heshmat augmented this with things that she thought would be interesting to learn more about.

Having other researchers work on the Moments project was extremely valuable as it brought additional help and varied perspectives into creating the technology and understanding the design space. But it did mean that autobiographical design was more challenging to use as a design research approach. In other autobiographical design projects that I have undertaken [25, 26], I have taken on multiple roles, including the designer, developer, and researcher of the system. That is, I have figured out what to build, I have built it, and I have studied its usage. Maintaining multiple roles meant that I gained a tremendous amount of deep understanding as to what was needed in the systems and why it was needed. In many moments, this knowledge was hard to articulate. And, given that I was the only person doing the work, I often did not need to. I could simply iterate the design based on how I was using it. However, with Moments it was different. I had to pay particular attention to convey my understanding of the design space to the two students I was working with, at different points in time. We had to create boundary objects that helped us share our understanding. For DeBrincat's design and development work, it included sketches and write-ups of features and experiences. It also included one-on-one conversations (undocumented) of what both DeBrincat and I thought of the design and its features. For Heshmat's study work, boundary objects included study protocols, interview questions, and subsequent analysis documents with transcripts, labels, and codes depicting results. The lesson we learned throughout the experience with Moments was that autobiographical design can be used with multiple people where not all have a genuine need for the design and not all use it. However, the takeaway message is that *all team members must be invested in the design process and be able to find ways to share knowledge and understanding across multiple roles in the project.*

2.2.3 Connecting Across Time Periods

With Moments, we were able to use the design over what one might consider in the field of HCI to be a very long time, two years. Many field studies are conducted over a period of weeks, in comparison. Because I was designing for myself and my family, it was easy to have a long-term investment in the work. Moreover, the genuine need we had for the system meant that it was worth any additional efforts that might be needed to keep the system going and maintained over a long time period. Because Moments tried to tie family moments together across time, it was the long-term usage of Moments that raised additional curiosity and insights. We found that the most interesting point in time for Moments was once we had used the design for a full year. At that point, rather than allow users to pick a certain day to view, we could set it to automatically show our family's activities from exactly one year ago, by default. On holidays like Christmas, New Year's and birthdays, my family members and I would look to see how we were celebrating the holiday last year, e.g., who was at our house, what we were eating, and what the birthday cake looked like. Because the system itself tied its usage to time, we were able to more deeply learn about how our family changed over time. Of course, long-term usage can be extremely challenging to achieve. The system needs to stay running, and, in our case, it needed to have enough storage space to keep recording video. As a family, we needed to ensure the benefit of the system continued to outweigh possible privacy concerns. Team members may also easily come and go in an academic environment as students graduate. Thus, the lesson is that *long-term usage can be very valuable to see behavior changes, yet many real-world pragmatic constraints could make it difficult to achieve long-term usage.*

2.2.4 Ending the Autobiographical Design Study

In academia, every project comes to an end at some point. Students move on. Research grants finish up. Professors decide to move on to new interests. After two years, I decided that it was the right time to complete the project. The hardware that we were using was becoming obsolete and we were running out of storage space for video. The camera was not capturing video at a fidelity that seemed sufficient for continued use. We could have conceivably purchased new equipment, yet it would have been hard to properly integrate it within the system, especially considering that DeBrincat was no longer a student. Updates would have been costly in personnel and equipment. I also asked myself as a researcher, even though I valued the system for my family and our ability to capture a record of our lives, had I learned as much as we could about the design space that it was time to move on? This was a difficult question to answer, but ultimately, I decided that I had an obligation to the research funding to end the work and move on. A challenge with autobiographical design in academia is that *one's genuine need for a system becomes intermixed with research funding, graduate student training and completion, and the pragmatics of research.* This is somewhat of an ethical dilemma as one is often publicly funded as an academic, and there are needs to properly use resources as part of research. I was fortunate in that this project did not require much funding to conduct. Equipment was reused from prior projects, and much of the student efforts were a part of course work. In other autobiographical design works, I have done, I have similarly had to weigh options around resources and time, and whether it is worth continuing on a project [25, 26].

2.3 Autobiographical Design: Living in a Prototype

The last case we present is an autobiographical design project called 'Living in a Prototype' [8]. Since 2013, I (Audrey Desjardins) have been engaged in the long and slow process of converting a cargo van into a livable space: a camper van. In October 2013, my partner and I bought a new Mercedes Sprinter van (Fig. 6 left) which offered an empty space of 10 feet long, 6 feet wide and 6 feet tall behind the seats. In 2016, I wrote about the van to show an alternative to top-down visions of one-size-fits-all smart homes, a topic often discussed in the HCI community. While the van itself and our builds are not using emerging technologies such as Internet of Things devices or wearables, the way in which we 'made home' allowed me to think and write about the home as an invariably unfinished space—a space that relies on the ongoing development of trust, care, intimacy, and sense of ownership between the home, things in the home, and home dwellers.

Living in a Prototype followed an autobiographical design approach. This means that as a researcher, I was also playing the roles of designer, maker, observer, writer, user, and partner. The study was conducted by analyzing the design decisions we

Fig. 6 Cargo van on day 1 (left) and interior of the van in 2016, after wall insulation and paneling, and storage and bed construction

made about how to build the van, the process of fabrication, as well as our ongoing use of the space. In terms of autobiographical design, I built off of Neustaedter and Senger's definition: *'design research drawing on extensive, genuine usage by those creating or building the system'* [13]. The documentation I collected to build my analysis included:

- Tutorials on the Instructables web platform for each important fabrication stage.
- Photos of each step in the making, including tools and materials. Those photos also show the finished product at each step.
- Seventeen time-lapse videos of each day of building. Photos were taken every 30 s and then assembled to make short videos.
- The Instructables tutorials also hold a record of readers' comments and questions, and my answers.
- Short diary logs that record the dates, places, and important events of the trips made in the van.
- Photos of the van's interior while on trips, focusing on different activities like cooking, eating, playing games, sleeping, and getting ready for outdoor activities.

Since the 2016 paper was published, my partner and I have continued to make additions to the van, for instance, adding a sink and water pump, building more storage above the seats, adding solar panels and alternative batteries, installing ceiling lights, and adding a heater. We are also continuing to use the van, mostly for weekend trips (almost every weekend), and longer vacation trips a couple times a year.

Below, I share three main reflections with regard to its longitudinal first-person methodological approach.

2.3.1 Moving in and Out of 'Research' Mode

Using the van project as a site of inquiry gave me the opportunity to investigate how the 'making of home' might evolve over time. The goal was to look at that practice over time, but the nature of autobiographical design meant that research was not always centered: my research life and personal life blurred and rhythms emerged over time.

While this project started as a personal project, it aligned with my doctoral research interests: I was studying ways in which people live with technology in their homes and how they transformed artifacts through DIY approaches and everyday design [27]. Once I saw the connection, it was a fluid, slow, and slightly ambiguous move to transition from a personal project to a research project. With the help of my advisor Ron Wakkary, I was able to conduct a rigorous retrospective analysis of the design and making process, based on the materials I had already been gathering about the van (i.e., photos, tutorials, time-lapse videos, etc.).

When I finished writing about the project for the CHI 2016 conference and for my dissertation, I felt like I slowly started to think of the van less as research and more as personal (the fact that we lived in it for 2 months on a road trip after my PhD helped with that!). And yet, now and again, reflections about the process, the method, and the living in the van came in waves and led me to continue to write about the van project as a research project. The first was a collaboration on a book chapter about sustainability and longer-term implications of the 'unfinishedness' of the van, thoughts that continued to bubble up for me as we continue to build the van [28]. The second was a collaboration with a master student at my new university. Aubree Ball, for her master thesis, decided to engage in an autobiographical design project as well. Together, we wrote about the experiences of doing autobiographical design as a meta-reflection around the method [7]. With this paper, it became clear that the long-term nature of autobiographical design allowed me to continue to do research work not only with the making of the van, but also through the writing and the reflecting.

A year or two passed, and I realized my partner and I were in building mode again, adding electricity, a water pump, a heater, and a ladder. As making and designing ramped up, I fell back into my earlier habits of photographing tools, materials, and steps in the making, and I took screen shots of discussions we had over text messaging and chats. I was not sure what I would use this data collection for, but I knew that they might become useful. I continue to have a haunting sense that I will write 'Living in a Prototype II'. Stay tuned.

The lesson here is that *longitudinal first-person research projects have fuzzy boundaries in time and scope. While Neustaedter talked about choosing to conclude the Moments project, I chose to continue to live in this ambiguous and ongoing state of potential research.*

2.3.2 Time Allows for New Modes of Making to Emerge

When we started the van fabrication in 2013, #vanlife was just starting, and there was not much information online about how to convert a van into a camper van. Since then, many tutorials have been created, many YouTube channels have emerged, and #vanlife definitely has a presence on social media. Between 2013 and 2015, we chose to document extensively our process for making the van because we thought we could contribute to this emerging community online.

However, as time went by, in addition to amateurs sharing their processes online, small companies started to emerge to support people in their making process. For instance, Adventure Wagon,[2] a company based in Portland, Oregon, started to create parts and frames that can easily be added to Sprinter Van conversions. This opened up new options for us. Instead of having to build everything from scratch, their battery tray kit allowed us to install alternative batteries and bring electricity in the van, an area we did not have much expertise in (Fig. 7).

In addition to new kits and instructions, I also gained easier access to new tools: we bought a small (and cheap) 3D printer for the home. With it, we were then able to print small parts to fix a few problems in the van. For example, when the heater was installed, the vent did not fit properly. I measured the vent and the angles of the

---

[2] https://adventurewagon.com/.

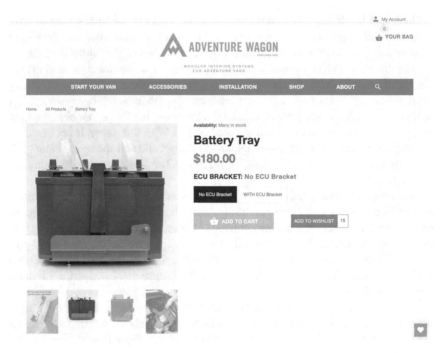

Fig. 7 Adventure Wagon Battery Tray kit and instructions now available online

surface it was resting on, designed a new custom-made buffer, printed it at home, and installed it. The proximity and ease to print at home made this process very easy.

Of course, in 7 years, personal changes also happened which also supported new modes of making. I moved from being a PhD student to an assistant professor, gaining more financial means and better stability. For a while we had been dreaming of an integrated diesel heater to replace our portable propane heater (which was less convenient and more dangerous). In 2019, we decided that it was the right time to buy the heater and have an expert install it for us (we did not feel comfortable working directly with the van's diesel tank). The cost of the heater (around US$1000) and the cost of installation (around US$500) would have been difficult to rationalize when I was a student, but not anymore. These changes in personal life meant that new materials and expertise became available.

In my case of longitudinal first-person research, *the slowness of the process and the fact that we still see the van as a prototype allowed for communities to grow and knowledge infrastructures and tools to emerge around us. This is interesting when trying to study how practices of making evolve over time: it means that we cannot study practices in isolation, but that we need to consider how the circumstances of designing and making also change.*

2.3.3   Opportunity for Changes in Theoretical Framings

The research project of Living in a Prototype started from the theoretical under-pinnings of everyday design [27], where everyday people are seen as designers of their own artifacts once they leave the manufacturer's and professional designers' hands. In 2016, I framed the project through the perspective of smart homes [8]. In the collaborative chapter from 2018, we used sustainability as a lens to look at place making in the van [28]. Over time, I have found myself revisiting this project through various theoretical framings, producing new insights and new understandings that are relevant to the field.

In the last year, again, I have looked at the van in a new light through new readings and theories I have encountered. In the 2016 paper, I wrote about 'reciprocal shaping' [8] to describe the ways in which we gave form to the van, physically, but in return, its materiality reshaped our ideas of what a van ought to be (does it need electricity right away? Does it need a polished kitchen?). Four years later, thinking alongside new materialism, in particular the book *Vibrant Matter* [29], I can articulate more precisely how artifacts may have as much of an impact on systems or events as humans. In her book, Bennett talks about the notion of 'thing-power' or the liveliness of matter. She writes about the active participation of non-human forces and entities, and she describes how agency is distributed between humans and nonhumans. With this new theoretical lens, I can write about cedar paneling, electricity, skis, tea, my partner, cups, infrastructure, the road, and wilderness landscapes as all the elements that shaped the van. The matter of the van has a vitality of its own that plays an important role in how it comes to be—perhaps as important as our human actions.

Similarly, in thinking alongside feminist theorists (e.g., [30–35], I am able to deepen discussions around authorial perspective and voice in the Living in a Proto-type project. From a methodological perspective, autobiographical design renders explicit who the researcher is and forces us to recognize that the knowledge gener-ated from a project is entangled with this person. Feminist theorists have long argued that human knowledge is situated and partial—that knowledge is not abstracted or decontextualized, but instead that it is learned, applied, and understood in situ. In fact, Donna Haraway cautions against knowledge that is disembodied, or, in her words: 'from everywhere and so nowhere' [36]. Understanding the importance of using 'I' when writing about the van project is something I had a hard time articulating at first. However, through a feminist theoretical perspective, I am able to express why it is important to respect (and celebrate) who these insights are coming from, clarifying whose lived experience has formed these new findings. Yet, when I wrote about the van project in 2016, I wrote with the pronoun 'we' to recognize the participation of my partner in the making and living with the van and to also acknowledge the analytical work my advisor contributed to while I was writing. Finding the right tone and voice to respect whose perspective is being shared in longitudinal first-person research is a difficult work, but with a new theoretical framing, I am now able to refine the position I take.

Similar to my previous point, *not only did the making circumstances change over time, but theoretical lenses can also change with time. When working with an autobiographical project, so much of the felt experience of living with a prototype needs to be unpacked and finding different theories is often welcome to help sharpen the contribution of a project.*

3   Discussion and Conclusions

Across the three projects, we see several main themes emerging in terms of how one should think about and consider first-person methods such as auto-ethnography and autobiographical design in the context of longitudinal research methods.

First, the projects illustrate that there can be a range of participation by individuals when it comes to longitudinal first-person approaches, despite that they focus heavily on an individual's perspective. For example, in *Living Without a Mobile Phone*, as an auto-ethnography, there is a strong emphasis on just one person's perspective. With *Living in a Prototype*, there was a single researcher; however, this role was coupled with the researcher being part of a domestic relation. As a result, Desjardins adjusted her writing practice to include the pronoun 'we' to acknowledge her partner's participation. In *Capturing Memories of Family Life*, Neustaedter was part of a design team with students. Across the projects, there was no one 'right solution' and the nature of who was involved depended on the real-world situation being explored. Participation was also greatly affected by the longitudinal nature of the studies. For Neustaedter, participation changed based on students and graduations over time. For Desjardins, her participation included her partner and her Ph.D. advisor more strongly at some points. And, for Lucero, his non-use of a mobile phone came about from having different situations, students, and activities before him. This was not direct participation per se, but the people around him did, to some extent, influence decisions to not use a phone or suggest that others do the same (e.g., his students). Together, these points illustrate the flexibility of using longitudinal first-person research methods over extended periods of time.

Second, longitudinal first-person research can amount to data collection that is tedious in nature yet highly important. Projects go on for months and years at a time, rendering evident that relying solely on memory is not enough to offer rigorous data. *Living Without a Mobile Phone* included multiple forms of data, including retrospective accounts, reflections-in action, and field notes. *Living in a Prototype* involved media of the design process and ever-changing van, web tutorials, and diary entries. *Capturing Memories of Family Life* utilized design boundary objects due to challenges with working among a small team of researchers that included students in addition to Neustaedter. In all cases, data collection was important for reflections and writing about the projects. Data collection was sometimes for the sole purposes of research. Other times, it was data that was collected for other reasons (e.g., communicating with friends and family, sharing information with an online community). Clearly, data collection is vital for longitudinal first-person research if it is to be understood as being credible, just the same as for other research methods. Yet unlike studies that are of a shorter duration in time, researchers using longitudinal first-person research methods may need to collect data over very long periods of time, as was the case for the projects reported on in this chapter. Long-term data collection comes with the potential for data collection fatigue, losing data, and challenges by analyzing data across time.

Third, it can be highly valuable to reflect on one's experiences as a part of longitudinal first-person research. Sometimes, it can take time to understand what is happening and why when using longitudinal first-person methods. This might be akin to how a researcher must often 'step back' and think critically about what they are seeing while they analyze their study data. Similar approaches are needed when it comes to longitudinal first-person research. For *Living Without a Mobile Phone*, this came from Lucero's retrospective accounts of his life across the years when he was not using a mobile phone. For *Capturing Memories of Family Life,* reflection came, in particular, once Neustaedter and his family had used Moments for an entire year. This allowed them to look back at their life one year ago and what they were doing with Moments. For *Living in a Prototype*, Desjardins was able to reflect as she moved between her roles of researcher and domestic partner. In all three cases, reflections were made stronger because the researchers participated in the research over a long period of time, building up their understanding as time progressed. This brings added complexity and commitment, yet additional value and experiential understanding. It also means that it can be challenging to write about and tell 'the story' from such a deep, interpersonal level.

Lastly, the three projects reveal opportunities and tensions around when to continue longitudinal first-person research and when to see it to a conclusion. Ultimately, decisions about concluding a research project will depend on the researcher and the particular context being studied. Our chapter reveals several ways to think about it and different perspectives to consider. *Living Without a Mobile Phone* concluded based on personal circumstances and needs to re-engage with a mobile phone. *Capturing Memories of Family Life* concluded based on student training needs and grant funding. And, it would be fair to say that *Living in a Prototype* has temporarily finished, yet there are possibilities for the work to continue moving forward with the use of various theoretical lenses, new additions to the van, and life changes for the couple. We suggest that researchers consider a mixture of their research needs coupled with their own personal needs when it comes to such longitudinal first-person research projects. Researchers should also consider the pragmatics of conducting first-person research, given that first-person research methods tend to naturally involve studies lasting a long time period. This can make it more difficult to fund a project and stay committed to it.

Overall, our three cases have illustrated several lessons and reflections when it comes to conducting longitudinal first-person research. Through these long periods of time, we are able to inquire about how our lives with technologies change. In addition, with this longitudinal first-person position, we can also observe and remark on what else around us changes with time: our families, our jobs, our communities, theories we engage with, and the tools we may use. This is a unique place to be: It opens up the possibility of looking at transformations in the mundane and the everyday within the broader context of fully lived lives, as complex and tangled as they are.

References

1. Cain CC, Eileen T (April 2017) Black men in IT: theorizing an autoethnography of a black man's journey into IT within the United States of America. SIGMIS Database 48(2):35–51. https://doi.org/10.1145/3084179.3084184
2. Cecchinato ME, Anna LC, Jon B (2017) Always On(line)? User experience of smartwatches and their role within multi-device ecologies. In: Proceedings of the 2017 CHI conference on human factors in computing systems (CHI '17). pp 3557–3568. https://doi.org/10.1145/302 5453.3025538
3. Chamberlain A, Mads B, Konstantinos P (2017) Mapping media and meaning: autoethnography as an approach to designing personal heritage soundscapes. In: Proceedings of the 12th international audio mostly conference on augmented and participatory sound and music experiences (AM '17), Article 32, pp 1–4. https://doi.org/10.1145/3123514.3123536
4. Jain D, Desjardins A, Findlater L, Froehlich JE (2019) Autoethnography of a hard of hearing traveler. In: The 21st international ACM SIGACCESS conference on computers and accessibility (ASSETS '19), pp 236–248. https://doi.org/10.1145/3308561.3353800
5. Lucero A (2018) Living without a mobile phone: an autoethnography. In: Proceedings of the 2018 designing interactive systems conference (DIS '18), pp 765–776. https://doi.org/10.1145/3196709.3196731
6. O'Kane AA, Rogers Y, Blandford AE (2014) Gaining empathy for non-routine mobile device use through autoethnography. In: Proceedings of the SIGCHI conference on human factors in computing systems (CHI '14), pp 987–990. https://doi.org/10.1145/2556288.2557179
7. Desjardins A, Ball A (2018) Revealing tensions in autobiographical design in HCI. In: Proceedings of the 2018 designing interactive systems conference (DIS '18). pp 753–764. https://doi.org/10.1145/3196709.3196781
8. Desjardins A, Wakkary R (2016) Living in a prototype: a reconfigured space. In: Proceedings of the 2016 CHI conference on human factors in computing systems (CHI '16), pp 5274–5285. https://doi.org/10.1145/2858036.2858261
9. W. Gaver (2–3 Jan 2006) The video window: my life with a ludic system. Personal Ubiquitous Comput 10:60–65. https://doi.org/10.1007/s00779-005-0002-2
10. Helms K (2017) Leaky objects: implicit information, unintentional communication. In: Proceedings of the 2017 ACM conference companion publication on designing interactive systems (DIS '17 Companion). pp 182–186. https://doi.org/10.1145/3064857.3079142
11. Heshmat Y, Neustaedter C, DeBrincat B (2017) The autobiographical design and long term usage of an always-on video recording system for the home. In: Proceedings of the 2017 conference on designing interactive systems (DIS '17), 675–687. https://doi.org/10.1145/306 4663.3064759
12. Mackey A, Wakkary R, Wensveen S, Tomico O, Hengeveld B (2017) Day-to-day speculation: designing and wearing dynamic fabric. In: Proceedings of the conference on research through design. pp 439–454
13. Neustaedter C, Sengers P (2012) Autobiographical design in HCI research: designing and learning through use-it-yourself. In: Proceedings of the designing interactive systems conference (DIS '12), pp 514–523. https://doi.org/10.1145/2317956.2318034
14. Denzin NK, Lincoln YS (2011) The SAGE handbook of qualitative research. Sage
15. Ellis C, Adams TE, Bochner AP (2011) Autoethnography: an overview. Hist Soc Res/Historische Sozialforschung 36, 4(138):273–290. http://www.jstor.org/stable/23032294
16. Sengers P (2011) What I learned on Change Islands: reflections on IT and pace of life. Interactions 18, 2 (March + April 2011), 40–48. https://doi.org/10.1145/1925820.1925830
17. Williams K (2015) An anxious alliance. In: Proceedings of the fifth decennial aarhus conference on critical alternatives (AA '15). Aarhus University Press pp 121–131. https://doi.org/10.7146/aahcc.v1i1.21146
18. Duncan M (2004) Autoethnography: critical appreciation of an emerging art. Int J Qual Methods 3:4. https://doi.org/10.1177/160940690400300403

19. Efimova L (2009) Weblog as a personal thinking space. In: Proceedings of the 20th ACM conference on hypertext and hypermedia (HT '09). pp 289–298. https://doi.org/10.1145/155 7914.1557963
20. Schultze U (2000) A confessional account of an ethnography about knowledge work. MIS Q 24(1):3–41. https://doi.org/10.2307/3250978
21. Ha Y, Karyda M, Lucero A (2020) Exploring virtual rewards in real life: a gimmick or a motivational tool for promoting physical activity? In: Proceedings of the 2020 ACM designing interactive systems conference (DIS '20), pp 1847–1858. https://doi.org/10.1145/3357236.339 5477
22. Sawyer R, Norris J (2013) Duoethnography: understanding qualitative research
23. Spry T (2001) Performing Autoethnography: an embodied methodological Praxis. Qual Inq 7(6):706–732. https://doi.org/10.1177/107780040100700605
24. DeBrincat B, Carman N (2015) Moments: family video recording right here, right now, on that day extended proceedings of graphics interface. New York, NY, USA, ACM
25. Carman Neustaedter, Tejinder Judge, and Phoebe Sengers (2014) Autobiographical design in the home. IN Studying designing technol domest life: lessons from home
26. Neustaedter C (2013) My life with always-on video. IN Elect J Commun: Spec Issue Video Conferencing 23:38
27. Wakkary R, Maestri L (2007) The resourcefulness of everyday design. In: Proceedings of the 6th ACM SIGCHI conference on Creativity & Cognition (C&C '07). pp 163–172. https://doi.org/10.1145/1254960.1254984
28. Desjardins A, Wang X, Wakkary R (2018) A sustainable place: everyday designers as place makers. In: Hazas M, Nathan L (eds) Digital technology and sustainability: engaging the paradox, 1 edn. Routledge, Abingdon, Oxon ; New York, NY
29. Bennett J (2009) Vibrant matter: a political ecology of things. Duke University Press. https://doi.org/10.1215/9780822391623
30. Haraway DJ (2016) Staying with the trouble: making kin in the chthulucene. Duke University Press Books, Durham
31. de la Bellacasa MP (2017) Matters of care: speculative ethics in more than human worlds. University of Minnesota Press, Minneapolis. Retrieved March 13, 2020 from http://site.ebrary.com/id/11357818
32. Rosner DK (2018) Critical fabulations: reworking the methods and margins of design. MIT Press
33. Suchman L (2005) Agencies in technology design: feminist reconfigurations. Gendered innovations in science and engineering. pp 15–1
34. Anna Lowenhaupt Tsing (2015) The mushroom at the end of the world: on the possibility of life in capitalist ruins. Princeton University Press, Princeton
35. Bardzell S (2010) Feminist HCI: taking stock and outlining an agenda for design. In: Proceedings of the SIGCHI conference on human factors in computing systems (CHI '10). pp 1301–1310. https://doi.org/10.1145/1753326.1753521
36. Haraway DJ (1988) Situated knowledges: the science question in feminism and the privilege of partial perspective. Fem Stud 14(3):575–599

Imagining the Future of Longitudinal HCI Studies: Sensor-Embedded Everyday Objects as Subjective Data Collection Tools

Armağan Karahanoğlu and Geke Ludden

Abstract Automated data collection has a significant role in collecting reliable longitudinal data in human–computer interaction (HCI) studies that involve human participants. While objective data collection can be obtained by and mediated through personal informatics, subjective data is mostly collected through labour-intensive tools. The potential of sensor-embedded everyday objects as subjective data collection tools is underexplored. Hence, in this chapter, we investigate the use of such products for subjective data collection purposes in longitudinal studies. First, we demonstrate current practices on subjective data collection tools and examine the aforementioned research gap. Following that, we discuss the results of three discussion sessions in which we collected insights from six expert researchers on the enablers and barriers of using sensor-embedded everyday objects as subjective data collection tools. We present our insights with use-case scenarios to communicate what possible roles sensor-embedded everyday objects could have in collecting subjective data in future longitudinal HCI studies and discuss how they could be further developed within the field.

Keywords Subjective data collection · User research · Everyday objects · Sensor-embedded objects · Longitudinal data

1 Introduction

The HCI community has studied the impact of interactive systems on people's daily lives for decades [1, 2]. While a focus on user experience after first time use has been dominant for a long time, since the earliest call for more experience-focused longitudinal studies [3], long-term user experience of interactive systems has been

A. Karahanoğlu (✉) · G. Ludden
Interaction Design Research Group, Faculty of Engineering Technology, University of Twente, Enschede, Netherlands
e-mail: a.karahanoglu@utwente.nl

G. Ludden
e-mail: g.d.s.ludden@utwente.nl

© Springer Nature Switzerland AG 2021   101
E. Karapanos et al. (eds.), *Advances in Longitudinal HCI Research*,
Human–Computer Interaction Series, https://doi.org/10.1007/978-3-030-67322-2_6

examined by various scholars [4–7]. In one of the earlier studies, Kujala et al. [4] propose "UX Curve" that aims to support people in recalling the details of their experience and draw a free-hand curve to describe it. In another example, Karapanos et. al. [7] propose "iScale", an online survey tool with a similar purpose, in which participants are asked to recall and sketch their most impactful experiences with a product. Both studies address the necessity of developing tools to explore and evaluate long-term user experience.

Scholars agree that to reliably study experience over time, as well as processes and effects of change, we need longitudinal studies that investigate user experience beyond the first time use [8]. An observable characteristic of longitudinal studies is that a minimum of three repeated observations on a construct of interest is carried out [9] that provides data in a series of time points [10]. In order to arrive at actionable data sets, most studies involving human participants, rely on two types measurements: objective (i.e. number of steps taken) and subjective (i.e. the perceived effort or confidence of the user).

Advances in personal informatics tools offer sensor-based, almost effortless objective data collection practices. These tools equip both the users of such tools, as well as researchers interested in their data, with an immense number of possibilities. Today, personal informatics help people to automatically track the number of steps they take, or the quality of their sleep [11]. It also supports people to arrive at meaningful information about their health status [12]; and supports decision-making on actions to take to improve their health [13]. For researchers, the same sensors bring new possibilities to collect and study objective data about the behaviour of large populations. One of the most well-known examples of this approach is probably the use of physical activity trackers to unobtrusively collect physical activity behaviours [14, 15]. Because tracking physical activity is now a practice that is available to almost every individual, the data gathered could even be used to study how the lockdowns due to the COVID-19 pandemic in 2020 affected physical activity of populations at country and city level [16]. While regular personal informatics tools are usually embedded in smartphones and smart watches, researchers have recently also started using different types of everyday objects as data collection tools. For instance, Bogers et al. used a sensor-embedded baby bottle to collect the baby-feeding behaviour of mothers [17].

These developments manifest effort-free, reliable objective data collection possibilities. The challenge here is no longer to collect data, but to make sense of the collected data. Although personal informatics provide researchers with easy to use tools to collect objective data, this does not always mean that the data collected gives them all the answers they are looking for. There are things that these sensors cannot capture automatically, such as the subjective experience of participants. For example, how did a person's mood or emotion affect their physical activity? Did the low quality of sleep affect feeding behaviour? How did that person experience their recent walk or run? These are all questions where sensors cannot provide a full and decisive answer and that require subjective measurement tools.

For subjective longitudinal data collection (SLDC) purposes, HCI studies involving human participants borrow various methods from different disciplines in the social sciences. Most commonly, studies use paper artefacts (such as questionnaires or diaries) or digital data collection tools (such as ecological momentary assessment applications). For instance, ecological momentary assessment (EMA) is usually implemented as an electronic diary on a smartphone or on a separate device. The goal of EMA is to obtain subjective, ecologically valid, real-life data [18]. Next to these tools that were specifically developed for research purposes, people have started to devise and use self-tracking tools for mood and emotion. For instance, Ayobi et al. [19] found that people are willing to use bullet-journaling to track their habits and mood. In another study, Sarzotti [20] found that people are interested in tracking their emotions especially when the way of tracking is combined with wearable trackers, such as a bracelet, a necklace or a smart watch. These are interesting findings which show that people are also interested in collecting data about their own subjective experiences. However, there still is no automatic way of collecting this type of data.

Collecting data in-the-wild requires participants' active and conscious involvement to collect reliable subjective data about their experience [21]. While researchers may applaud involvement of participants in their studies, it also places a burden on participation that may cause boredom or frustration with the participants, which eventually may limit the quality of the data collection. Therefore, in this chapter, we will explore how sensor-embedded everyday products can play a role in smarter subjective data collection and overcome the challenges that current subjective data collection tools face.

We propose that sensor-embedded everyday objects can be employed for collecting reliable subjective data purposes. To support this proposal, in the following section, we first analyse available tools and put forward the challenges of collecting subjective data in longitudinal HCI studies. Following that, we provide the results of three discussion sessions that we conducted with six design researchers. In these sessions, we aimed to discover the broader potential of sensor-embedded everyday objects as alternative means of collecting subjective data in longitudinal HCI studies. Accompanied with visualizations made by five industrial design engineering students, we refine and present the emerging subjective data collection possibilities for different contextual data collection case. We discuss how the ideas presented can contribute to the future of data collection in the HCI community.

2 Subjective Data Collection Tools in Longitudinal Studies

Commonly used retrospective and real-time data collection methods and tools in HCI have their origins in social science domains such as psychology and anthropology. The use of self-reports is widespread both for collecting subjective data about one time use and for collecting longitudinal data. Schwarz [22] suggests that a combination of open-ended questions (such as asking the participant "what did you do today?"), closed formats (such as a list of activities from which the participant can pick) and rating scales (such as questionnaires) can help the participants to better

Table 1 Overview of retrospective subjective data collection tools

Tools	Forms of data collection	Advantages	Challenges
Diary studies	Participants' own insights and narratives	Powerful in collecting real-life insights	Depends on participants' memory Decreased response rate Individual biases
Experience sampling method (ESM)	Combines objective data with ecologically valid assessments	More ecologically valid data than diary studies	
Ambulatory assessments (AA)	Combines self-reports with observational, physiological and behavioural methods	Reduce retrospective biases	Fatigue in responding
Ecological momentary assessment (EMA)	Mostly used in collecting behavioural assessment which the researcher may not reach easily	Mobile and less labour intensive	Require strong infrastructure

clarify on their experiences. Often, self-reports have been criticized to be less reliable, because the method highly relies on the memory of the subjects in reporting their recalled experience [23]: the participants might self-select what to report [24]. On the other hand, research shows that when planned carefully, self-reports can turn into powerful self-tracking tools for HCI researchers [19]. To come to a good understanding of the current practices in subjective data collection, we provide an overview of and discuss commonly used tools for retrospective data collection (see Table 1).

Diaries are the most frequently used tools for self-report studies [e.g. 25], that provide researchers with participants' own insights and narratives [26]. The diaries can be both paper-and-pencil and digital formats. Green et al. [27] compared the compliance of participants in these two designs by employing them in the same study. They found that regardless of the format, the compliance of the participants changed when a very narrow time window was applied. Therefore, the time window must be carefully defined depending on the research question.

A more structured and less time-consuming version of self-reports is experience sampling method (ESM), which originally focuses more on sampling of experience at random times [28]. It usually combines objective indices and contents [29] and grants "ecologically valid" assessments of human behaviour [30]. With an aim of minimizing the retrospective biases, ambulatory assessments (AA) compound self-reports with observational, physiological and behavioural methods and study people in their natural environment [31]. The common trait of these tools is that all can easily be applied both in physical and digital forms.

Recently, technological advancements have enabled researchers to develop easy to use and more advanced digital tools for self-report [32, 33]. For instance, ecological momentary assessment (EMA) [34] is an effective tool used to collect people's experiences, behaviours and moods in real-time and in real-world settings [35]. The emphasis in EMA is in collecting people's current state, that aims to avoid the biases of other subjective data collection tools [34]. Asking closed questions, this form of assessment corroborates to reliably collect momentary behavioural data of (i.e.) physical activity [36], dietary intake [37] or smoking cessation [38] very well. Nevertheless, especially the longer EMA studies require participant compliance [39] and strong infrastructure when it comes to collection of data flow and monitoring of the assessment completion [35].

Although self-reports can reveal insights about participant's experience over time, there are several drawbacks of self-reports. The report rate of the participants can decrease considerably over time, in correlation with the formulation (i.e. having too many questions asking for text input) [40] and length of the questions in self-reports (i.e. having too long questions) [41], resulting in fatigue effect (such as getting tired of answering the same questions over time) [42] and individual biases. Still, data collection in-the-wild can result in unexpected technical issues [21], such as interruptions in sensor recording [43] and variations in sensor placement in mobile devices [44].

One of the issues that emerge from these findings is that the forms of longitudinal subjective data collection can be perceived as labour-intensive by both the participants and the researchers. Most of the tools still rely on text-based input. We see that development of these tools has stayed very close to the original practices in the social sciences. However, there are other ways to express our experiences than using text that technology is able to capture. In addressing especially the report rate, which creates reliability problems for most commonly used methods, we find it promising to investigate alternative ways of subjective data collection. Considering the above-mentioned challenges, we propose that sensor-embedded everyday objects that participants wish to interact with can be utilized as a tool for SLDC purposes. The potential use of these objects as subjective data collection tool in longitudinal studies is still open to exploration, as advances in technology do not yet provide a definitive solution for capturing subjective experiences. In the next section, we discuss how our ideas can have broad implications in designing and developing the future of subjective data collection tools.

3   Imagining the Future of SLDC Tools

Considering the capabilities of HCI researchers, we argue that HCI research has the competencies to overcome the presented challenges (see: Table 1) of SLDC methods. To imagine the future of SLDC tools, we studied the enablers and barriers of using everyday objects to collect subjective data in longitudinal studies. For this purpose, we conducted three video conference sessions with duos of experienced researchers. In the following parts, we explain the details of these discussion sessions. The outcomes of the discussion sessions were input for imagined scenarios presenting alternative means for subjective data collection that can help overcome current challenges in this field.

Participants

To select the participants, we set the following criteria: the researcher must have been involved in at least one longitudinal study that involved human participants in HCI or adjacent fields as a hands-on researcher. One of our goals was to reach out to researchers with diverse research interests in terms of both research methodologies and application fields. With these criteria we scanned our network and preselected 13 researchers. We reached out to these researchers, informed them about the goals of our research and invited them to participate in an online discussion session. Six researchers responded positively. The other invitees, despite their interest in the topic, were not able to participate due to time limitations.

Of the participants, two were pursuing a Ph.D. degree, while four were working as post-doctoral faculty members in three different universities. The background and research interest of each researcher is presented in Table 2. The researchers had 3–7 years of experience in research involving human participants. The methods the researchers are familiar with are also listed in the below table. In the end, we were

Table 2 Participants of the discussion sessions

Session	# Researcher	Researcher background	Academic position	Research interest	Experience in research methods
1	R1	Computer science	Assistant professor	Physical activity behaviour change	Automatic (sensor) data collection and reflective interviews
	R2	Psychology	Ph.D. researcher	Well-being technologies in forensic mental health care	Questionnaires
2	R3	Design engineer	Assistant professor	Research methodologies in the process of design	Paper-based self-reports
	R4	Interaction design	Ph.D. researcher	The effect of nature on mental well-being of hospital patients	Paper-based self-reports, observations
3	R5	Industrial design	Post-doctoral researcher	User experience of emerging and future technologies	Self-reports, diary studies and reflective interviews
	R6	Industrial design	Assistant professor	Integration of user experience research methods in design process	Paper-based and online diary studies

able to include researchers with different backgrounds who are all working in diverse application fields and active in HCI research.

Flow of the Discussion Sessions

We prepared a 15 slides' PowerPoint presentation to facilitate the discussion sessions. The slide stack consisted of three parts. The first part was for welcoming the participants, introductions and explaining the aim of the session. The second part was for presenting an overview of existing subjective data collection tools and challenges of employing those in longitudinal HCI studies. The third part was explicitly for illustrative and discussion facilitation purposes. This part is built up on two slightly challenging subjective data collection scenarios. Those scenarios highlighted possible needs of future researchers to effortlessly and reliably apply subjective data collection tools in longitudinal HCI studies. The first scenario was urging the need of collecting participants' *perceived effort* in an exertion activity. For this scenario, we illustrated a runner from whom future researchers would collect *perceived increase in effort* data during a high-intensity workout. The challenge of the scenario is that due to the intensity of the workout, the runner is not able to speak, nor stop to provide feedback. In the second scenario, we illustrated an elderly person, from whom future researchers would collect *satisfaction* data in a home context. We raised the challenge of this scenario as the incapability of the elderly person in using emergent technologies. While preparing these scenarios, we put forward several aspects of connected everyday objects as enablers of subjective data collection. These were exemplified as "having physical affordances, material properties and spatio-temporal relationships" as suggested by [45].

The online sessions started with presenting the first part of the presentation and getting acquainted with each other. For this part, first author shared her screen with the researchers. After the first three slides, screen sharing was disabled, and each participant was invited to tell more about their prior experience in participant research, and the connection they see between their research and the subject of the current research. Afterwards, the first author reshared her screen and presented second and third parts of the presentation.

Researchers were informed that after the presentation, the discussions were envisioned to evolve around the two illustrated scenarios. We also invited the participants to feel free to ask any questions that came up during the presentation. Where necessary, to clarify what we mean by sensor-embedded everyday objects, we gave existing examples such as smart watches or the previously mentioned Phillips Baby Bottle [17]. In the end of the third part, the screen share was disabled again and the discussion started. The discussions were formed around our two goals: (1) collecting inspiring ideas for using everyday objects as data collection tools in the scenarios proposed and (2) discovering potentials of using everyday objects as subjective data collection tools for researchers' own research projects.

4 Results

After each discussion session, we transcribed the voice recordings into Word documents. We analysed researchers' experiences of current subjective data collection separately. The rest of the data was thematically analysed. These themes were then discussed among the authors who ultimately arrived at four themes, that were covering the separate discussions completely and exclusively.

We recognized two directions in the results: (1) capturing subjective experiences through objective measures; (2) discussions around new directions for subjective data collection. We also found promising suggestions made by the researchers. To better conceptualize the results, we asked five second year industrial design students to visualize the results. We present our findings next to these visualizations in the following parts.

4.1 Capturing Subjective Experiences Through Objective Measures

During the sessions, researchers discussed important differences, benefits and drawbacks of collecting both objective and subjective data. Moreover, they discussed how they could be combined. We briefly present this discussion here before moving on to new SLDC tools.

It was suggested that automatically captured data could transform into a powerful subjective data collection tool. Over the three discussion sessions, we observed consensus among the researchers on this. Researchers described three stages in this type of data collection. First, objective data on research-significant moments would be captured by sensors. Collecting research-significant data was indicated to be important in order to eliminate the burden of analysing non-tagged research data. Second, this data would be shared with the people. Finally, the people would be asked to reflect on what the collected data means for them. This way, subjective data collection could be less repetitive and less boring for participants because they are only asked to reflect on relevant use-episodes. As an example, R1 explained a previous study of measuring perceived fatigue over multiple running trainings. In that specific study, the researchers wanted to reliably capture "perceived effort" by using repeated measures of several sensors. Following, the researchers asked the participants to reflect on their own data and report their perceived effort during and in between several workouts. While this provides a way to combine objective with subjective data, this type of research setting might lead participants to overinterpret the data because they feel pressured to make sense of it.

R6 suggested that using a method similar to the one explained above, fluctuations in heart rate measurements collected by smart sensors could be shown to runners to gather their subjective reflections after a running workout. Combining objective data with self-reflections collection is not completely new. For instance, in an explorative study, Gouveia and Karapanos [24] investigated the effectiveness of camera-captured memory cues during diary studies. They found that visual cues, such as pictures from the context of experience, is the most effective memory trigger in recalling activity tracking experiences. However, this way of capturing data does not eliminate the retrospective challenges of longitudinal HCI studies completely. Retrospective investigation still has the pitfall that the reports of the participants about the moment they are reflecting on are influenced by their present feelings.

The participants in our study stated that emotions, as a subjective measurement outcome, are interesting, yet challenging to reliably capture. R2 shared her knowledge in validated studies of emotion capturing by technology. A large body of work on emotion recognition by technology has been studying how to reliably capture people's emotional states through their tone of voice [e.g. 46]. R5 suggested to make use of the knowledge available in this field by using vocal interaction with smart objects as a natural way of objective data collection over subjective experiences. She suggested that in the near future, products like Alexa or Google Home could be programmed to understand the feelings of participants in home context (Fig. 1, left image). This was found to be a pleasant way of collecting emotional states, especially for people who have problems with sight or using hands. However, R1 and R3 criticized these and similar attempts to use technology to capture emotions. These researchers recommended refraining from automatic capturing of emotions, not only because it is hard to reliably capture emotions, but also because it may be more important to understand how a person actually looks back on and memorizes a certain experience.

Alternatively, R5 recommended that people could be asked to interact with a smart object (a lamp in this case, Fig. 1, right image) to select a colour that best expresses their emotional states, at certain moments of the experiment. Achieving this could lead to a labour-free way of reflecting on participants' mood or emotional state. Although this was not specifically mentioned in the discussion with participants, we believe that the body of work on the relation between colours and emotions [i.e. 47] could be used to build future studies on.

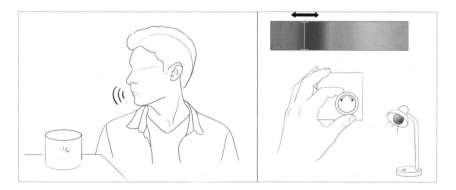

Fig. 1 Examples for "selecting" and "vocal interaction"

Researchers also agreed that the HCI domain can benefit from the capabilities of the field to create "fun" (R2, R4) and "interactive" (R1, R5, R6) ways of subjective data collection. Designers could also assist HCI researchers in developing more "user-friendly" (R3), "intuitive" (R5) and "engaging" (R3, R5, R6) subjective data collection tools. Researchers pointed out the importance of understandable, intuitive interactions in collecting reliable subjective data collection through everyday objects. These exemplify simple ways of interacting, such as touching. A domain of HCI that has recently been developed, affective haptics, deals with the skills of smart surfaces to identify the characteristics of touch (such as an angry touch or a comforting touch) [48]. This possibility could be further elaborated on for subjective data collection purposes as we will also see in the examples proposed in Sect. 2.

We noticed that the importance of SLDC was acknowledged by the researchers. The topic was found to be "timely" (R3) and "significant" (R1 and R5) for the HCI domain. These researchers agreed that the existing subjective data collection tools could be extended with or merged into artefacts that human participants could more easily use to express their experience. R3 and R6 indicated that sensor-embedded everyday objects could be "promising" and "effective" next-generation subjective data collection tools. As an example, R4 expressed her experience of patient-research in hospital setting. Her biggest challenge was that the participants were not comfortable in speaking about their feelings, while it was easier for them to communicate those when family members came to visit. This researcher stated that, even though it is fundamentally different from interacting with people, interacting with everyday objects could well be utilized as subjective data collection tools. She imagined that the patients could use the sensor-embedded everyday object for story telling purposes throughout the day. R4 did not provide any further insight about how a patient would interact with everyday objects or what they should look like but others did offer such ideas as we shall discuss in the next section.

4.2 Discussions Around New Directions for Subjective Data Collection

We observed several recurring ideas in the results. We categorized these ideas under the categories that we asked during the video discussion sessions: "physical affordances, material properties and spatio-temporal relationships" [45] of everyday objects. We combine the emergent ideas with scenarios to come to a more clear image of potential scenarios for using the sensor-embedded everyday objects as subjective data collection tools.

Sen and Sener [45] discuss above-mentioned three dimensions as the sources of sensorial enrichment in product interactions. Gibson explains affordances as all the possible actions that physical capabilities of products supported [49, 50]. Physical affordance covers the physical qualities of interactive products such as the physical alterations in size, weight, colour as well as the position of the interactive controls on the products [45]. Material properties are as the descriptive properties of the materials, such as rigidity, elasticity of the materials, which are inherent to the materials and can naturally enhance the physical affordances [45]. The difference between physical affordances and material properties is that physical affordances is all about what type of interaction products afford, material properties is about how we can interact with the materials [e.g. 51]. Spatio-temporal relationships of interactive products are about the change of places, proximity between the controls and speed and repetition of physical manipulations [45].

Physical Affordances

In two of the video sessions, it was suggested that physical properties of everyday objects could be a labour-free way of data collection for participants. In all three discussion sessions, researchers suggested multiple ways of using the physical properties of objects as a way of collecting subjective data from people. Tactile interactions with objects such as pressing, tapping, touching or stroking could be used, where the amount of "pressing", "tapping" "touching" or "stroking" or the mere presence of one type of interaction over the other would inform the researchers about the subjective patterns in an experience. For instance, R6 suggested using photo frames as a subjective data collection tool. A smart photo frame could display a range of images and, in a research context, "touching" or "hugging" a photo frame could be natural way to express varying "emotions" towards pictures presented in smart photo frames where hugging would for example communicate love for the image on display and mere touching would indicate interest (Fig. 2).

It was suggested that subjective data collection through using physical affordances of everyday objects could also be implemented into sensor-embedded clothes. For

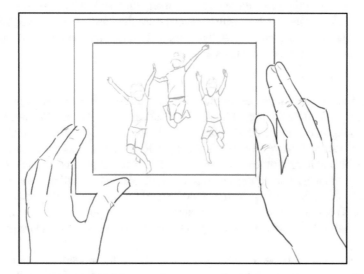

Fig. 2 Touching smart photo frame as a subjective data collection method

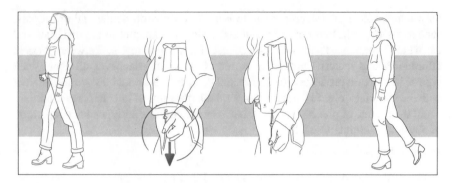

Fig. 3 Pulling buckle of jacket for subjective data collection

instance, R5 suggested that a "pulling" function could be implemented into a certain garment of a participant, and the person wearing the garment could be requested to provide subjective data by interacting with the embedded sensors. In the same discussion session, R6 suggested that this idea could be applied to different scenarios. R5 and R6 built up a scenario in which this function was implemented. In this scenario, it was assumed that the goal of the research is to explore how often participants experience pleasant moments during city walks over time, participants could be asked to report those moments by interacting an accessory of a sensor-embedded jacked. Aligned with their suggestion, in the example, we illustrated below, the participant can pull the buckle of their jacket to the right to report positive experiences while pulling the buckle to the left can be used for reporting negative experiences (Fig. 3).

This way of data collection can also be an alternative for real-life data collection tools. Relevant initiatives are coming to market, such as Levi's commuter trucker jacket [52], that uses touch-sensitive, copper-core threads, woven directly into the fabric. This example alone shows that similar types of interaction could soon be implemented into research contexts as well.

Material Properties

Ideas for using material properties in subjective data collection arose as a possibility for measuring certain feelings (Fig. 4). For instance, R2 articulated that referring to the flexibility of certain materials, some type of "stress ball" could be an unobtrusive way of measuring "stress" experience of people. R2 suggested that participants could squeeze the ball in case of feeling stressed, and the fluctuations in data could provide frequency and length of feeling stress. In this type of research setting, data about the length and the strength of squeezing could be used to compare within person subjective data. This type of interaction is already accessible in physical and occupational therapy studies [53] and could be employed for subjective data collection purposes as well.

Another possibility would be using elasticity of the materials. For instance, stretching the fabric of clothes would be a way of providing data about feelings at a certain moment. This idea emerged while R5 was talking about measuring the

Fig. 4 Using material
qualities for subjective data
collection

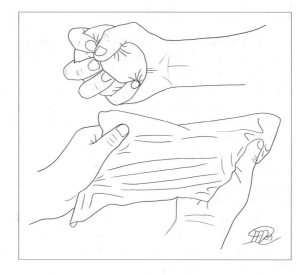

tiredness level of runners. Especially in the studies where performance athletes such
as runners or cyclists, are the participants, material properties of clothes could be
used for subjective data collection purposes (Fig. 5). In this use case, athletes could
be asked to provide subjective feedback about the level of exertion they feel during
the workout, by stretching the fabric of the t-shirt they wear. R5 suggested that using
the elasticity of the fabric, the type of data that is challenging to collect during the
activity can be collected by using the material properties of clothes.

While we see the potential of expanding the research with material properties of
objects, we acknowledge, that especially in this example, material properties and the
physical affordances of sensor-embedded everyday objects can be complementary
and intertwined: the elasticity of the material of the object could be combined with
the physical affordances (the degree of elasticity).

Fig. 5 Smart t-shirt as data collection tool

Spatio-temporal Relationships

Another possibility of using sensor-embedded everyday objects in subjective data collection is to reappraise the spatio-temporal relations of objects with their use contexts. R6 stated that moving (Fig. 6) a simple and data-related object from one place to another could be used for collecting subjective data This idea emerged during the discussions about collecting subjective data in a home context. R5 and R6, emphasizing their experience of longitudinal studies, especially in kitchen and home contexts, suggested that the objects that people use frequently at home could be transformed into subjective data collection tools. Considering the diversity of people they interviewed within the longitudinal studies, they argued that especially in home contexts, people should feel comfortable about using (products) and should not be forced to use tools they might not be familiar with. For example, in a study on the experience and effectiveness of a virtual coach for lifestyle change, participants might be asked to place a sensor-embedded bottle on a kitchen cabinet if they did not like the particular coaching message they were given and on the kitchen counter if they did like the message.

In our final example, we discuss a scenario that shows how collecting subjective data could be implemented into studies that require the input of older adults. During the session with R5 and R6, it was suggested that garments or accessories that participants carry could be used to collect subjective data outside the home contexts. To clarify their proposition, these researchers developed an idea in which subjective data from older adults was collected through a sensor-embedded everyday object such as a scarf (Fig. 7). It must be noted that these researchers suggest "scarf" as an example, rather than a "must-use" product like a coat, allowing the person the freedom not to use the sensor-embedded garment. The test objects could also be things like an umbrella or a hat. R5 and R6 emphasized that the data collection objects must be selected from the range of products that participants are familiar with. These objects must also make sense in the context of data collection.

In the scenario that was developed in session 3, that we visualize below, wearing the scarf could be taken as an indication that the elderly person is willing to provide subjective data. The researchers portrayed a research set-up in which older adults

Fig. 6 Example
"spatio-temporal relations"

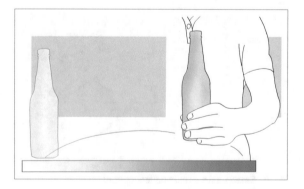

Fig. 7 Scarf as a subjective data collection tool

are encouraged to take more steps while the researchers monitor their fatigue level. In such a set-up, older adults could be asked to interact with the scarf to provide subjective data (fatigue during physical activity). The data collection moments could be emerged by detecting the most research-significant moments such as when the person sits on a bank in a park to take a rest. In such a scenario, the data collection tool, a scarf in this case, must be dedicated only for the data collection purposes, in order to avoid conflicts of use.

5   Discussions and Conclusion

In this chapter, we presented sensor-embedded everyday objects as promising future subjective data collection tools in longitudinal HCI studies. Since the beginning of the last decade, understanding user experiences has been interesting for HCI researchers to be able to design interactive systems that fulfil users' needs [4, 7]. Recognizing the necessity of capturing experiences over a period of time, HCI researchers were challenged with finding ways to explore people's experiences in-the-wild [21]. While collecting objective data is relatively smooth with very well developed personal informatics tools, collecting subjective data is still a considerable challenge in longitudinal HCI studies.

For subjective data collection purposes, the HCI field adopted various methods and tools from social science research domains such as psychology and anthropology. As we explained in Sect. 2, these tools include several forms of self-reports, such as diaries, experience sampling method, ambulatory assessment and ecological momentary assessment. We portrayed one of the main challenges of these methods as increasing participants' fatigue in responding over time, and therefore decreasing the reliability of the studies. Besides this, for digital data collection tools, technical problems in sensor recording may result in interruptions of data collection. Overcoming the infrastructure hurdles is something that can eventually be solved, while the other challenges need all the creativity the HCI community has to offer. We argue that going beyond adopting existing tools in other research domains, HCI researchers can design their own research tools for subjective data collection purposes.

The findings presented in this paper highlighted several new directions for subjective data collection in longitudinal studies. Some of the directions we propose have similarities with exiting studies that use everyday objects as data collection tools such as the work of Giaccardi et al. [54]. In their work, they suggest using things as data collection tools and using sensor-embedded objects as data collection. However, the difference is that we ask for active participation of people for subjective data collection, but in a more intuitive and automatic way.

We see the opportunity that the directions presented in Sect. 4.2 could alleviate some of the mental burden that research set-ups put on people. In current practices of subjective data collection methods, the participants are asked to fill in text-based questionnaires by using smartphones or paper-based data collection tools. Conversely, we propose that data collection tools can be selected from everyday objects that make sense in the context of data collection and that the people are familiar with. One way to employ this method is familiarity with objects (e.g. a scarf), and the other is meaning attributed to the interaction (e.g. hugging or mere touching). People's familiarity with data collection objects (similar to the example of scarf) as well as the connotations that these tools elicit in use context (such as wearing the scarf while going for a walk) can help researchers to reduce the mental burden that longitudinal studies can induce on people. With this approach, using sensor-embedded objects as a data collection tools may partly overcome lower response rates and biases due to the formulation of the questions that traditional data collection tools impose [31–33].

We believe that sensor-embedded everyday objects have the potential to be developed into a new category of data collection tools. We have presented a number of interactions with subjective collection tools that are the first to think of, when considering the use of this type of objects in daily life. To come to smart solutions for interactions, the field may make a link with shape-changing interfaces [55]. This type of interfaces has so far mostly been used to provide status feedback, but they could also be interfaces for subjective feedback.

Despite the need and opportunity for sensor-embedded everyday objects in longitudinal HCI studies, we see some weaker points. In order to successfully implement these objects in research studies, we invite researchers to consider the following points carefully. These points are especially important in order not to overwhelm people with the ambitions of the researchers' goals, but rather engage the people with the longitudinal studies.

1. *Reduce participant effort*: The perceived effort of the participant influences the participants' responsiveness in repetitive measures studies. In the case of using everyday objects for subjective data collection purposes, it is essential to make the participants comfortable about the demanded time and cognitive effort for participating. This connects to points 2 and 3.

2. *Collect one type of data at one time*: Researchers should prioritize the importance of subjective data being collected from participants. After all, with the type of

interactions that we propose in the scenarios, only one question can be answered with one object. If there is an interest of collecting multiple data, using multiple sensor-embedded everyday objects could be considered or perhaps the object could be designed in a way that it allows for response on two variables. However, researchers should be very cautious not to complicate the use of the objects for data collection.

3. *Find friendly ways of using sensor-embedded everyday objects*: Not every form of everyday object might be suitable for subjective data collection. The researchers should review the objects that participants use within the context of experience (such as a t-shirt during a running experience). The researchers should find the most relevant everyday object that is meaningful for the experience to embed sensors in.

4. *Consider user privacy*: Using sensor-embedded objects pose the danger of easily violating the privacy of individuals. Therefore, the ethics of using these objects in data collection should be well elaborated. Researchers should think carefully about the perceptions of participants and other individuals within the context of data collection, to avoid giving the impression of "big brother is watching us".

5. *Consider frequency of data collection moments*: It is still probable that the set-up of the research results in participants dropping outs. In that sense, the research should be flexible enough so that the frequency of data collection moments could be adapted. For instance, when it becomes clear that at a certain phase of the research the participants become idle, a clear reframing of data collection moment could be planned to reduce the burden on participants. This obviously demands flexibility of the studies in the way everyday objects are used for subjective data collection purposes.

One limitation of the present study is that the set-up of our video sessions with researchers might have affected the outcomes, as we had presented predefined roots and scenarios. On the other hand, our findings showed that the participants already had experience and knowledge about the directions we proposed and did not feel restricted to only those scenarios.

We believe that the directions we proposed in this chapter are promising, yet still might be difficult to develop. The proposed subjective data collection directions require extensive work for developing reliable sensors and strong infrastructures. While reducing the burden on the participants, those tools have the danger to increase the time investment of researchers on tackling the technical challenges of proposed subjective data collection tools. In that respect, the ideas might still align with the challenges of EMA [34]. Future research can explore ways to overcome these challenges, by collaboration of multiple HCI researchers and sharing their experiences in a platform that the tools developed for subjective data collection purposes are showcased.

The ideas presented in this chapter should be considered as envisioned possibilities for future studies, rather than reliable and valid subjective data collection tools. We hope that these ideas will inspire the HCI researchers to discover new opportunities of collecting subjective data in longitudinal HCI studies.

References

1. Hassenzahl M (2018) The thing and I: understanding the relationship between user and product. In: Funology 2. Springer, pp. 301–313
2. Shin Y et al (2017) Design for experience innovation: understanding user experience in new product development. Behav Inf Technol 36(12):1218–1234
3. Kjeldskov J, Skov MB, Stage J (2005) Does time heal?: A longitudinal study of usability. In: OZCHI
4. Kujala S et al (2011) UX Curve: a method for evaluating long-term user experience. Interact Comput 23(5):473–483
5. Ledger D, McCaffrey D (2014) Inside wearables: how the science of human behavior change offers the secret to long-term engagement. Endeavour Partners, Cambridge, MA, USA
6. Karapanos E, et al (2009) User experience over time: an initial framework. In: Proceedings of the 27th international conference on human factors in computing systems. ACM: Boston, MA, USA, pp 729–738
7. Karapanos E et al (2010) Measuring the dynamics of remembered experience over time. Interact Comput 22(5):328–335
8. Gerken J (2011) Longitudinal research in human-computer interaction. Universitat Konstanz
9. Ployhart RE, Vandenberg RJ (2010) Longitudinal research: the theory, design, and analysis of change. J Manag 36(1):94–120
10. Gerken J, Bak P, Reiterer H (2007) Longitudinal evaluation methods in human-computer studies and visual analytics. In: InfoVis
11. Ravichandran R, et al (2017) Making sense of sleep sensors: how sleep sensing technologies support and undermine sleep health. In: Proceedings of the 2017 CHI conference on human factors in computing systems
12. Lupton D (2017) Self-tracking, health and medicine. Taylor & Francis
13. Rooksby J, et al (2014) Personal tracking as lived informatics. In: Proceedings of the SIGCHI conference on human factors in computing systems
14. Harrison D, et al (2014) Tracking physical activity: problems related to running longitudinal studies with commercial devices. In: Proceedings of the 2014 ACM international joint conference on pervasive and ubiquitous computing: adjunct publication
15. Coskun A (2019) Design for long-term tracking: insights from a six-month field study exploring users' experiences with activity trackers. Des J 22(5):665–686
16. Narici M, et al (2020) Impact of sedentarism due to the COVID-19 home confinement on neuromuscular, cardiovascular and metabolic health: Physiological and pathophysiological implications and recommendations for physical and nutritional countermeasures. Eur J Sport Sci 1–22
17. Bogers S et al (2016) Connected baby bottle: a design case study towards a framework for data-enabled design. In: Proceedings of the 2016 ACM conference on designing interactive systems
18. Robbins ML, Kubiak T (2014) Ecological momentary assessment in behavioral medicine. The handbook of behavioral medicine. Wiley, Ltd, pp 429–46
19. Ayobi A, et al (2018) Flexible and mindful self-tracking: design implications from paper bullet journals. In: Proceedings of the 2018 CHI Conference on Human Factors in Computing Systems
20. Sarzotti F (2018) Self-monitoring of emotions and mood using a tangible approach. Computers 7(1):7
21. Vaizman Y, et al (2018) Extrasensory app: data collection in-the-wild with rich user interface to self-report behavior. In: Proceedings of the 2018 CHI conference on human factors in computing systems
22. Schwarz N (1999) Self-reports: how the questions shape the answers. Am Psychol 54(2):93
23. Gerald JH, George SH (2010) Self-report: psychology's four-letter word. Am J Psychol 123(2):181–188
24. Gouveia R, Karapanos E (2013) Footprint tracker: supporting diary studies with lifelogging. In: Proceedings of the SIGCHI conference on human factors in computing systems

25. Blaynee J, et al (2016) Collaborative HCI and UX: longitudinal diary studies as a means of uncovering barriers to digital adoption. In: Proceedings of the 30th international BCS human computer interaction conference 30
26. Blandford A, Furniss D, Makri S (2016) Qualitative HCI research: going behind the scenes. Synth Lect Human-centered Inf 9(1):1–115
27. Green AS et al (2006) Paper or plastic? Data equivalence in paper and electronic diaries. Psychol Methods 11(1):87
28. Larson R, Csikszentmihalyi M (2014) The experience sampling method. Flow and the foundations of positive psychology. Springer, pp 21–34
29. Nehrkorn-Bailey AM, Reardon MS, Hicks Patrick J (2018) Some methodological and analytical issues related to real-time data capture studies. Transl Issues Psychol Sci 4(4):349
30. Pejovic V, et al (2016) Mobile-based experience sampling for behaviour research. Emotions and personality in personalized services. Springer, pp 141–161
31. Trull TJ, Ebner-Priemer U (2013) Ambulatory assessment. Annu Rev Clin Psychol 9:151–176
32. Youngs A, Graf AS (2017) Innovating the innovation: Applying mobile research methods to experience sampling. J Soc, Behav, Health Sci 11(1):8
33. Van Berkel N, Ferreira D, Kostakos V (2017) The experience sampling method on mobile devices. ACM Comput Surv (CSUR) 50(6):1–40
34. Shiffman S, Stone AA, Hufford MR (2008) Ecological momentary assessment. Annu Rev Clin Psychol 4:1–32
35. Burke LE et al (2017) Ecological momentary assessment in behavioral research: addressing technological and human participant challenges. J Med Int Res 19(3):e77
36. Dunton GF (2017) Ecological momentary assessment in physical activity research. Exerc Sport Sci Rev 45(1):48
37. Rangan AM, et al (2015) Electronic Dietary Intake Assessment (e-DIA): comparison of a mobile phone digital entry app for dietary data collection with 24-hour dietary recalls. JMIR mHealth uHealth 3(4):e98
38. McCarthy DE et al (2015) An experimental investigation of reactivity to ecological momentary assessment frequency among adults trying to quit smoking. Addiction 110(10):1549–1560
39. Stone AA, Shiffman S (2002) Capturing momentary, self-report data: a proposal for reporting guidelines. Ann Behav Med 24(3):236–243
40. Sahar F, et al (2014) Identifying the user experience factors of a multi-component sports product. In: Proceedings of the 18th international academic MindTrek conference: media business, management, content & services
41. Yang T, Linder J, Bolchini D (2012) DEEP: design-oriented evaluation of perceived usability. Int J Human-Comput Inter 28(5):308–346
42. La Bruna A, Rathod S (2005) Questionnaire length and fatigue effects. Bloomerce White Paper# 5, Accessed 15 July 2007
43. Stisen A et al (2015) Smart devices are different: assessing and mitigating mobile sensing heterogeneities for activity recognition. In: Proceedings of the 13th ACM conference on embedded networked sensor systems
44. Kunze K, Lukowicz P (2014) Sensor placement variations in wearable activity recognition. IEEE Pervasive Comput 13(4):32–41
45. Şen G, Şener B (2019) Enriching the aesthetics of mobile music player interactions through the use of personal clothing and accessories as interfaces. METU JFA 2:141
46. Garcia-Garcia JM, Penichet VM, Lozano MD (2017) Emotion detection: a technology review. In: Proceedings of the XVIII international conference on human computer interaction
47. Naz K, Epps H (2004) Relationship between color and emotion: a study of college students. College Student J 38(3):396
48. Jiao Y, Xu Y (2020) Affective haptics and multimodal experiments research. In: International conference on human-computer interaction. Springer
49. Gibson JJ (1977) The theory of affordances. Hilldale, USA 1(2)
50. Greeno JG (1994) Gibson's affordances
51. Karana E, Pedgley O, Rognoli V (2015) On materials experience. Des Issues 31(3):16–27

52. Designing the Levi's commuter trucker jacket with jacquard by google. Available from: https://www.ideo.com/case-study/designing-the-levis-commuter-trucker-jacket-with-jacquard-by-google
53. Vandenberghe B (2020) Squeeze interaction in physical & occupational therapy. In: Companion publication of the 2020 ACM designing interactive systems conference
54. Giaccardi E, et al (2016) Thing ethnography: doing design research with non-humans. In: Proceedings of the 2016 ACM conference on designing interactive systems
55. Kwak M, et al (2014) The design space of shape-changing interfaces: a repertory grid study. In: Proceedings of the 2014 conference on designing interactive systems

Experiments, Longitudinal Studies, and Sequential Experimentation: How Using "Intermediate" Results Can Help Design Experiments

Maurits Kaptein

Abstract This chapter formalizes the traditional randomized experiment as a sequential decision problem in which treatments are allocated to units sequentially to achieve a specific goal. This problem description is known as the multi-armed bandit (MAB) problem and we describe it in detail and relate it to the methodological considerations that arise when designing longitudinal studies in HCI. Subsequently, the chapter reviews multiple treatment allocation policies—attempts to solve the MAB problem—and analyzes their properties. Next, we discuss utility of a sequential perspective on experimentation for various methodological purposes such as early stopping, best arm selection, and powerful testing. We demonstrate how in many cases, and particularly in longitudinal studies, the "intermediate" results of an experiment can be used to improve the experimental design. We close off by discussing several recent software packages that allow readers to implement and analyze sequential experiments.

Keywords Sequential experimentation · Multi-armed bandits · Thompson sampling · StreamingBandit · Contextual

1 Introduction

Within HCI experiments are common: in the classic experiment, participants (or users) are randomly allocated to one of multiple treatments to allow for the estimation of the causal effect of the treatment (see, e.g., [24, 49], for more details on the rationale behind randomized experiments). A simple example of an experiment in HCI would be the random allocation of users to different versions of a mobile exercise application (see, e.g., [30]) to examine which version of the application is most successful. In this context, the term *longitudinal research*—which is the sub-

M. Kaptein (✉)
Professor of Data Science & Health, The Jheronimus Academy of Data Science (JADS), Tilburg University,
Tilburg, The Netherlands
e-mail: m.c.kaptein@uvt.nl

© Springer Nature Switzerland AG 2021
E. Karapanos et al. (eds.), *Advances in Longitudinal HCI Research*,
Human–Computer Interaction Series, https://doi.org/10.1007/978-3-030-67322-2_7

ject of this book—is frequently used to refer to the practice of measuring the usage (and the effects thereof) of the different application versions over a longer period of time. In this chapter, we will discuss an alternative view on longitudinal experiments which is better captured by the name "sequential experiments"; in this framework of designing experiments the aim is not necessarily on longitudinal effects (i.e., effects over a longer period of time), but rather on the ability to, over time, as opposed to in one single shot, allocate participants to treatments. Thus, when planning sequential experiments we assume that participants arrive one by one, and that for each participant we can choose which treatment to administer, *possibly using data collected on earlier participants to drive our treatment allocation decisions*. This chapter aims to introduce this sequential view on experimentation and distills lessons from the rich literature on sequential experiments that are useful for planning, designing, and analyzing HCI studies. Furthermore, we discuss how a sequential view on experimentation might be particularly insightful when designing longitudinal experiments.

To better introduce the conceptual idea behind sequential experiments, let us start from a very simple—and not necessarily longitudinal—HCI study: a researcher aims to evaluate the usability of three different versions of a new desktop application by randomly assigning prospective users of the app to one of the three versions and having them carry out a simple task in the usability lab. Thus, one by one, users are allowed into the lab, placed behind the screen, and they carry out the task. After carrying out the task, users rate the usability using a simple rating scale. Earlier power calculations by the researcher demonstrated that 35 users per group would be sufficient for a sufficiently powerful test; thus, the researchers recruit and allocate a total of $n = 105$ users and subsequently analyze the resulting data. Now, there are two ways of thinking about this data-generating process:

1. *The traditional experiment view*: First, we can think about this experiment as effectively creating three groups of users $g = 1, \ldots, g = 3$, each providing $n_g = 35$ datapoints. Our final dataset simply consists of $n = 105$ rows each with a group indicator (1, 2, or 3) and an outcome measure for each user i, y_i. The main analysis would consist of simply comparing the means of the three different groups, i.e., comparing $\bar{y}_1$ to $\bar{y}_2$ and $\bar{y}_3$.
2. *The sequential experiment view*: Second, we can think of the experiment as a sequence of treatment decisions followed by measurements. In practice, all the $n = 105$ respondents arrived in the usability lab *one by one*, thus we can think about our data as consisting of $t = 105$ timepoints, each generating a data-tuple consisting of the treatment allocation decision or *action a*, and the associated outcome y. Thus, we have $(a, y)_{t=1}, \ldots, (a, y)_{t=105}$ observed tuples that arrived in *sequence*.

Note that the above two views regarding the data-generating process in this simple HCI experiment both lead to a dataset that allows the researcher to compare the means of the usability scores in the three different groups. When this is the sole aim of the experiment, the first, traditional, view on the experiment usefully abstracts away from the fact that users in actuality arrive one by one and allows the researcher to focus on the three groups of interest in the analysis. The second view on the data generating process however provides an additional richness that is often overlooked by those thinking about experiments along the lines of the first view: the second view opens up the possibility that a treatment decision at some timepoints t' is affected by the observed treatment decisions and outcomes up to that time-point (i.e., $(a, y)_{t=1}, \ldots, (a, y)_{t=t'-1}$). Since this is not the case in the traditional experiment—in which treatments are assigned uniformly at random and thus not related to earlier measurements—the second view is often not even considered. In this chapter, however, we argue that the second view on experimentation is useful in many cases: it often allows researchers to achieve higher statistical power (or conversely make decisions based on smaller samples sizes), and it is advantageous when the experiment comes at a cost (e.g., when an experiment is conducted *in situ* and some outcome values are to be prevented as much as possible). The first view on the problem is merely a special case of the second that we can always resort to if the additional richness is not sought after.

The second, sequential, view on experiments is not only relevant for simple between subjects experiments such as the investigation of the two different versions of a desktop application. On the contrary, a sequential view on experimentation has already benefitted many longitudinal HCI studies. For example, while the experiment presented by Kaptein et al. [30] starts out as a simple randomized experiment, the longitudinal effects of the different versions of the different persuasive messages are measured during the experiment and used for subsequent treatment assignment: over time the most effective messages for each user are "learned", and subsequently, users are assigned to new treatment groups (i.e., effectively using a within-subjects design) that are directly affected by the earlier measurements. Thus, to fix terminology: the experiment by Kaptein et al. [30] is *longitudinal* as it tracks the effects of different interventions over a longer period of time (two weeks in this specific case). It is however also *sequential* in the sense that results obtained earlier in time affect the treatment allocation(s) at later points in time. It is exactly this latter mechanism that we explore in this chapter: How can "intermediate results"—either over time within a single subject, or between subjects when the subjects arrive in a sequence—be used when designing experiments. For simplicity, we focus primarily on the sequential arrival of subjects, but the main concepts presented in this chapter generalize to obtaining multiple measurements from individual subjects over time.

In the remainder of this chapter, we first introduce the so-called Multi-Armed Bandit (MAB) problem which serves as the canonical mathematical representation for sequential experiments [2, 9, 48]. We provide motivating examples and a formal description of the problem. Subsequently, we discuss various "solutions" to the MAB problem: we highlight that the traditional experiment itself is merely one potential solution to a MAB problem and we demonstrate potentially appealing alternatives. Next, we discuss utility of a sequential perspective on experimentation for various methodological purposes such as early stopping, best arm selection, and powerful testing. We close off by discussing several recent software packages that allow readers to implement and analyze sequential experiments.

2 Multi-armed Bandits: A Model for Sequential Experimentation

The sequential view on experimentation is often studied under the name: "the multi-armed bandit (MAB)" problem [3, 38, 44]. The MAB provides a description of the problem setting and is derived from one of its early motivating examples: consider facing a set of slot machines (also called one-armed bandits), each with a potentially different payoff. Next, given some fixed amount of money, decide how you will *sequentially*—after every play observing the outcome of that specific machine—play the machines such that you make as much money as possible [17]. As the payoffs of the machines potentially differ, the player has to balance learning which machine has the highest payoff (effectively by *exploring* all the machines), with frequently playing the machine that she/he believes has the highest payoff (effectively *exploiting* the most promising machine).

Mapping the canonical slot-machine problem back to our HCI example, we would formulate the problem as follows: given a fixed amount of users (105 in the simple study described above), the experimenter should decide *sequentially* which user receives which version of the desktop application. Thus, the sequentially arriving users take the position off the sequential plays of the machine, while the different experimental conditions map to the different one-armed bandit machines that are played. Mapping back from the HCI study to the MAB problem, the traditional experiment effectively dictates to put $\frac{1}{3}$ of the money in each slot machine (i.e., play each machine 35 times in our numerical example) after which the gambler will have some clue as to which machine is the best since she/he will have explored all the arms, but the traditional experiment does not include any exploitation.

It is important to note at this point that the original aim of the MAB problem is not the exact same as the aim of the traditional experiment: while closely related, the traditional experiment often focusses on "finding the best arm", i.e., finding the version of the application that has the highest usability score. The MAB problem, in its original formulation, conversely focusses on maximizing the outcome over all interactions (i.e., making sure that the usability score over all $n = 105$ users is high as possible). Clearly, these problems are closely related; the outcome over all interactions is maximized by selecting the best arm at each point in time. However, these problems are not the exact same: while in the experiment we aim to learn, as exactly as possible, the average outcome of each treatment, in the canonical MAB problem the experimenter would be tempted to quickly disregard treatments that seems suboptimal without caring about "how suboptimal" the treatment is exactly. We will revisit this distinction later in the chapter, for now we will focus on the canonical MAB problem in which the aim is to maximize the average outcome over all interactions.

2.1 Bandit Problems in Practice

Bandit problems—even in their original form—appear throughout the social and behavioral sciences [17, 27, 31]. Here we briefly highlight examples in political science, medicine, and educational psychology. Examples include, but are not limited to:

- *Donation requests to political campaign email list.* A political campaign has a list of email addresses of likely supporters and is trying to raise money for the campaign. Staffers have written several versions of emails to send to supporters and there are many different photos of the candidate to use in those emails. The campaign can randomize which variant of the email is sent to a supporter and observe how much they donate. Thus, the sequentially send out emails correspond to the sequential plays of the machines, the versions of the emails to the specific machines, and the donations to the payoffs.
- *Chemotherapy following surgery.* Following surgery for colon cancer, some guidelines recommend adjuvant chemotherapy, but there is substantial uncertainty about which patients should be given chemotherapy [20, 56]. For example, should older patients still be given chemotherapy? Continuing to randomize treatment of some types of patients even as the best treatment for other types is known could help discover improved treatment guidelines that reduce, e.g., five-year mortality. Here, the sequentially arriving patients correspond to the plays of the machines, the specific treatments to the specific machines, and the health outcome to the payoffs.
- *Psychological interventions in online courses.* Interventions designed to increase motivation and planning for overcoming obstacles are sometimes used in educational settings, including online courses where students begin and complete the course at their own pace. There are many variations on these interventions and students may respond differently to these variations. For example, motivational interventions might work differently for students from collectivist versus individualist cultures [35]. The learning software can randomize students to these interventions while learning which interventions work for (e.g., result in successful course completion) different types of students. In this case, the sequentially arriving students correspond to the sequential plays of the machines, the different interventions to the specific machines, and the student learning constitutes the payoff.

The omnipresence of the MAB problem throughout the sciences, and also in HCI, hopefully highlights that while the traditional experimental view on these problems is valuable, potentially other approaches might exists that are worth exploring.

At this point in the text, it is worth relating our examples back to longitudinal studies: while the three examples listed above seem like between-subject experiments with little longitudinal methodology (other than potentially outcomes that manifest over longer periods of time), this need not at all be the case for a sequential view on experimentation to be useful and open up new research designs. Consider the last example of students learning based on different online courses: In this case, we could approach the problem longitudinally (i.e., within-subjects) and map each, e.g., month of the students learning to the different plays of the machine, the learning program in place that specific month to the specific machine, and the learning outcome that month to the payoff: setup this way we have a longitudinal study, running over multiple months, that is potentially sequential in the sense that the performance of an individual student in earlier months might affect the choice of intervention in later months. It is this flexibility—that of using intermediate outcomes when assigning treatments—that we explore in this chapter.

2.2   A More Formal View Toward the MAB Problem

It is useful to describe the MAB problem a bit more formally. In the multi-armed bandit problem, a set of actions (the machines, often called *arms*) are assumed to have potentially heterogeneous stochastic payoffs and an experimenter aims to maximize the payoff over a sequence of selected actions. Multi-armed bandit problems can thus be formalized as follows [17, 38]: At each time (or interaction) $t = 1, \ldots, T$, we have a set of possible actions (i.e., arms, machines, treatments, interfaces) $\mathcal{A}$ at our disposal. After choosing an arm $a_t \in \mathcal{A}$ we observe reward r_t (it is common in the MAB literature to use r as the "dependent" measure as opposed to y in most of the traditional experimental methodology literature). The aim of the experimenter is to select actions so as to maximize the *cumulative reward*[1]:

$$\mathcal{R}_c = \sum_{t=1}^{T} r_t. \tag{1}$$

$\mathcal{R}_c$, in the gamblers example, simple denotes the sum of all the payoffs the gambler received. Toward the final purpose of maximizing the cumulative reward, much of the literature on the MAB problem focusses on developing, and examining the performance off, different treatment allocation *policies*. A treatment allocation policy in this setting can formally be defined as a mapping from all historical data D_{t-1} (all data until time point $t - 1$) to a new action a_t: $\pi(x_t, \mathcal{D}_{t-1}) \rightarrow a_t$. Informally, a policy is nothing more than the strategy the gambler uses at each point in time to determine which machine to play next. Different policies will lead to different (expected) outcomes: for example, always choosing the same action without regards for its outcome, while theoretically a valid policy, will, in expectation, lead to selecting a suboptimal arm with probability $\frac{1}{K}$ where K is the total number of possible actions. Effective policies perform much better than such naive random selection; we will review a number of policies below.

---

[1] Again note that this is the canonical aim in the MAB literature; it is often not how we think about designing experiments where the aim is often thought of as finding the action a that has the highest associated reward r (or even just learning which reward is associated with which arm).

Note that for the theoretical evaluation of policies, instead of assessing the performance using the cumulative reward $\mathcal{R}_c$, we often evaluate policies based on their (expected) cumulative *regret* [2, 10, 18]. The regret is the sum of the differences in reward between the most optimal policy (i.e., the policy that always plays the arm with the highest expected reward—this is in practice not known) and the allocation policy that is being assessed. Regret is defined as:

$$\mathbb{E}[R(t)] = \mathbb{E}\left[\sum_{i=1}^{t} r_i^* - r_i\right] \qquad (2)$$

where r^* is the reward of an optimal policy and is theoretically useful as it has a clear lower bound: a regret of 0 implies that the policy is acting optimally. Note that while the notation might look a bit daunting, regret is simply the expected performance of a gambler executing a specific strategy, compared to the performance of an oracle who knows which machine has the highest payoff.

2.3 Common Extensions: The cMAB Problem

In many social science applications, the outcome distribution likely depends on observable variables of the units being allocated. For example, in HCI, it is common that the computer literacy (e.g., [14]) of a user might affect their performance using a specific interface. Such differences between participants are not included in the traditional MAB formulation as each unit is supposed to be independent and identically distributed [8]. A common extension of the MAB problem, the *contextual* MAB problem, releases this assumption. In the contextual bandit problem [7–9, 15, 39], the set of past observations $\mathcal{D}$ is composed of triplets $(x, a, r)_t$, where the x denotes the context (i.e., covariates): additional information that is observed prior to the decision, rather than assigned by the experimenter.

The cMAB problem provides an extremely rich problem formalization that is used in many real-world applications. For example, the allocation of online content to users that have different properties is often approached as a cMAB problem [50]. Also, the allocation of medical treatments to patients, when treatment heterogeneity is expected, is often approached as a cMAB problem (see [21, 28, 29, 43], for examples). Below we discuss different policies to address the traditional MAB problem; note however that for most of these solutions extension to the cMAB problem are readily available.

3 Common Policies and Their Performance

In this section, we examine the performance of various bandit policies. Using the expected regret, as defined above, allows us to investigate the behavior of allocation policies and derive so-called regret bounds that describe how the regret of an allocation policy behaves in the long run (i.e., as T grows larger). This long-run behavior is an object of theoretical study, and for many policies, the asymptotic regret is known [10, 48, 57]. Also, for various problem descriptions (i.e., with specific reward distributions), to optimal regret any policy could achieve is known [38, 57]. Here however we do not focus on these theoretical result, but rather on the practical performance of various often used policies.

3.1 Common Policies

To make our discussion regarding the performance of various policies in practice more accessible, we ran a small simulation examining the performance of various bandit policies in a setting in which there are three arms available, each with a unit reward according to some probability. We choose success probabilities [0.9, 0.1, 0.1] for the three arms respectively, and thus any reasonable policy should, rather rapidly, converge toward choosing the first arm.

Figure 1 shows the performance of the five policies that we will discuss below; the lower the regret the better the performance of the policies. We discuss each policy and its behavior in detail below.

3.1.1 ϵ-First

As a first example, we discuss ϵ-first. ϵ-first can be described as follows: first, for n interactions, the policy chooses an action randomly with probability $\frac{1}{K}$ for each arm; this period is often called the *exploration phase*. In the remaining $T - n$ interactions, coined the *exploitation phase*, the policy chooses whichever arm achieved the highest reward during this exploration period [12].

Figure 1 clearly demonstrates the average behavior of ϵ-first over multiple simulation runs.[2] During the exploration phase, the policy incurs so-called linear regret as it is just randomly selecting actions and hence it has a $\frac{2}{3}$ probability of selecting one of the two suboptimal arms. Next, in the exploitation phase, the policy will select the arm that performed best during the (admittedly small in this case) exploration stage. The policy is most likely to select the optimal arm (the arm with a payoff probability of .9, but there is a non-zero-chance that a suboptimal arm is selected,

---

[2] In individual runs the policy will either select the correct arm after the exploration phase and thus incur 0 regret, or it will select one of the two suboptimal arms and incur $.9 - .1 = .8$ regret each round.

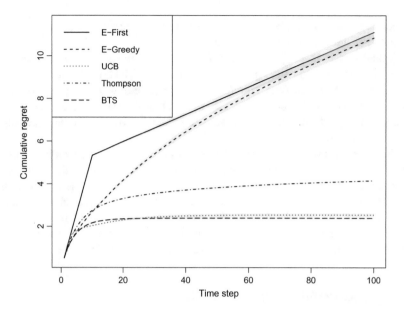

Fig. 1 The expected cumulative regret of five different policies on a 3-armed Bernoulli bandit

and hence this happens occasionally. Therefore, the expected regret is not zero after n rounds but rather the regret grows linearly. This linear growth of the regret of ϵ-first is asymptotically suboptimal: one can conceive policies that incur sub-linear regret and these will, in the long run, always outperform policies that have linear regret.

ϵ-First is often related to the traditional experiment. Consider the HCI experiment examining different interface versions as introduced earlier. In this case, the experiment itself constitutes the exploration phase of the ϵ-first policy: during the experiment we aim to learn which interface version is most usable. After the experiment, we likely make a choice and deploy the interface version that was most successful: the users that follow after the experiment are, in a way, part of the exploitation phase. The linear regret in Fig. 1 effectively shows that if our aim is to maximize the usability score over all users—thus both those included in the experiment as those downloading the software after we made our choice—ϵ-first can be outperformed.

3.1.2 ϵ-Greedy

Instead of having a separate exploration and exploitation phase, it is also possible to mix exploration and exploitation continuously. The simplest version policy that implements this idea is called ϵ-greedy [12, 39]. The ϵ-greedy policy effectively explores with probability ϵ, and with probability $1 - \epsilon$ the best performing arm— that that specific iteration t—is selected. Thus, if $\epsilon = 0.1$ (a common choice), in expectation, one every 10 plays an arm is selected at random, while the other 9 out of ten plays the arm that performed best in previous rounds is selected. Note that often, to get started, each arm is played once.

Typically, ϵ is fixed. This implies that there is a fixed, and clearly non-zero, probability of choosing the wrong arm at each point in time, even after a large number of interactions. Thus, similar to ϵ-first, ϵ-greedy will asymptotically incur linear regret as can also be seen clearly in Fig. 1. It is possible to decrease ϵ as a function of, e.g., the number of iterations to reduce improve upon the linear regret incurred when fixing ϵ.

This latter idea provides a nice intuition toward understanding policies that have sub-linear regret: To achieve sub-linear regret a policy has to steadily decrease its rate of exploration as the number of interactions—and thus the available information—grow. However, as we learned from discussing ϵ-first, setting the probability of exploration to zero too early also ensures linear (expected) regret, as the policy is bound to select a wrong arm occasionally. A careful balancing act between exploration and exploitation is thus necessary to create asymptotically optimal policies.

3.1.3 Upper Confidence Bound Methods

One of the most famous (class of) policies that is asymptotically optimal are the Upper Confidence Bound (UCB) methods [2]. The intuition for these policies is simple: after playing every arm once to get some information, the policy estimates the expected reward of each arm (i.e., simply the mean of the observations), and the associated confidence interval. Subsequently, the policy chooses the arm that has the highest upper confidence bound (i.e., the arm for which the top of the confidence interval is the highest) at that interaction. Note that the exact computation of the confidence interval depends on the problem at hand (e.g., distributional assumptions regarding the arms) but often depends on the total number of interactions, the number of times the respective arm was played, and—again depending on the distributional assumptions—the observed variance in the rewards. However, the intuition remains in each case: At each interaction, we pick the arm with the highest upper confidence bound where the bound includes both the expectation of the reward of the arm (effectively driving exploitation) and our uncertainty regarding the arm as provided by the confidence interval (effectively driving exploration).

UCB methods nicely formalize the intuition that arms are of interest when they have a high observed reward (for exploitation purposes) or when they have high uncertainty (for exploration purposes). UCB policies are said to be "confident in the face of uncertainty"; a heuristic that overall seems to be effective in many decision problems. A large body of work exists determining the exact confidence intervals necessary for specific instantiations of the MAB problem to walk the thin line between exploration and exploitation (see, e.g., [2, 3, 18, 38], for examples). Figure 1 shows that UCB has no trouble learning the three armed bandit setting and has a regret that is close to zero (and endlessly getting closer) after only a few interactions.

3.1.4 Thompson Sampling

UCB methods are inherently frequentist as the confidence bounds are motivated from a frequentist perspective. A simple Bayesian approach to the MAB problem is provided by a policy called Thompson sampling [1, 19, 33]. Thompson sampling is intuitively appealing: play each arm with a probability that is proportional to your belief that specific arm is the best performing arm. Thus, when starting and no data is available, each arm should be played with equal probability. However, as data start "streaming in" [25], we can model which arm we believe has the highest reward. From a Bayesian point of view—assuming reasonably uninformative priors that span the full range—no arm will ever be fully certain to be the best, but, as successes are observed for one arm and not for the others, our confidence that that specific arm is the best keeps increasing. And, subsequently, when implementing Thompson sampling, the probability of selecting that specific arm keeps increasing.

Thompson sampling is a rather old idea [54] and surprisingly easily implemented as long as we can quantify a posterior distribution for the estimated reward of each arm (in the Bernoulli bandit case introduced above by simply putting a Beta prior on each arm and updating our inferences accordingly (see [16], for details), than all we need to do at each interaction is generate a random draw from the respective posteriors and play the arm for which we obtained the highest draw. This simple scheme will ensure that indeed, "each arm is played with a probability that is proportional to the belief that specific arm is the best performing arm". Figure 1 shows that Thompson sampling performs competitively, and its regret seems sub-linear. It however took quite some time before proofs started emerging that the indeed Thompson sampling is asymptotically optimal [33].

3.1.5 Bootstrapped Thompson Sampling

Although Thompson sampling is easy to implement when sampling from the posterior distribution is easy, there are situations in which directly sampling from posterior distributions is not feasible. In that case, we would have to resort to approximations using, e.g., Markov chain Monte Carlo (MCMC) sampling methods. The huge drawback of using MCMC sampling in a bandit setting is that these can be computationally too inefficient to carry out at each interaction. This situation often occurs in online marketing [31]: In this field, the cMAB problem formalization is often used to think about selecting advertisements for users as they arrive to a Web site sequentially over time. In this scenario often thousands of users are observed each hour and it is infeasible if every next choice of advertisement takes considerable time to compute. Bootstrapped Thompson sampling (BTS) tries to solve this problem by replacing the Bayesian posterior distribution by a bootstrap distribution around the point estimates of the expected rewards [16, 46]. The bootstrapping trick makes Thompson sampling computationally appealing, especially in complex contextual bandit problems. However, this computational advantage comes at a cost: although in Fig. 1 BTS seems to be the best performing policy, its zero regret is an artifact of the simulation: Theoretically, the (expected) regret of Thompson sampling is bounding by the number of bootstrap replicates and will be, albeit often with an extremely small constant, linear.

3.2   Policy Evaluation

In this section, we discussed several treatment allocation policies and their performance. We hope to have highlighted that the traditional experiment (or the exploration phase of ϵ-first) is—once we allow ourselves to look at experiments in a sequential fashion—just one of the many options we have available to choose treatments at each interaction. Depending on the purpose of the data collection effort, the traditional experiment might not be the best choice: our regret analysis showed that, if the aim is to maximize the cumulative rewards, ϵ-first is actually a pretty poor solution. Before we discuss alternative purposes (such as estimation precision and best-arm selection), it is worthwhile to briefly discuss how the (expected) performance of different policies can be compared. There are effectively four methods to do so (each often with multiple flavors, we highlight the main strands):

1. *Theoretical analysis*: One way of ranking the performance of different policies is by carrying out a theoretical analysis of the performance of a policy; this is the approach that has given us a notion of asymptotical optimality of policies (see, e.g., [33]). Although the MAB problem is notoriously hard, a large number of theoretical advance have been made in recent year covering both the MAB and the cMAB problems. The theoretical analysis approach is appealing as it gives mathematical certainty regarding the performance of different polices, a property impossible to attain by any other method. However, this comes at a cost: First, most theoretical work has focussed on the asymptotic case, ignoring regret constants (i.e., parts of the expected regret that do not depend on the number of interactions). While these constant might be uninteresting from a theoretical viewpoint, they can be essential in applications of different treatment allocation policies. Second, theoretical analysis is only possible by making strict assumptions regarding the true data generating process (e.g., the reward distributions of the arms); these assumptions are likely not to hold in applied problems.
2. *Simulation studies*: Figure 1 provided an example of how we can use computer simulations to examine the performance of different bandit policies [12]. We simply create a data generating process ourselves and we have a policy "play against" the data generating policy multiple times. This process is often easy to implement, and modern computers allow for examining very complex data generating mechanisms and policies. That said, simulations never provide a proof of the performance of a policy and can be misleading: for example, on relatively simple bandit problems, ϵ-first with a sufficiently large exploration phase might seem to have zero regret during the exploitation phase as in each simulation run the optimal arm is selected hiding the fact that there is a non-zero (albeit small)

probability that a wrong arm is selected. Furthermore, one can always debate whether the data generating mechanism implemented in a simulation is realistic.

3. *Empirical (or "online") evaluation:* A third method of examining the performance of bandit policies is by simply "deploying them in the wild" and observing their outcomes empirically. A relatively recent manifestation of bandit problems is in the selection of content (e.g., advertisements) online: for each Web site visitor (the interactions) we select one out of a set of available advertisements, and subsequently see the potential click on the advertisement (the binary reward). In this case, it is now customary to try out various bandit policies "in the wild", i.e., by deploying a bandit policy for a period of time on a live Web site and iteratively trying out various policies.[3] Evaluation in the wild is appealing for its external validity, but it is costly and often technically challenging [31].

4. *"Offline" evaluation:* Finally, a now popular method is based on the simple idea that data collected using one policy in the wild (and thus externally valid), can be used to evaluate other policies [8, 42, 43]. This sounds esoteric, but we actually do this quite routinely: when setting up a traditional experiment we subsequently use the data to compute the mean outcome $\bar{y}_1$ to $\bar{y}_2$ for each arm which can be regarded as the estimate of the expected reward under the policy of playing arm one or arm two respectively. There is a large literature discussing when and how (using various methods), data collected using one policy in the wild can be used to provide a valid estimate of the performance of other policies. Essentially this is possible if two criteria are satisfied; first, the data collection policy needs to have a random "aspect" to it (i.e., at each interaction the probabilities of selecting an arm should not be exactly 0 or 1), and second these probabilities should be known at each interaction. These criteria are clearly satisfied for ϵ-first, but also ϵ-greedy and Thompson sampling satisfy these requirements. Offline evaluation methods are appealing as they are externally valid (since there are based on a real-world data generating mechanism) but still allow for the evaluation of various policies.

We will return to these different evaluation methods in Sect. 5 when we discuss several available tools for simulation, offline analysis, and empirical analysis of the performance of bandit policies. Before we do so we however first discuss the broader use of sequential experimentation: what are the benefits of a sequential view toward experimentation when the aim of the experimenter is not to maximize the expected cumulative reward?

---

[3] Please note that interestingly at this point the "iteratively trying out" of various bandit policies has become a bandit problem on its own, with policies replacing the initial arms.

4 The Broader Use of Sequential Experimentation: Methodological Advantages and Challenges

In the previous sections, we have introduced the (c)MAB problem and analyzed the performance of various treatment allocation policies in terms of their expected regret. This allowed us to rank the performance of policies when the main goal of the experimenter is to maximize the overall reward gained when executing a sequence of treatment allocations. We discussed how the traditional experiment—including the guideline that follows the experiment—is often suboptimal for this aim: other policies, such as Thompson sampling will, in the long run, have a higher expected reward than the traditional experiment.

However, the aim of maximizing the reward of a sequence of treatment allocations is distinct from the aim of most experimenters in HCI: although we do often want to select "the best arm" eventually (i.e., select the version of our interface that performs best), our (longitudinal) experiments often focus on precisely estimating the effect of each arm, as opposed to selecting the arm that maximizes the outcome. In this section, we will briefly review alternative uses of a sequential view on experimentation that provide useful treatment allocation policies when the aim of the experimenter is not to maximize rewards.

4.1 Early Stopping

An often encountered problem in medical research is declaring superiority of a novel treatment over a control (or existing treatment). To do so, researchers often setup a Randomized Clinical Trial and determine some cut-off to declare superiority based on the outcomes. Traditionally, the size of these experiments, i.e., the number of patients who are randomly assigned to either treatment or control, is computed a priori using power calculations. These a priori calculations are often imprecise as they rely on estimates of, e.g., the effect size which are unknown prior to starting the experiment. A sequential view on experimentation in this case can often greatly improve the experimental design: by actively using the data collected during the experiment to assess whether the cut-off is met it is often possible to convincingly declare superiority using a smaller number of patients: thus, the experiment can be stopped early [5, 6].

This approach can be considered sequential as, effectively, the information collected during the experiment is used to make a more efficient decision. Note that a large literature exists on how to do this properly: simply re-testing a null hypothesis using frequentist tests is strongly advised against as the error rates of these tests under naive repeated administration are very poor. Often, Bayesian methods are used for early stopping in which, repeatedly throughout the experiment, the evidence in favor of superiority of the treatment is (re)computed based on the collected data [40].

Early stopping is potentially interesting for many HCI studies in which there are either substantial costs associated with running the study (as is often true in longitudinal studies), or there are potential negative effects of participating in the study: In both cases, one would like to stop the study once sufficient evidence has been collected. The rich early stopping literature provides a sequential view on experimentation that allows researchers to terminate (longitudinal) experiments once sufficient evidence has been collected.

4.2 Best Arm Identification

An alternative, but related, problem to the MAB problem is that of "best arm selection": given an (often fixed) number of interactions T, and given a set of treatments k (where $k > 2$), select the best performing treatment. Here, contrary to the traditional bandit problem, the aim is not to maximize rewards throughout the sequence, but rather to maximize the probability that after T interactions the treatment that indeed has the highest mean reward is selected after the experiment. This slightly changes the dynamic of the problem. While in the traditional MAB problem it does not pay off for the experimenter to actively try to decide between two arms that both seem to have a high expected reward, in the best arm identification the crux is precisely understanding which of these two promising arms is the best. Thus, contrary to the traditional MAB problem, an experimenter in a best-arm identification setting would, especially in the latter interactions, choose to collect as much information as possible regarding the well-performing arms to make sure that the final decision is as accurate as possible [34].

A recently advanced, and very well-performing treatment allocation strategy for the best arm identification problem is provided by a slight variation on Thompson sampling: Instead of choosing the arm with the highest posterior draw, the experimenter randomly selects between the two arms that have the highest posterior draws. This additional randomization ensures that all competitive arms are played often and thus their expected rewards can be estimated precisely [26].

Best arm identification is easily related to HCI research: often our (longitudinal) experiments aim to identify which interface, app, or message is most effective out of a set of different messages. It is interesting to see that even in the literature on (sequential) best arm selection ϵ-first (or just the traditional experiment) is not considered effective when more than two alternatives are present. This finding strengthens the main thesis of this chapter that in longitudinal HCI studies (and beyond) a sequential view on experimentation (thus one in which intermediate results are used to make changes to the experimental design as the experiment is still running) is beneficial.

4.3   Powerful Comparisons

Another slight variation on the aim of running an experiment—which also benefits from a sequential approach—is that of so-called "optimal design". In the literature on the optimal design of experiments, the main aim is often formulated as minimizing the standard error of the estimates resulting from the experiment given a (often fixed) number of interactions (i.e., one wants to design an experiment such that the quantities of interest are estimated as precisely as possible). There is a rich literature on this topic (see, e.g., [22]), and often the problem is approached in the "traditional" view: an experiment is planned beforehand while making assumptions regarding the outcome distributions in such a way that treatments are allocated to minimize the resulting standard errors. However, also in this case a sequential view on treatment allocation can help: exploiting the information gained during the experiment to refine one's assumptions and improve the treatment allocation is often beneficial. For example, Kaptein [27] shows that in the simple case of estimating the difference between two means—in a situation in which the variances of the two groups are unequal—it pays off to allocated more interactions toward the arm with a higher variance. A simple variation on Thompsons sampling in which not the posterior distribution of the mean but rather that of the variance is used to select treatments improves the precision of the resulting estimates and thus increases the power of the comparison. This latter work is directly relevant for HCI studies: the work implies that if we are designing a study that aims to make the most powerful comparison between two different conditions in any experiment, assigning subjects to treatments inversely proportional to the variance in the outcome associated with the treatment improves power.

4.4   Active Learning

A final related problem which benefits from a sequential view is that of active learning. In a traditional active learning, setting a learning is presented by a set of examples composed of features and labels. The aim of the learner is to learn a relationship between the features and labels, however, uncovering the label for a specific example comes at a cost. To minimize the costs the learning has to actively select which examples it wants to learn from (thus, the features are available, but the labels are not; this problem is common in many machine learning situations where, e.g., images are available but their classification is not and obtaining this classification is labor intensive and thus costly). The traditional view toward this problem selects a (single) batch of examples for which the features should be revealed. It is however relatively easy to show that a sequential view, in which new examples are selected one by one and the learning from that example is explicitly used to select new examples, is beneficial. The literature on active learning is too large to properly review in this chapter, but it provides an interesting literature in which the benefits of sequential experimentation are immediately clear [13, 23].

The actively learning literature might seem far from any HCI example, but even here strong links can be made. For example, consider designing an interface for a heterogeneous group of users (i.e., users with various backgrounds), and further consider that recruiting users into your evaluation is costly. The active learning literature can directly help to determine sequentially which types of users you already know sufficiently about—and hence it is not necessary to recruit more similar users—and for which types of users you need more information. Here a sequential view on data collection can greatly improve the efficiency of an experimental design.

4.5   Challenges of Sequential Experimentation

Although a sequential view on experimentation can increase the overall rewards of an experiment, make the choice for a best arm more informed, more powerful, or based on a smaller number of subjects as we have explored above, some things are also complicated by adopting a sequential approach to experimentation. Predominantly, many traditional statistical (frequentists) test assume on a fixed experimentation scheme to be able to compute type I and type II errors. By changing the design of an experiment based on "intermediate" results these assumptions are violated, and thus, e.g., p-values use their exact meaning.[4] Thus, "traditional" statistical methods need to be used with care when analyzing sequential designs.

Another often encountered challenge with sequential experimentation concerns the broader acceptation of the "novel"—although many are decades old—methods in the field. For example, when considering early stopping, the experimenter often finds her-/himself in the dilemma of having sufficient evidence—quantified, e.g., by the Bayesian posterior distribution of a treatment difference—to stop the experiment, but potentially having too little evidence—quantified by, e.g., a p-value—to convince peers.

5   Sequential Experimentation in Empirical Studies: Available Software

In this section, we introduce two software packages that allow readers to easily experiment with different sequential treatment allocation policies. We first introduce `contextual`, an [R] package that allows user to easily run simulations of various bandit policies and to run offline evaluations (i.e., evaluate the performance of a policy on an existing dataset). Next, we discuss `streamingbandit`, a python

---

[4] This exact meaning of p-values is often lost in non-sequential designs as well, but due to the violation of other assumptions.

package that allows for easy deployment of sequential treatment allocation policies in empirical studies. The former software package is primarily useful for readers who would like to learn more about sequential experiments by running simulations. The latter software package effectively allows for endowing standard survey packages (such as Qualtrics or SurveyMonkey) with extremely flexible treatment allocation policies that depend on intermediate results. Admittedly, the descriptions provided are a bit technical; they aim to inform the reader aspiring to implement distinct bandit policies and thus assume a quick familiarity with the notation involved.

5.1 Contextual

CMAB policies' have proven successful in many different areas: from recommendation engines [37] to advertising [52] and (personalized) medicine [32, 53], healthcare [47], and portfolio choice [51]—inspiring a multitude of new bandit algorithms or policies. However, although CMAB algorithms have found more and more applications, comparisons on both synthetic, and, importantly, real-life, large-scale offline datasets [43] have relatively lagged behind. To address this problem, the R package `contextual` facilitates such offline analysis of various bandit policies [55].

The class structure or of the R package stays close to the formal roots of the contextual bandit problem: in `contextual`, a Bandit B is defined as a set of arms $k \in \{1, \ldots, K\}$ where each arm is itself described by some reward function that maps d dimensional context vector $x_{t,k}$ to some reward $r_{t,k}$ [4, 36, 39] for every time step t until horizon T. A Policy π seeks to maximize its cumulative reward $\sum_{t=1}^{T} r_t$ (or minimize its cumulative regret) by sequentially selecting one of bandit B's currently available arms [11], here defined as taking action a_t in $\mathcal{A}_t \subseteq K$ for $t = \{1, \ldots, T\}$.

At each time step t policy π first observes the current state of the world as related to B, represented by d-dimensional context feature vectors $x_{t,a}$ for $a_t \in \mathcal{A}_t$. Next, making use of some arm-selection policy, π (i.e., the treatment allocation policy) then selects one of the available actions in $\mathcal{A}_t$. As a result of selecting action a_t, policy π then receives reward $r_{a_t,t}$. With observation $(x_{t,a_t}, a_t, r_{t,a_t})$, the policy can now update its arm-selection strategy. This cycle is then repeated T times. That is, for each round $t = \{1, \ldots, T\}$:

(1) Policy π observes current context feature vectors $x_{t,a}$ for $\forall a \in \mathcal{A}_t$ in bandit B
(2) Based on all $x_{t,a}$ and θ_{t-1}, policy π now selects an action $a_t \in \mathcal{A}_t$
(3) Policy π receives a reward r_{t,a_t,x_t} from bandit B
(4) Policy π updates arm-selection strategy parameters θ_t with $(x_{t,a_t}, a_t, r_{t,a_t})$

Overall, it is Policy π's goal to minimize *cumulative regret* or optimize *cumulative reward* $R_T = \sum_{t=1}^{T}(r_{t,a_t,x_t})$. The `contextual` package is setup such that each of the four steps defined above can easily be implemented by the user of the package to implement various data generating mechanisms and evaluate various (c)MAB policies.

5.1.1 Class Diagram and Structure

The current section will show that `contextual`'s structure does indeed closely mirror the previous section's formal description of the CMAB problem. In `contextual`, the Bandit and Policy superclasses expose respectively `contextual`'s reward generation and its decision allocation strategy API. For custom of Bandits or Policies, these are the two classes to subclass and extend:

- `Bandit`: R6 class `Bandit` is the parent class of all `Bandit` subclasses. It exposes k arms and is responsible for the generation of a chosen arm's `reward`, and, in the case of contextual policy evaluation, current d dimensional or k x d dimensional `context`.
- `Policy`: R6 class `Policy` is the parent class of all `Policy` subclasses. For each $t = \{1, ..., T\}$ it has to choose one of a `Bandit`'s k arms and update its parameters `theta` in response to the resulting `reward`, and, in the case of contextual policy evaluation, the current d dimensional or k x d dimensional `context` (Fig. 2).

The four remaining classes constitute contextual's parallel evaluation, logging and visualization routines, and are generally not subclassed or extended:

- `Agent`: R6 class `Agent` is responsible for the running of one `Bandit`/`Policy` pair. Multiple `Agents` can be run in parallel, where each `Agent` keeps track of t for its assigned `Policy` and `Bandit` pair. To keep agent simulations replicable and comparable, starting seeds are set equal and deterministically for each agent.
- `Simulator`: R6 class `Simulator` is the entry point of any `contextual` simulation. It encapsulates one or more `Agents`, creates a `Agent` clones (each with its own deterministic seed) for each to be repeated simulation, runs the `Agents` in parallel, and saves the log of all `Agent` interactions to a `History` object.
- `History`: R6 class `History` keeps a `data.table` based log of all `Simulator` interactions and several performance measures, such as policies' cumulative reward and regret. Optionally, it also keeps context and theta logs. It allows several ways to interact with these logs, provides summaries, and can save and load simulation logs.
- `Plot`: R6 class `Plot` generates plots from `History` logs. It is usually invoked by calling the generic `plot(h)` function, where h is an `History` class instance.

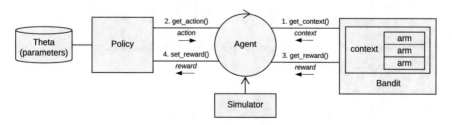

Fig. 2 Diagram of `contextual`'s basic structure. The context feature vector or matrix returned by get_context() is only taken into account by contextual policies, and may be ignored by context-free policies

5.1.2   Example Code: Running Context-Free and Contextual Policies

The following code brings all of the classes described in the previous section together by comparing the performance of a number of different cMAB policies using an existing dataset. The code clearly highlights how `contextual`'s comprehensive class structure enables researchers to construct offline policy comparisons with ease.

```
library(contextual); library(data.table)

# load data, 0/1 reward, 10 arms, 100 features, arms
    always start from 1
dt <- fread("http://d1ie9wlkzugsxr.cloudfront.net/
    data_cmab_basic/data.txt")

#        z  y  x1 x2 x3 x4 x5 x6 x7 x8 x9 x10 x11 x12 x13
    x14 x15  .. x100
#    1: 2  0  5  0  0 37  6  0  0  0  0  25   0   0   7
         1  0  ..    0
#    2: 8  0  1  3 36  0  0  0  0  0  0   0   0   1   0
         0  0  ..   10
#    3: .  .  .  .  .  .  .  .  .  .  .   .   .   .   .
         .  .  ..   .

# Set up formula:            y        ~ z      | x1 + x2 + ..
# In bandit parlance:    reward ~ arms | covariates or
    contextual features

f          <- y ~ z | . - z

# Instantiate Replay Bandit (Li, 2010)
bandit   <- OfflineReplayEvaluatorBandit$new(formula =
    f, data = dt)

# Bind Policies withs Bandits through Agents, add
    Agents to list
agents   <- list(
  Agent$new(UCB2Policy$new(0.01),                bandit, "
    UCB2    alpha = 0.01"),
  Agent$new(LinUCBDisjointPolicy$new(0.01), bandit, "
    LinUCB alpha = 0.01"),
  Agent$new(LinUCBDisjointPolicy$new(0.1),  bandit, "
    LinUCB alpha = 0.1"))

# Instantiate and run a Simulator, plot the resulting
    History object
history <- Simulator$new(agents, horizon = nrow(dt),
    simulations = 5)$run()
plot(history, type = "cumulative", regret = FALSE,
    legend_border = FALSE)
```

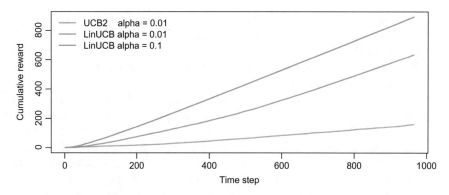

Fig. 3 Cumulative reward for a context-free UCB2 [4] and two contextual LinUCB policies [41] with differing α-values (determining the width of the Upper Confidence Bound) when evaluated against a "Replay" Bandit using offline data

5.1.3 Conclusion

We have only briefly introduced the `contextual` package. The R package is openly available at https://github.com/Nth-iteration-labs/contextual where extensive documentation and multiple examples can be found. Effectively, the package allows users to implement distinct data generating processes or use existing data (for offline evaluation), and to implement various sequential treatment allocation policies. Subsequently, simulations of the performance of these policies can be run easily, and their results can be visualized. Thus, `contextual` provides an easy tool to rank bandit policies for various goals (Fig. 3).

5.2 Streaming Bandit

To take the next step and to start experimenting with policies "in the wild", `StreamingBandit` is a useful tool. `StreamingBandit` is an open-source RESTful web application for developing and deploying sequential experiments in field and simulation studies. It allows designers to easily and quickly implement a policy $\pi()$ on a webserver. It is designed such that when set up, it alleviates the technical hurdles for researchers to deploy different policies in the field and thus to enable sequential experimentation to be used within a broader research community.

Just as in `contextual`, in `StreamingBandit` we translate the cMAB problem into two important steps. To ensure the computational scalability of `Streaming-Bandit` we assume that, at the latest interaction $t = t'$, all the information necessary to choose an action can be summarized using a limited set of parameters denoted $\theta_{t'}$, the dimensionality of θ_t often being (much) smaller than that of the historical data $\mathcal{D}_{t-1}$. Given this assumption, we identify the following two steps of a policy:

1. The decision step: In the decision step, using $x_{t'}$ and $\theta_{t'}$, and often using some (statistical) model relating the actions, the context, and the reward, which is parametrized by $\theta_{t'}$, the next action $a_{t'}$ is selected. Making a request to StreamingBandit's *getaction* REST endpoint returns a JSON object containing the selected action.

2. The summary step: In each summary step $\theta_{t'}$ is updated using the new information $\{x_{t'}, a_{t'}, r_{t'}, p_{t'}\}$. Thus, $\theta_{t'+1} = g(\theta_{t'}, x_{t'}, a_{t'}, r_{t'}, p_{t'})$ where $g()$ is some update function. Effectively, all the prior data, $\mathcal{D}_{t-1}$ are summarized in $\theta_{t'}$. This choice means that the computations are bounded by the dimension of θ and the time required to update θ instead of growing as a function of t. Note that this effectively forces users to implement an online policy [45] as the complete dataset $\mathcal{D}_{t-1}$ is not revisited at subsequent interactions. Making a request to StreamingBandit's *setreward* endpoint containing a JSON object including a complete description of $\{x_{t'}, a_{t'}, p_{t'}\}$, and the reward $r_{t'}$, allows one to update $\theta_{t'+1}$ and subsequently to influence the actions selected at $t' + 1$.[5]

For the basic usage of StreamingBandit the experimenter—or rather an external server or mobile application—sequentially executes requests to the *getaction* and *setreward* endpoints (more details will follow next), and allocates actions accordingly. Using this setup, StreamingBandit can be used to sequentially select advertisements on webpages, for example, allocate research subjects to different experimental conditions in an online experiment, or sequentially optimize the feedback provided to users off a mobile eHealth application. The complete details of how the software is set up and how it should be installed, configured and prepared can be found in the original paper and the online documentation.[6] In the remainder of this section, we assume that StreamingBandit is installed.

5.2.1 Basic Example

When StreamingBandit is running, a researcher can use some of the default implementations of policies that are shipped with the software. As an example, we run through how ϵ-first would be deployed within StreamingBandit. We will show the code for the *getaction* and *setreward* endpoints and run through them line by line. The *getaction* code for ϵ-first looks as follows:

---

[5] It is also possible to use the *advice_id* functionality, but this is not discussed here for simplicity sake. Full details can be found in the paper.

[6] See https://nth-iteration-labs.github.io/streamingbandit for the complete documentation.

```
1  n = 100
2  mean_list = base.List(
3                self.get_theta(key="treatment"),
4                base.Mean, ["control", "treatment"]
5                )
6  if mean_list.count() >= n:
7      self.action["treatment"] = mean_list.max()
8  else:
9      self.action["treatment"] = mean_list.random()
```

This code uses a number of libraries implemented in StreamingBandit. First, the sample size n of the exploration phase of the experiment is set. The next line of code generates a list of *base.Mean* objects from the *libs.base* library. This object provides the functionality to compute streaming updates of sample averages, and the list contains one such average for each of the possible treatments specified by name, using *["control", "treatment"]*. The *self.get_theta()* call is used to retrieve $\theta_{t'}$, which in this case thus contains two *base.Mean* objects named "control" and "treatment". A count, n, and mean reward, $\bar{r}$, are contained within each *base.Mean* object.

The resulting *mean_list* object thus, in this case, contains two *base.Mean* objects, each of which contains a mean value and a count that can be updated and manipulated. In the next lines the total count of the number of observations over all mean elements in the list is retrieved. If this is larger than n, the treatment with the highest average value is returned, and otherwise, a random element of the list is returned.

Then we have the code for the *setreward* endpoint:

```
1  n = 100
2  mean_list = base.List(
3      self.get_theta(key="treatment"),
4      base.Mean, ["control", "treatment"]
5      )
6
7  if mean_list.count() < n:
8      mean = base.Mean(
9          self.get_theta(
10         key="treatment", value=self.action["treatment
       "])
11         )
12     mean.update(self.reward["value"])
13     self.set_theta(
14         mean, key="treatment",
15         value=self.action["treatment"]
16         )
```

First again a *mean_list* is created. After this, the θ_t that is associated with the played action is retrieved and the associated mean object is updated using *mean.update* as long as the exploration phase is ongoing. The last line stores $\theta_{t'+1}$ such that it can be retrieved again for future decision-making using the *self.set_theta* function. In this implementation, after the experiment when $n > t$, θ is no longer updated.

Once the experiment has been created with this code, it receives an $< exp\_id >$ and a key *<key>*. This enables the REST endpoints

```
http://HOST/getaction/<exp_id>?key=<key>&context={}
```

and

```
http://HOST/setreward/<exp_id>?key=<key>&context={}&
    reward={}&action={}.
```

Where HOST is the location of the hosted `StreamingBandit` instance. Within the {}'s we can supply the information that is needed by `StreamingBandit` to select actions and update parameters.

The returned object when making a call to http://HOST/<exp_id>/getaction?key= <key> and filling in the correct *exp_id* and *key* for the experiment with this ϵ-first appears as follows:

```
{"action":
       {"treatment": "control"},
"context": {}}
```

where the value of *treatment* changes randomly as long as $n \leq t$. Then if we would call the endpoint for the *setreward* with the action and reward filled in: http://HOST/<exp_id>/getaction?key=<key>&context=&action="treatment": "control"&reward="value":1 and this would return the following object:

```
{"action": {"treatment": "control"},
 "context": {},
 "reward": {"value": 1},
 "status": "success"}
```

And that is the beginning of your first experiment in `StreamingBandit`! We have now once requested an action and updated θ and would, in any applied setting, repeat this process for each treatment assignment.

5.2.2   Conclusions

`StreamingBandit` provides a platform that allows user to implement bandit policies "in the wild". We merely provided a simple example here, but, we hope it is clear that this tool is very flexible. It can be used to, e.g., implement AB tests on the web or in mobile applications. However, after implementing such an AB test, the treatment allocation mechanism can be altered without altering the surrounding system:

the random treatment allocation that is common in the AB test can be replaced by Thompson sampling or UCB methods pretty much instantly. StreamingBandit is available open-source and is actively developed and used by a growing team of contributors.

6 Discussion, Recommendations, and Conclusions

In this chapter, we tried to introduce an alternative view on both simple between subject experiment and longitudinal experiments: we have tried to introduce a sequential view regarding experiments. While often in experiments—even longitudinal studies—the treatment assigned are planned and fixed a priori, we have tried to highlight an alternative: In many situations, it might be possible to use data collected during the experiment to improve upon the design of the experiment itself. We started by introducing the canonical Multi-Armed bandit problem; a problem formalization that nicely captures the trade-off between exploration and exploitation that is present when an experimenter aims to—in sequence—select actions such that the expected rewards are maximized. We discussed various treatment assignment policies that the experimenter could use in this case and we tried to continuously relate our discussion to the traditional experiment. Next, we highlighted that a sequential view on experimentation can improve numerous design properties of experimental studies: it can be used for early stopping, actively learning, or improving power. We hope this overview has at the very least inspired interest for the large literature regarding sequential experimentation; we have tried to provide meaningful references throughout.

In the last section of this chapter, we introduced two software packages that readers can use to evaluate (contextual) and deploy (StreamingBandit) sequential treatment allocation policies. We hope these software packages lower the practical hurdles involved in approaching experimentation sequentially. The readily available simulation examples in contextual should allow the interested reader to develop a good intuition regarding the behavior of various treatment allocation policies.

6.1 Recommendations

Although admittedly the main body of this chapter is predominantly methodological—the advantages of sequential experimentation can be reaped in any field—it is useful to reflect specifically on the opportunities that arise for sequential experimentation in longitudinal HCI studies:

1. It is often useful to consider that in many longitudinal studies not all users start the study at the same time, and thus "intermediate" results from participants who started earlier might be used to inform the design of the experiment in later stages.

   For example, if a specific version of an interface has already shown sufficiently
   poor performance compared to other interfaces in the first few months of an
   experiment, the experimenter can choose not to confront newly enrolled users
   with the poor performing interface.

2. Longitudinal HCI studies often lend themselves well for a sequential approach
   as each time-epoch happens in a sequence, and whatever happened to a (single-)
   user at earlier points in time potentially could (and perhaps should) affect the
   design of the experiment in later points in time. For example, if a user is asked
   to complete a task of medium difficulty and fails, it is likely not informative to
   ask that same user at a later point in time to perform a highly difficult task.

3. It is often good to consider explicitly the aims of the experiment: is the aim
   to have precise estimates of the outcomes of all the "treatments" involved, or
   is the aim to select the best treatment (or even maximize the outcome over
   various treatment selections)? Especially in longitudinal experiments, we might
   be seeking to maximize some outcome for each user as she/he interacts with a
   system over time. In such a case all the different version/variants of the system
   can be considered arms, and we are seeking for a strategy to interact with the
   user over time such that the outcome of interest is maximized. In a sense, the
   experiment seeks the most efficient policy.

4. As we move more and more toward "adaptive" systems, i.e., systems that in one
   way or another adapt to the behavior of users, we often find that it is beneficial
   to think about a strategy for adaption (i.e., how a system responds to historical
   interactions) as a (bandit) policy: when designing an interactive system that over
   time adapts to the user to reach a certain goal we are often effectively designing
   a good bandit policy.

6.2 Conclusions

We are aware that we have only been able to scratch the surface of sequential experimentation in this chapter. However, we hope that by providing a sequential view to
standard experiments and longitudinal studies, one in which "intermediate" results
might influence the design of the experiment, we have provided the reader with
novel inspiration for setting up experiments using more flexible treatment assignment schemes.

Acknowledgements I would like to thank both Robin van Emden and Jules Kruiswijk for their
input regarding this chapter (and their work on Contextual and StreamingBandit respectively). I
would also like to thank all the members of the *Computational Personalization* lab at the Jheronimus
Academy of Data Science for their input and valuable discussions.

References

1. Agrawal S (2012) Further optimal regret bounds for Thompson sampling. CoRR none:1–14
2. Audibert J-Y, Munos R, Szepesvári C (2009) Exploration-exploitation tradeoff using variance estimates in multi-armed bandits. Theor Comput Sci 4100(19):1876–1902. https://doi.org/10.1016/j.tcs.2009.01.016
3. Auer P, Ortner R (2010) UCB revisited: Improved regret bounds for the stochastic multi-armed bandit problem. Periodica Mathematica Hungarica 610(1):1–11
4. Auer P, Cesa-Bianchi N, Fischer P (2002) Finite-time analysis of the multiarmed bandit problem. Mach Learn 470(2–3):235–256
5. Berry DA (1991) Experimental design for drug development: a Bayesian approach. J Biopharm Statist 10(1):81–101
6. Berry DA (2006) Bayesian clinical trials. Nat Rev Drug Discovery 50(1):27–36
7. Beygelzimer A, Langford J, Li L, Reyzin L, Schapire RE (2011) Contextual bandit algorithms with supervised learning guarantees. In: Proceedings of the fourteenth international conference on artificial intelligence and statistics (AISTATS-11), pp 19–26
8. Bietti A, Agarwal A, Langford J (2018) A contextual bandit bake-off. arXiv preprint arXiv:1802.04064
9. Bubeck S (2012) Regret analysis of stochastic and nonstochastic multi-armed bandit problems. Found Trends Mach Learn 50(1):1–122
10. Bubeck S, Liu C-Y (2013) Prior-free and prior-dependent regret bounds for Thompson sampling. In: Advances in neural information processing systems, pp 638–646
11. Bubeck S, Cesa-Bianchi N et al (2012) Regret analysis of stochastic and nonstochastic multi-armed bandit problems. Found Trends® Mach Learn 50(1):1–122. https://doi.org/10.1561/2200000024
12. Chapelle O, Li L (2011) An empirical evaluation of Thompson sampling. In: Advances in neural information processing systems, pp 2249–2257
13. Cohn D, Atlas L, Ladner R (1994) Improving generalization with active learning. Mach Learn 150(2):201–221
14. Dray SM, Siegel DA, Kotzé P (2003) Indra's net: HCI in the developing world. Interactions 100(2):28–37
15. Dudík M, Erhan D, Langford J, Li L et al (2014) Doubly robust policy evaluation and optimization. Statist Sci 290(4):485–511
16. Eckles D, Kaptein M (2014) Thompson sampling with the online bootstrap. arXiv preprint arXiv:1410.4009
17. Eckles D, Kaptein M (2019) Bootstrap Thompson sampling and sequential decision problems in the behavioral sciences. SAGE Open 90(2):2158244019851675
18. Garivier A, Cappé O (2011) The KL-UCB algorithm for bounded stochastic bandits and beyond. Bernoulli 190(1):13
19. Gopalan A, Mannor S, Mansour Y (2014) Thompson sampling for complex online problems. In: Proceedings of The 31st international conference on machine learning, pp 100–108
20. Quasar Collaborative Group et al (2007) Adjuvant chemotherapy versus observation in patients with colorectal cancer: a randomised study. The Lancet 3700 (9604): 2020–2029
21. Hauser JR, Urban GL, Liberali G, Braun M (2009) Website morphing. Market Sci 280(2):202–223. ISSN: 1526-548X. https://doi.org/10.1287/mksc.1080.0459
22. Herzberg AM, Andrews DF (1976) Some considerations in the optimal design of experiments in non-optimal situations. J R Statist Soc: Ser B (Methodol) 380(3):284–289
23. Hoi SCH, Jin R, Zhu J, Lyu MR (2006) Batch mode active learning and its application to medical image classification. In: Proceedings of the 23rd international conference on machine learning, pp 417–424
24. Imbens GW, Rubin DB (2015) Causal Inference in Statistics, Social, and Biomedical Sciences. Cambridge University Press. ISBN 9780521885881. Google-Books-ID: Bf1tBwAAQBAJ
25. Ippel L, Kaptein M, Vermunt J (2016) Dealing with data streams. Methodology

26. Jamieson K, Nowak R (2014) Best-arm identification algorithms for multi-armed bandits in the fixed confidence setting. In: 2014 48th annual conference on information sciences and systems (CISS). IEEE, New York, pp 1–6
27. Kaptein M (2015) The use of Thompson sampling to increase estimation precision. Behav Res Methods 470(2):409–423
28. Kaptein M (2019) Personalization in biomedical-informatics: methodological considerations and recommendations. J Biomed Inform 90
29. Kaptein M (2019) A practical approach to sample size calculation for fixed populations. Contemp Clin Trials Commun 14
30. Kaptein M, De Ruyter B, Markopoulos P, Aarts E (2012) Adaptive persuasive systems: a study of tailored persuasive text messages to reduce snacking. ACM Trans Interact Intell Syst (TiiS) 20(2):1–25
31. Kaptein M, McFarland R, Parvinen P (2018) Automated adaptive selling. Euro J Market 520(5/6):1037–1059
32. Katehakis MN, Derman C (1986) Computing optimal sequential allocation rules in clinical trials. Lecture Notes-Monograph Series, pp 29–39. https://doi.org/10.1214/lnms/1215540286
33. Kaufmann E, Korda N, Munos R (2012) Thompson sampling: an asymptotically optimal finite-time analysis. Algorithmic learning theory. Springer, Berlin, pp 199–213
34. Kaufmann E, Cappé O, Garivier A (2016) On the complexity of best-arm identification in multi-armed bandit models. J Mach Learn Res 170(1):1–42
35. Kizilcec RF, Cohen GL (2017) Eight-minute self-regulation intervention raises educational attainment at scale in individualist but not collectivist cultures. Proc Nat Acad Sci 1140(17):4348–4353
36. Kruijswijk J, van Emden R, Parvinen P, Kaptein M (2016) Streamingbandit; experimenting with bandit policies. arXiv preprint arXiv:1602.06700
37. Lai TL, Robbins H (1985) Asymptotically efficient adaptive allocation rules. Adv Appl Math 60(1):4–22. ISSN 01968858. https://doi.org/10.1016/0196-8858(85)90002-8
38. Lai TL (1987) Adaptive treatment allocation and the multi-armed bandit problem. Ann Statist 150(3):1091–1114. ISSN 2168-8966. http://projecteuclid.org/euclid.aos/1176350495
39. Langford J, Zhang T (2008) The epoch-greedy algorithm for multi-armed bandits with side information. In: Advances in neural information processing systems, pp 817–824
40. Lecoutre B (2001) Bayesian predictive procedure for designing and monitoring experiments. In: Bayesian methods with applications to science, policy and official statistics, pp 301–310
41. Li J, Zhang C, Doksum KA, Nordheim EV (2010) Simultaneous confidence intervals for semiparametric logistics regression and confidence regions for the multi-dimensional effective dose 20:637–659
42. Li L, Chu W, Langford J, Moon T, Wang X (2012) An unbiased offline evaluation of contextual bandit algorithms with generalized linear models. In: Proceedings of the workshop on on-line trading of exploration and exploitation, vol 2, pp 19–36
43. Li S, Montgomery L (2011) Cross-selling the right product to the right customer at the right time. J Market Res , XLVIII0 (August): 683–700. ISSN 00222437. https://doi.org/10.1509/jmkr.48.4.683. http://search.ebscohost.com/login.aspx?direct=true&db=bsh&AN=62970998&site=ehost-live
44. Macready WG, Wolpert DH (1998) Bandit problems and the exploration/exploitation tradeoff. IEEE Trans Evol Comput 20(1):2–22. https://doi.org/10.1109/4235.728210
45. Michalak S, DuBois A, DuBois D, Vander Wiel S, Hogden J (2012) Developing systems for real-time streaming analysis. J Comput Graph Statist 210(3):561–580. ISSN 10618600. https://doi.org/10.1080/10618600.2012.657144
46. Osband I, Van Roy B (2015) Bootstrapped Thompson sampling and deep exploration. arXiv preprint arXiv:1507.00300
47. Rabbi M, Aung MH, Zhang M, Choudhury T (2015) MyBehavior: automatic personalized health feedback from user behaviors and preferences using smartphones. In: Proceedings of the 2015 ACM international joint conference on pervasive and ubiquitous computing. ACM, pp 707–718. https://doi.org/10.1145/2750858.2805840

48. Robbins H (1952) Some aspects of the sequential design of experiments. Bull Am Math Soc 580(5):527–535
49. Rubin DB (2005) Causal inference using potential outcomes: design, modeling, decisions. J Am Statist Assoc 1000(469):322–331
50. Scott SL (2010) A modern Bayesian look at the multi-armed bandit. Appl Stochast Models Bus Industry 260(6):639–658
51. Shen W, Wang J, Jiang Y-G, Zha H (2015) Portfolio choices with orthogonal bandit learning. IJCAI 15:974–980
52. Tang L, Rosales R, Singh A, Agarwal D (2013) Automatic ad format selection via contextual bandits. In: Proceedings of the 22nd ACM international conference on Conference on information & knowledge management. ACM, pp 1587–1594. https://doi.org/10.1145/2505515.2514700
53. Tewari A, Murphy SA (2017) From ads to interventions: contextual bandits in mobile health. In: Mobile health. Springer, Berlin, pp 495–517. https://doi.org/10.1007/978-3-319-51394-2_25
54. Thompson WR (1933) On the likelihood that one unknown probability exceeds another in view of the evidence of two samples. Biometrika 250(3–4):285–294. https://doi.org/10.1093/biomet/25.3-4.285
55. van Emden R, Kaptein M (2020) Nth-iteration-labs/contextual: v0.9.8.3, March 2020. https://doi.org/10.5281/zenodo.3697236
56. Verhoeff SR, Van Erning FN, Lemmens VEPP, De Wilt JHW, Pruijt JFM (2016) Adjuvant chemotherapy is not associated with improved survival for all high-risk factors in stage ii colon cancer. Int J Cancer 1390(1):187–193
57. Whittle P (1980) Multi-armed bandits and the Gittins index. J R Statist Soc: Ser B (Methodol) 420(2):143–149

Reviews of, and Case Studies On
Longitudinal HCI Research

Tensions and Techniques in Investigating Longitudinal Experiences with Slow Technology Research Products

William Odom

Abstract How can technologies be created that take on a long-term place in people's lives and that coevolve with them over time? What kinds of qualities should designers consider in crafting such kinds of computational things? And, how should we study and evaluate such new technologies through a longer temporal frame? In this chapter, we draw on examples of longitudinal field studies of the Photobox and Olly research products to explore these questions and to detail tensions and techniques that emerged across these two cases. Our findings reveal key tensions that researchers ought to be wary of when conducting longitudinal field studies of slow technology research products and techniques that can be applied to mitigate them.

Keywords Research products · Slow technology · Research through design

1 Introduction

The convergence of social, cloud, and mobile computing has created a world in which people generate, access, manipulate, and share personal digital data at larger scales and faster rates than ever before. From digital photo albums to online music streaming services, these new technologies have enabled people to create vast archives of digital data that capture their life experiences. These shifts raise complex questions for the HCI community as we critically look to the future and consider their longer-term implications. As archives continue to grow, what roles can personal data play in supporting people's evolving understandings of self as they change over time? What kinds of qualities should designers consider in crafting a longer-term place for computational things in everyday life? How should we study and evaluate such new technologies through a longer temporal frame?

These questions are motivated by the fact that the form of contemporary personal data generation opens up new opportunities to enable people to re-experience past life experiences, relationships, tastes, patterns, and idiosyncrasies in new and potentially

W. Odom (✉)
School of Interactive Arts and Technology, Surrey, BC, Canada
e-mail: wodom@sfu.ca

© Springer Nature Switzerland AG 2021
E. Karapanos et al. (eds.), *Advances in Longitudinal HCI Research*,
Human–Computer Interaction Series, https://doi.org/10.1007/978-3-030-67322-2_8

valuable ways. They also point to how little is known about what design strategies might be effective in designing meaningful experiences with personal data archives over time, and what concepts could help productively frame design inquiries in this emerging research territory. More generally, there are growing calls in the HCI community to develop design approaches that enable people to interact with their personal data in reflective, contemplative, and curious ways (e.g., [1, 2]). However, examples illustrating how such rich, open-ended engagements with personal data can be supported through the creation and longitudinal evaluation of new design artifacts remains sparse in HCI.

Photobox and *Olly* are two projects that aim to contribute precisely to this inter-section. Photobox is a domestic technology embodied in the form of an antique wooden chest that prints four or five randomly selected photos from the owner's Flickr collection at random intervals each month (see [3, 4]). Three Photoboxes were deployed through longitudinal field studies in three different households simultane-ously for fourteen months. Olly is a domestic music player that enables people to re-experience digital music they have listened to previously. Olly works by making use of its owner's Last.FM [5] personal music listening history archive to occasionally randomly select a song from its owner's past and make it available to be played (see [6, 7]). Three Ollys were deployed through longitudinal field studies in three different households simultaneously for fifteen months. In the case of both Photobox and Olly, study participants had no control over when the artifact would decide to select and surface personal data from their past or when. The behaviors of both Photobox and Olly occurred randomly and somewhat seldomly, but continued indefinitely. Taken together, these design artifacts investigate how new forms of interaction and experi-ence design might enable personal data archives to be more materially present and temporally expressive in people's everyday lives to support ongoing experiences of reflection and reminiscence. These projects also aim to investigate the application of *slow technology* [8] and how this concept could challenge the idea of domestic technology being always on and accessible and lead to an interaction pace that might sustain longer-term experiences with personal data.

The design qualities of Photobox and Olly raise key questions for longitudinal HCI research: How should researchers approach conducting longitudinal field studies of design artifacts that intentionally aim to operate slowly, in the background of everyday life? What are effective techniques for opening a space for discussion on a slow technology with study participants, while also balancing the need to not force too much attention onto it? How should researchers explore participants' potentially changing relations with a slow technology that they may only occasionally interact with directly?

In this chapter, we draw on examples from the longitudinal field studies of Photobox and Olly to explore these questions and to detail tensions and techniques emerged across the two cases. Next, we offer a brief background on the *research product* methodology [9] that in part emerged out of the Photobox project and that subsequently influenced the Olly field study. Then, we describe and reflect on key examples from each longitudinal field study. This chapter concludes with a discussion and reflection on lessons learned across these projects and techniques that can be mobilized in future HCI research.

2 Background and Approach: Research Products

Prototypes have had a long and important history in the HCI community. Prototyping has, and continues to be, an instrumental practice in supporting HCI researchers to develop, refine, and test theories, concepts, and interactive systems through an iterative, human-centered approach. The use of prototyping and prototypes to elicit feedback from people plays a significant role in pursuing the question of how new technologies can be created that are intelligible, usable, and enjoyable to interact with. Yet, prototypes are often of a limited fidelity and robustness which introduces challenges in using them in longitudinal field studies.

In parallel, the kinds of questions that HCI researchers are pursuing continue to expand. The focus of a growing portion of recent research in the HCI community has moved beyond designing for efficient use to investigating complex matters of human technology relations that often involve messy, intimate, and contested aspects of everyday life. These kinds of questions include: What roles could—or *should*—interactive technology play when we consider it as a long-term, evolving component of everyday life? How do technologies mediate between humans and their actions in the world? How do choices that go into the materials, form, and computation of interactive systems shape human relations to them? And, how do these relational qualities change over time?

While the fidelity of prototypes can range, they remain references to future products, systems, or services. In this way, prototypes are placeholders for *something else*; they are an instantiation of a future outcome [10]. Within HCI research, a prototype may be the manifestation of a theoretical concept not to be judged for its actuality or present state, but rather its potential [11]. Prototypes are also often assumed to be a point on a trajectory toward a fully realized commercial product used to test specified needs or unmet requirements. In either case, new knowledge and insights are produced through the use of research prototypes that has clear value. From a high level, the research product concept helps extend the capacity for developing new knowledge through the longitudinal study of design artifacts.

The concept of a research product emphasizes the nature of the engagement that people have with an artifact predicated on *what it is* as opposed to what it *might become*. It is this core distinction that led to the term 'research product' in reference to the final and actual nature of the artifact. This is in contrast to a 'research prototype' that refers to a final concept but the artifact itself may be transitional or in-progress. The term 'research product' emphasizes the actuality of the design artifact helping to overcome the limitations of prototypes when investigating complex matters of human technology relations over time. Importantly, the term 'product' does not aim to suggest these kinds of artifacts are intended to be commercial products, or produced at commercial scale and volume. Research products exhibit key qualities that can help productively support longitudinal field studies of design artifacts in people's everyday lives. The conceptualization of the research product concept emerged through the ongoing design, deployment, and analysis of design artifacts (see [9] for more details). These qualities include the following:

Inquiry driven: A research product aims to drive a research inquiry through the experience of a design artifact in a longitudinal study. Research products are designed to ask particular research questions about potential alterative futures. They embody theoretical stances on a research issue or set of issues. Photobox and Olly aimed to inquire into how the conceptual framing of slow technology could open up new ways of supporting rich, ongoing experiences with personal data for each of our respective field study participants.

Finish: A research product is designed such that the nature of the engagement that people have with it is predicated on *what it is* as opposed to what it *might become*. It emphasizes the actuality of the design artifact. Photobox and Olly operated largely on their own, occasionally presenting elements from our respective participants' personal digital archives (e.g., in the form of a printed photo or a song from their past). Both of these design artifacts needed to have a high quality of finish such that participants could encounter these recurrently over a long period of time (more than one year) and reflect on their evolving relation to the them as well as the personal data that they slowly, yet continually surfaced.

Fit: The aim of a research product is to be lived with in an everyday environment over time. Under these conditions, nuanced dimensions of human experience can emerge and be studied. In the cases of both Photobox and Olly, achieving a quality of fit was essential to investigating our participants situated experiences with and their perceptions of living with a slow technology. Fit requires the artifact to balance the delicate threshold between being neither too familiar nor too strange, such that cycles of direct engagement and interaction can emerge and while also enabling the design artifact to fade into the background of everyday life. Photobox was embodied in the form of an antique wooden chest that required a user to actively decide to open it up to see if a photo from their past was waiting for them inside. Olly was embodied in a more teardrop-like form factor that enabled it to operate in any orientation (i.e., lying flat on either side or in any orientation standing up). We anticipated this design feature would enable end users to integrate their Olly into wherever they deemed most appropriate in their home and to adapt it to new domestic environments and situations over time. In the case of both design artifacts, design decisions around their form were carefully guided by the need to achieve a high quality of fit in our participant's respective households.

Independent: A research product operates effectively when it is freely deployable in the field for an extended amount of time. This means that from technical, material, and design perspectives, a research product can be lived with for a long duration in everyday conditions. The quality of independence was crucial for studying Photobox and Olly as they needed to remain robust and independently functioning even though they may only enact their computational behavior (e.g., printing a photo, or beginning to rotate when a song is selected) relatively rarely.

In summary, Photobox and Olly are research products—artifacts designed to drive a research inquiry and that have a high quality of finish such that people engage with them as is, rather than what they might become; and, that operate independently in everyday settings over time. Low-volume batches of Photobox (3 total) and Olly (3 total) were produced for longitudinal field studies of each. Next, we describe each case with a focus on how lessons learnt from the Photobox study productively influenced how we conducted the longitudinal field study of Olly.

3   Case 1: The Photobox Longitudinal Field Study

The Photobox is a WiFi-connected domestic technology embodied in the form of a well-worn antique chest that prints four or five randomly selected photos from the owner's Flickr [5] photo collection at random intervals each month.

We intended the Photobox form to appear familiar to other non-digital cherished things, aiming for its material aesthetics to evoke a sense of warmth associated with older domestic artifacts. We settled on the final design because of its distance from contemporary 'technology' (i.e., oak compared to plastic). The two main components of Photobox are an antique oak chest and a Bluetooth-enabled Polaroid Pogo printer (which makes $2'' \times 3''$ prints). We decided on using a chest that had already gathered a healthy amount of patina as it seemed to symbolize a well-aged artifact that could support the idea of revisiting past experiences whose materials could inspire a sense of *perceived durability* [12]. To this end, we decided to use a printer to make digital photos material, contrasting the potential durability of paper prints with digital files. We augmented the oak chest with an upper panel to hide the technological components. The printer was installed behind the upper panel with a laser cut and press fitted acrylic case securing it to a small opening in the panel (to allow a photo to drop onto the central platform of the box). This helped integrate all technology used to print photos into a form that enabled it to be opened up and later put away. This choice was influenced by prior work articulating the value of *designing technologies to be put away* [13] (Fig. 1).

Every month, the Photobox prints four or five photos randomly pulled from its owner's Flickr archive. To do this, at the beginning of each month, the participant's Flickr archive is indexed. The.NET Photobox service application we developed then enacts the following set of procedures (which we call *layered randomness*). It randomly makes a binary decision to print either four or five photos that month. Then, it randomly selects four (or five) photos from the index and generates four (or five) randomly selected 'future print times tamps,' which specify the print time and date for each photo. Each photo is uniquely associated with a time stamp, respectively. When the date and time arrive associated with a time stamp, the matching photo is printed. This application runs on a laptop that communicates wirelessly with the Photobox printer via Bluetooth. We lived with the three Photobox prototypes for a four-month period to debug the system prior to deployment and to develop a general sense for how many photos should be printed each month.

Fig. 1 Photobox occasionally randomly selects photos from its owners past and prints them. A wireless printer is mounted above the black rectangular opening in the upper cabinet; when a photo prints, it drops onto the bed of the chest. No information is provided to signal when or if a photo has printed

Photobox's behavior was intentionally designed to be autonomous, not requiring input from the user. This choice was partly influenced by prior work describing how ceding autonomy to a system can enable new ways for people to meaningful experience their digital content [14] and, more generally, open a space for pause and contemplation [15]. We could have curated a special selection of photos from a person's collection to appear in their Photobox. However, randomness was selected to introduce a potentially unfamiliar and disruptive machine behavior. We wanted to explore how people might confront a technology delving into their personal archive and how their perceptions might change over time.

3.1 Field Study Method

We deployed three nearly identical Photoboxes in three different households for 14 months from early 2012 to mid-2013 (see [3] for more details). Similar to the aim and ambition of the original technology probes paper [16], and several field studies since then (e.g., [17–19]), a smaller selection of households was initially selected to focus on in order to gain a richer descriptive understanding of the space as a whole to inform what might be salient issues for future research.

We recruited participants from three different households in the greater Pittsburgh, Pennsylvania (USA) metropolitan area for our field study. We use the term 'primary participant' to differentiate between the main 'owner' of the Flickr account that is embodied in a Photobox and 'secondary participant' as other household members that also lived with the Photobox during the study. All primary participants were familiar with technology, owned digital cameras, and at least one member of each household owned a Flickr account with unlimited storage. Pseudonyms are used to describe household members.

Household 1 (H1) consisted of Tim (aged 48, bookstore clerk) and Britt (42, librarian), a married couple who had lived in their current home for ten years. Tim and Britt shared their Flickr account, contributing photos to it nearly equally; they had approximately 4,500 photos in their 7-year-old archive at the start of the study. **Household 2** (H2) consisted of five roommates (two female, three male): Heather (31, massage therapist), Zack (28, grocery store employee), Thomas (30, technician), Jenn (29, postal service employee), and James (29, barista). They had been living together for 18 months. Heather was the primary participant in household two and the sole owner of the Flickr account; several of her roommates are featured in many photos in it. She had approximately 2500 photos in her 5-year-old archive at the start of the study. **Household 3** (H3) consisted of Samuel (35, insurance salesman) and Shelly (34, legal clerk), a couple who had been living together in the same apartment for nearly two years. Samuel was the primary participant and the sole owner of his 6-year-old Flickr account. He had approximately 3000 photos in it at the start of the study (Fig. 2).

Participants owning the Flickr accounts used in this study all reported similar shifts in interaction with that service over time. Initially, they had been active members in the Flickr community, using the service to support social relationships, and as an outlet for self-expression (these trends in behavior match findings from prior research on Flickr) [20]. However, all account owners had become much less active in the Flickr community. At the time of this study, participants' primary use of their Flickr accounts was as storage for their digital photo collections (approximately between five to sixty photos were uploaded each month). Consequently, our participant pool helped support our goal of exploring how people might more meaningfully revisit their photo archive on a general level.

Fig. 2 From left to right. H1's Photobox after the laptop was moved under a living room couch (in month six of the study). H2's Photobox kept alongside many electronics and entertainment technologies. H3's Photobox kept near the kitchen and living room

We recruited participants with large Flickr photo archives for a few key reasons. First, these large archives would enable us to provide participants with glimpses into past experiences that stretched over several years. During preliminary research, we found many people's locally stored photo archives were fragmented across various hard drives and physical media (e.g., DVDs). As a result, we decided against using locally stored digital photographs, as the effort required to make these archives cohesive would have complicated our goal to easily introduce a prototype into the home. Second, at the time we created the Photoboxes, the Flickr API emerged as the most flexible and robust option for the.NET application we developed.

Through our longitudinal field study, we aimed to collect rich accounts from participants about the rhythms and activities of the home through semi-structured interviews that took place bimonthly. This interview schedule included an introductory interview when installing the Photobox and a final interview at the end of the deployment. During our initial home visit (which lasted 2–3 h), the research team aimed to develop an understanding of members' everyday lives, common domestic activities, perceptions of their photo collections, and technology usage trends. Household members gave us a home tour and decided where the Photobox should be installed (all Photoboxes were installed in or near living rooms). We deliberately gave brief descriptions of the Photobox, noting it will occasionally print a photo from the owner's Flickr archive. We wanted participants to develop their own interpretations over time. We did not explicitly encourage participants to interact with their respective Photobox, and all were aware they could drop out of the study at any time.

All interview sessions over this fourteen-month period were audio recorded, producing 40+ hours of content. Relevant segments of recordings were transcribed. We also took field notes and documentary photographs during each interview. Field notes were reviewed immediately following each interview, and tentative insights were noted in reflective field memos [21]. Weekly meetings were held among the research team to discuss emergent findings. Analysis of the data was an ongoing process. After each home visit, we conducted preliminary analysis, searching for emergent (and shifting) patterns across recordings field notes and photos to draw out underlying themes [22]. We coded raw data documents with these themes. We also created conceptual models and affinity diagrams to reveal unexpected connections and differences among households.

3.2   Reflections on the Field Study of Photobox

Our field study of the Photoboxes was highly influenced by Gaver et al.'s [17] concept of the *trajectory of appreciation* to analyze how new technology design artifacts might (or might not) be accepted by people living with them. Through the lens of this trajectory, a new technology may initially be embraced with excitement because it is novel. As novelty wears off and if expectations are unmet, people may become frustrated. Over time, the technology should normalize into a state of understanding for people—it is either abandoned or accepted. If accepted, people's experiences with it may improve as they develop ways to work around the difficulties they faced, and the technology can be integrated into everyday life.

While individual trajectories somewhat varied, all three households followed a similar path in the Photobox study: a period of initial excitement in the first few weeks, which were followed by tensions that emerged around a lack of control Photobox as well as broader confusion (and even disbelief) over the goal of our research project. Eventually, key moments of acceptance occurred with the Photobox, yet it took a considerable amount of time (e.g., 4–7 months) for participants to fully understand the nature of Photobox as a design artifact and integrate it into their lives.

3.3   The First Home Visits: Miscalibration of Photobox's Initial Description

Prior to initially visiting households, we asked participants to consider where in their home they would like to have their Photobox installed. In the first visit to each household, participants gave us a brief tour of their home to help the research team develop a sense of their everyday lives and interests. We then configured and deployed a Photobox in the location participants desired it to be in their respective homes. During this time, we manually triggered the Photobox to print one randomly selected photo from its owner's Flickr archive to ensure it was working properly with participants' home network system and to generally demonstrate how it works. Here, we noted that when a photo prints it will drop onto the internal bed of the chest and that the main 'interaction' with the Photobox would be opening the chest to see whether or not a photo from one's past is there. We also mentioned that the Photobox will 'occasionally' print a photo from their past. At the time, we did not want participants to know that their Photobox prints either four or five photos per month because this could have changed their impression that Photobox has an ongoing, slow yet perpetual behavior. For example, we anticipated that if a participant had already received five photos in a month, they may lose interest entirely in the device. We also wanted participants to come to their own impressions and interpretations of their Photobox over time. Thus, we did not want to overly discuss how it is engineered to operate. We described that our field study was open-ended and exploratory and noted that our research goal was to understand participants' experiences with their Photobox. We made sure participants were aware that the study would last for approximately fourteen months and that they could drop out of the study at any time.

In hindsight, during this point of the initial deployment, it would have been advantageous for us to have spent more time communicating and reinforcing the motivations for our study and its uniqueness. All participants were avid digital photographers, and it was clear that the ability to re-experience photographs from their past in an unpredictable and tangible way through Photobox was appealing to them. Although Photobox seemed like an 'easy' design artifact to live with, it was hard for participants (and the research team) to imagine how they would react to living with it over time. When we departed from the initial deployment and interview sessions, participants seemed content to begin living with their Photobox and did not have many questions for us. They were aware that the research team would visit their household again in two months to interview them about their experiences with Photobox.

3.4   Emergent Tensions and Skepticisms as the Field Study Progresses

In returning two months later for our first bimonthly interview, the research team found tensions had emerged in each household. On the surface, these tensions appeared to stem from participants living with a slow technology that they wanted to have more control over. Across participants, there was a desire to increase the 'speed' of the system such that they would receive more photos from their past or even have the ability to receive them on demand (e.g., having a button that, when pressed, would print a photo from the past). These were exactly the kinds of tensions we expected might emerge. We wanted to understand how people would react to living with a system that exhibited an intentionally slowed down pace and if this might ultimately to valued cycles of an anticipation. A key motivation for conducting our longitudinal study was to explore if such tensions would eventually fade away and the Photobox would be accepted, or if they would be too great and Photobox would be viewed in a negative light and rejected. Thus, it was interesting to find that in month two of our field study participants described the complex trade-off around wanting to have more control over the Photobox while equally recognizing that ceding autonomy to it played a key role in the surprising, anticipatory, and, at times, serendipitous experiences that were slowly emerging with it. Better understanding the experiential qualities around these tensions and how they might change over time was core to our research and conversations with participants on these tensions were highly insightful across our study.

However, we were surprised to find an emerging skepticism across participants about the genuineness of our field study. In wrestling with the tensions described above and prospectively considering the longitudinal duration of the field study, participants had begun to question if our project had ulterior motives that we had not initially been forthcoming about. Could academic researchers *really* be interested in people's experiences with such a slow acting system? Or was the study they were participating in about something entirely different?

These sneaking suspicions had led to participants developing various folk theories to explain how and why the Photobox operated and, in some cases, to speculate on what the 'real' study was about. The algorithm we designed for selecting which photo would print, when it would print, and whether four or five photos would print each month was completely random. However, by the end of month, two participants had started to think otherwise. For example, Tim (household 1) was convinced that his Photobox would only print photos of people if they were wearing a hat. He was unsure of what we, the research team, wanted to find out by implementing this into the algorithm. Two months into the study (and nine printed photos later), coincidentally only hat-wearing people had emerged in his photographs (only four of the nine photos had people in them). Tim speculated this must have had some significance in relation to the seemingly innocuous, but increasingly unusual research study he was participating in.

More extraordinarily, Heather (household two) speculated that her Photobox may have knowledge of and perhaps even be predicting her love life after a photo of her ex-lover was consecutively followed by one of her current boyfriend. Heather described that this surprising instance prompted her to consider if she had been secretly surveilled by the Photobox and that the field study actually aimed to focus on factors influencing her decision making in romantic relationships.

Interestingly, Samuel's (household 3) account of two months into the study also revealed anxieties over possible surveillance; he had considered that his Photobox might actually be designed to track his movements around the house as he passed by it daily. Motivated by these emergent concerns and general curiosity, Samuel confessed to having partially disassembled his Photobox to examine the internal components. He discovered a wireless printer, acrylic case, and electrical wiring inside. While this discovery countered his theory that there may be more sophisticated sensing technology for tracking his everyday movements, he remained skeptical of our field study's actual goal.

3.5 Addressing Our Initial Misstep: Re-emphasizing the Goal and Aim of Our Longitudinal Field Study

Collectively, the skepticisms experienced by our participants were not extreme enough to motivate them to drop out of the study. All participants reported highly positive experiences emerging from receiving photos from their past within their respective Photobox. The tensions participants reported on related to lack of control and the slow pacing of the printing rate were precisely what our field study aimed to explore. Yet, it was clear the skepticisms needed to be addressed. When we began our study, our hope was that through causally explaining what the Photobox is and what it does, and it would create a space for participants to come to their own inter-pretations of it. However, the combination of a somewhat ambiguous details on how the Photobox works, and the unusualness of participating in a longitudinal study of a largely inactive domestic technology had triggered participants to question the goal of our study and develop diverse speculations on its focus. During our month two interview, we re-emphasized the goals of our field study to participants. We also provided more specific details on precisely how the Photobox works and that the algorithm driving its behavior is purely random. This gentle reinforcement appeared to address our participants' emergent concerns around the focus, scope, and goal of our project.

However, these issues had drawn a high amount of attention to the Photobox. While we hoped participants would engage with the Photobox, we also aimed to explore the extent to which this slow technology could subtly fade in and out of the background of domestic life. This motivated us to explore developing a technique that would allow us to create a space for discussion with participants about their experiences with Photobox while not forcing it. Initially, we decided to adopt a bimonthly semi-structured interview approach in our field study because we felt that including a diary or camera study might overly require participants to engage with the Photobox (i.e., on our terms, not theirs). Conducting semi-structured interviews would provide an infrequent, but consistent format to have deep conversations about participants' experiences over time. Yet, in practice during our month two interview, this felt overly formal.

3.6   The Emergence and Application of 'Maintenance Visits'

Coincidentally, we had also decided on the bimonthly interview schedule because the Photobox came with a key constraint: The wireless photo printer embedded inside of the chest could only hold ten pieces of thermal photo paper that the photos are printed onto. We used this constraint as an opportunity to reframe our bimonthly interactions with participants to be 'maintenance visits' instead of planned interviews. This shift enabled us to have concrete times planned to visit each household where the primary goal would be to refill the Photobox's printer paper. In month 4, we found this technique was effective at creating a more informal atmosphere in our visits. Upon visiting each household, we first navigated to the Photobox and began servicing it (e.g., opening it, unscrewing the acrylic case in the upper cabinet of the chest, inserting a new module of photo printer paper, etc.). This provided time for participants to adjust to us being in their home and triggered informal conversation which often (but not always) segued into participants discussing their experiences with the Photobox over the past couple of months. If our discussions transitioned to talking about the Photobox, only then would the research team ask permission to start recording the discussion. At the conclusion of each visit, the research team immediately wrote in-depth field notes to capture the experience of the visit and details (e.g., changes to the spatial arrangement of the Photobox in relation to other physical artifacts in the home, the emergence of printed photos in the home and their movement to different locations, etc.). These field notes were paired with data from field discussions in an ongoing analysis which progressively built up to the final, in-depth concluding semi-structured interview with each household. These interviews typically lasted two hours, and we referred to emergent themes in our findings, specific discussions, and observations captured in field notes across the 14-month period. This approach was ultimately effective at capturing ongoing changes in participants' relations to their Photobox and then confirming and retrospectively exploring them in the final interview. We found that early tensions emerging from lack of control over the Photobox faded over time across households and that it was accepted as a valued artifact in our participants' everyday lives.

The 'maintenance visit' technique offered several important outcomes for conducting our longitudinal field study of the Photobox. It shifted expectations and softened the 'researcher–participant' dynamic. Participants could approach the research team to share their experiences with the Photobox if they desired. But, this was not a requirement since the ostensible goal of our bimonthly visits was to refill the photo printer paper. After all, the Photobox was a slowly operating technology; if participants did not engage with it frequently within a month or two, we did not view this as a failure. A key example of this was Samuel (household 1) going on holiday to subsequently to come back to a 'treasure trove' of photos capturing memories from the past that had accumulated over a month he was away. By utilizing a technique that did not 'force' participants to report on their experiences, we were able to more effectively balance the subtly and nuances of conducting a longitudinal study of a slow technology without drawing too much attention to it.

The maintenance visit technique also provided opportunities to have more interactions with other household members that lived with a Photobox but did not have their Flickr account linked to it. For example, several instances emerged in which the primary owner of a Photobox (that had their account linked to it) was unavailable and other household members greeted the research team for a maintenance visit. These interactions were valuable in providing additional perspectives on how the Photobox became integrated in the broader household over time. For example, during maintenance visits in months six and ten, various roommates of Heather (household two) shared impromptu reflections on their own experiences of the Photobox during and after it was serviced by our research team. In other households, similar situations emerged where the research team had opportunities to have open-ended discussions with members that lived with Photobox while primary participant was not present. This helped build rapport with all members in our households and, as a result, all members in each household opted to join the final, in-depth interview at the conclusion of our study. Importantly, this helped us better understand the experiences and interactions that the Photobox catalyzed among our primary participants and others living with it. In this, it provided a space for group reflection on how emergent tensions faded away, why Photobox was eventually accepted as a novel domestic technology in each household, and what kinds of social practices it catalyzed and mediated. Ultimately, the maintenance visit technique enabled us to obtain depth on various dimensions to understand the process through which the Photobox was ecologically adopted in and across households over time.

4   Case 2: The Olly Field Study

The next longitudinal field study in our research program focused on a design artifact named Olly. Olly is a domestic music player that explores how a framing of slowness might be applied to a person's digital music listening history to support reflective experiences with this data over time. Olly works by making use of its owner's personal music listening history metadata archive to randomly select a song from its owner's past and make it available to be played. The random selection algorithm we designed provides an interaction pacing of about nine random selections per week. Olly's central feature is its internal wooden disk encircled in aluminum (see Fig. 3). When a song is surfaced from the past, it is not immediately played. First, the disk begins rotating to subtly indicate a song has been selected and is available to be played (i.e., similar to a 'pending' state). The speed of the disk's rotation is relative to how deep into the past the song was listened to by Olly's owner (e.g., the deeper into the past, the slower the rotational speed). To play the song, the owner must tangibly spin the rotating disk. If the song is not played within a relatively brief time window (e.g., about 10 min), Olly will abandon it and stop spinning until another song is eventually surfaced. This process continues indefinitely (for more details on the design process, please see [6]).

A crucial part of Olly's implementation is its connection to its owner's Last.FM [23] online database. Last.FM is a commercial application and online service that runs across a user's devices (e.g., laptop, iPod, smartphone, etc.) and automatically creates a detailed, time-stamped log of each instance of when they listen to a song. In simple terms, Last.FM is a personal metadata repository of the digital music one has actively played and listened to in the past; it captures and logs when digital music is listened to locally (e.g., mp3 song files stored on one's phone or personal computer) and via streaming services (e.g., Spotify, Tidal, YouTube). In existence since 2002, Last.FM offers unusually rare access to extensive personal music listening histories, which Olly uses to surface songs from its owner's past. Thus, when Olly selects a song from one's past to be listened to, it is presenting a precise instance in the past of when that song was played (see Figs. 4 and 5).

Another important part of Olly's design is that it causes all instances in a user's Last.FM database to slowly age over time because their 'age' is relative to today's current date. For example, Olly's absolute fastest rotation could only be triggered

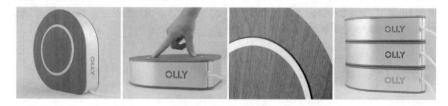

Fig. 3 Left to right. Olly can operate standing up (or lying flat); a pending song is played by gently spinning the rotating disk (pictured here when lying flat); woodgrains move in and out of alignment as the disk rotates; three Olly research products deployed with participants

Fig. 4 (1) Olly's algorithm has a 'success', and it randomly selects a specific listening instance from its owner's Last.FM library; in this case, the song Bittersweet Symphony that was listened to on 18:11 June 7, 2012, is selected. (2) The internal disk begins to rotate indicating that a song is availability to be played; in this case, the listening instance is quite old which causing the disk's rotational speed to be quite slow. (3) The user notices the rotation and manually spins the disk to trigger the song to play

Fig. 5 From left to right. Jim-H1's Olly, kept in his home office, was easily visible from the bed and living room; Suzie-H2's Olly kept in her living room with cat Terry; an earlier image of Tom-H3's Olly soon after he moved it from the living room into his bedroom

if it selected a listening instance that the user had listened to the previous week (and its slowest possible rotation would be triggered if Olly selected songs at the very beginning of the Last.FM archive). Thus, since the rotational speed is relative to today's date, all of the songs in the Olly database will continue to slowly grow older irrespective of the actions of its owner. These decisions made it possible to use Last.FM metadata to encode an added layer of temporal expressiveness into Olly's manifestation of songs listened to at precise points in a user's past. Beyond the speed of rotation, no other information is offered about the specific listening instance when it is surfaced and made available to be played. Understanding the rotational speed relative to each specific music listening instance will likely require the user to take time to interpret and make sense of. We speculated that, over time, these subtle differences might become more discernible and personally meaningful. We were interested in exploring if study participants' perceptions of Olly might evolve over time if they developed a sensibility for 'reading', interacting, and living with it. Similar to the Photobox field study, we also did not want to draw too much attention to these subtle design qualities and wanted participants to come to their own judgment of Olly's character over time.

4.1   Field Study Method

We created three nearly identical Olly research products, and they were deployed with three different households in a field study over the course of 15 months from early June 2017 to late August 2018. We recruited three participants from the greater Vancouver, British Columbia (Canada) metropolitan area, to participate in our study. All participants were familiar with technology, owned digital devices (e.g., music players, smartphones, computers), and had Last.FM accounts that were still in use. We recruited participants that had large existing Last.FM archives; coincidentally all three participants' accounts were started in 2006. This enabled us to provide participants with glimpses into music from their past that stretched over a decade (see Fig. 5). It is important to acknowledge that due to our participants' preexisting interest in using Last.FM, they likely already had some interest in exploring past music tastes and trends.

Household 1 consisted of Jim (mid-30 s, full-time bike mechanic and freelance graphic designer). Jim lived with his wife Sally in a two bedroom apartment. Jim was the primary participant in this household and had a Last.FM that account contained 82,230 entries (an average of 18 songs per day over 12 years). **Household 2** consisted of Suzie (mid-50 s, massage therapist). Suzie lived alone with her cat Terry in a one bedroom apartment. Suzie's Last.FM account contained 136,988 entries (an average of 30 songs per day over 12 years). **Household 3** consisted of Tom (mid-20 s, restaurant waiter and part-time college student). Tom shared a house with three roommates. Tom was the primary participant in this household; he had started his Last.FM account in early high school, and it contained 163,436 entries (35 songs per day over 12 years). The average amount of music participants listened to daily remained similar to their respective averages in our study.

We aimed to collect rich accounts from participants about the rhythms and activities of the home through semi-structured interviews that took place monthly. This interview schedule included an introductory interview when installing Olly and an in-depth final interview at the end of the 15-month longitudinal study. During our initial home visit (which lasted 1–2 h), we aimed to develop an understanding of participants' everyday lives, common activities, interests in music, music listening practices, and technology usage trends. Participants gave us a home tour and decided where Olly should be installed and where the Raspberry Pi for music playback should be connected. We designed Olly to be easily movable once connected to home WiFi, simply requiring it to be unplugged, moved, and plugged back in wherever desired. Using our web dashboard, we then manually triggered Olly to randomly select a listening instance to test for reliability and demonstrate how Olly works. All were aware they could drop out of the study at any time.

After the initial home visit, we conducted monthly interviews to probe and record participants' unfolding experiences with Olly in a structured, yet informal manner. We viewed Olly as a somewhat more sophisticated and unusual design artifact in comparison with Photobox. We desired to carefully capture and explore participants' potentially changing experiences with and perceptions of their respective Olly. Additionally, the Photobox field study had made us well aware of the potential pitfalls and tensions that can come with studying slow technology research product in situ over time. Thus, these reasons motivated our decision to conduct monthly interviews with participants (as opposed to the bimonthly interviews schedule in the Photobox study). Monthly interview sessions with participants typically lasted 30–60 min. At the conclusion of the study, we visited each household to conduct in-depth interviews (these sessions lasted 2–2.5 h). We commonly referred to field notes and recordings capturing participants' earlier experiences to explore possible changes in attitudes toward and experiences with Olly and participants Last.FM archives over time.

All interview sessions over this 15-month period were audio recorded. Relevant segments of recordings were transcribed. Researchers also took field notes and documentary photographs during each interview. Field notes were reviewed immediately following each interview, and tentative insights were noted in reflective field memos [21]. Analysis of the data was an ongoing process. After each home visit, we conducted a preliminary analysis, searching for emergent, stabilizing, and shifting patterns across recordings, field notes, and photos to draw out underlying themes [22]. We coded raw documents with these themes. We also created affinity diagrams to model connections and differences among households.

4.2 Reflections on the Field Study of Olly

Similar to our prior field study, we drew inspiration from the trajectory of appreciation [17] to map our participants' perceptions of Olly as they explored if it would be embraced and accepted into their everyday practices or be rejected and abandoned. Following lessons from the Photobox field study, we had the foresight to ensure participants understood how Olly worked and that the goal of our research project was clearly communicated and its legitimacy was reinforced. We also anticipated it would be important to create a space for participants to share their experiences and potentially shifting perceptions of Olly with us, while not forcing these interactions.

We asked participants to consider where they would like Olly to initially be placed within their home. In addition to requiring an electrical outlet and a wireless Internet connection, Olly also needed to be in proximity to an audio speaker system in participants' home so that they could easily listen to a song if they decided to trigger it to play when one was selected. When we arrived at participants' respective homes, we took a brief tour and then installed Olly in their desired location. During the installation period, we took care to do a demonstration of the system for participants. We manually triggered Olly to randomly select a song from their Last.FM archive, described to them that the rotational speed of the song that was just selected is relative to how deep into the past this specific instance had been listened to. We then invited them to tangibly spin the rotating disk to become familiar with the interaction that triggers the pending song to play.

We also made clear to participants that the song selection algorithm we designed is entirely random and will surface about nine songs per week, although precisely when this will happen is also random and thus unpredictable. We used the informed consent research ethics form as an opportunity to reinforce that this project is funded by a national research council, and our sole objective is to understand participants' experiences with Olly. Participants were made aware that two other Olly devices were simultaneously deployed in other households in the greater Vancouver area. Participants in particular appeared to positively respond to this point, both in terms recognizing our aim to develop comparative insights based on multiple empirical field studies conducted simultaneously as well as with curiosity around how others might experience re-encounters with respective personal music listening history.

In addition to demonstrating how Olly functions during our initial interview, we also opened up the exterior enclosure of Olly to visibly show participants the internal mechanics and engineering of the device as it operated in real time (see Fig. 6). We had intentionally designed Olly's enclosure to be easily openable to support long-term repair and modifications. We used this opportunity to show participants the internal timing belt and narrow tolerances that it physically operates within to produce the actuated rotation of the internal disk. In this, we primed participants with expectation that the research team will need to conduct bimonthly 'maintenance visits' to ensure that the internal belt is functioning properly or if it is in need of repair. We made participants aware that we would be conducting these lightweight bimonthly visits over the course of the field study, which would build up to an in-depth final interview at the study's conclusion. We also briefly described the Photobox field study and that this was a common practice in our prior work.

While these are seemingly lower-level methodological details, in practice we found they were highly effective at mitigating the unwanted tensions and distractions that we encountered in the Photobox study. Participants collectively had a clear vision of the goal and validity of the field study; and, suspicions about potential ulterior motives did not arise. Over the course of the fifteen-month field study, our maintenance visits worked reliably as a technique to subtly invite discussion about Olly without forcing it. We found that participants did experience some tensions triggered by Olly's slow pacing and their own lack of control over it. Interestingly, these tensions related to pacing and control faded away faster than in the Photobox study.

Fig. 6 From left to right. The exterior enclosure included a cabinet bracket for easy access to internal components during maintenance visits; the belt that actuates Olly's rotational movement using a stepper motor; Exploded view of various modular components that fit within Olly's alumni enclosure when assembled

Additionally, for both Jim (household 1) and Tom (household 3), the maintenance visits provided valuable opportunities to engage in discussion with secondary participants in the household about their perceptions of Olly. Over the course of our field study, all secondary participants eventually had direct experiences with Olly through listening to music it played back from the primary participant's Last.FM archive and, in some cases, through triggering it to play music by tangibly manipulating the disk when a song was pending. Similar to the Photobox study, all secondary participants across households decided to join the final in-depth interview at the conclusion of our study (with the except of household two where Suzie lived alone). The situated accounts of secondary participants proved invaluable to developing a deeper holistic understanding of how Olly mediated reflective experiences for our primary participants as well as triggered social interactions and practices around it with others. These group discussions also opened up to broader dialog on that questioned the motives and values that shape the design of contemporary consumer technologies which was unexpected but ultimately became an important part of our overall research findings and the design implications resulting from our study.

5   Discussion

Developing approaches to creating and studying new technologies that mediate people's practices of reflecting on their life experiences, sense of self, and desires for the future raises important opportunities and issues for the HCI community. With these new possibilities comes complex questions around what kinds of qualities researchers ought to consider when designing technologies that might take on a long-term place in people's everyday lives and how we might study these systems over time. The slow technology design philosophy offers a promising conceptual lens to frame inquiries into crafting longer-term relationships with computational things. Key to creating a slow technology that can be successfully taken up and sustained in people's practices is generating an interaction pacing that balances the design artifact's ability to it to be directly engaged with as well as to fade into the background of everyday life. Methodological approaches such as technology probes [16] and research products [9] offer important advances for guiding HCI researchers in conducting longitudinal field studies of design artifacts in the real and situated complexities of people's daily lives. Yet, longitudinal studies of slow technologies have particular concerns that can shape the potential for successfully conducting a longitudinal field study. As detailed in this chapter, implementing an approach that does not attract 'too much' attention to a slow technology deployed in a participant's everyday environment while maintaining implicit openings for discussion initiated by participants on their own terms are important parts of conducting a longitudinal field study. Next, we reflect further on experiences from our field studies of Photobox and Olly describe to distill practical considerations for conducting longitudinal studies of slow technologies in future HCI research.

5.1 Understanding Where Tensions are Occurring and What Triggers Them

In the case of the Photobox field study, our aim to create a situation in which participants can come to their own interpretations of the design artifact caused the research team to be somewhat ambiguous in the initial deployment installation when describing how it operated. We felt that such in-depth knowledge of the Photobox might adversely shape participants' unique subjective perspective of the design artifact and perceptions on how it might fit (or not fit) into their lives over time. We also anticipated this might draw too much attention to the Photobox. While well intentioned, this technique began to derail our study. It led to a 'guessing game' situation where participants' felt that part of the study might involve them determining what it was *really* about. This triggered participants to develop various folks theories that were used to explain how the Photobox 'actually' works and how such explanations tie to alternative conceptualizations of what the 'true' goals of the longitudinal study are. These experiences helped remind us that, from a study participant's perspective, receiving and living with a slow technology can be highly unusual because they operate relatively seldomly and often study participants have little control over them. After the initial adjustment period of living with the Photobox, its unpredictability and long periods of inaction paired with the longitudinal trajectory of the field study raised questions and introduced distractions for our participants. Ultimately, we were able to correct the course of field study early on by clarifying and reinforcing the aim of the Photobox project. We leveraged these insights in planning our protocol for the Olly project and were mindful to be highly transparent about describing its functionality and the specific questions that our study inquired into. As this study progressed, participants across households raised no skepticisms about the Olly design artifact or the broader aims of the research project itself. The lesson learned here is that taking extra care to clearly explain how a slow technology works, why it was designed to work this way, and reinforcing the legitimacy of the research project is important to establishing the scaffolding to conduct a successful longitudinal field study.

The lesson described immediately above must be treated with care. Conducting a successful longitudinal study of a slow technology does not mean or require that participants always 'enjoyed' living with the design artifact or did not encounter tensions. Slow technologies, like Photobox and Olly, aim to empirically explore conceptual propositions that are subtle and nuanced: They take time to understand, slowly move between the foreground and background of everyday life, and manifest change over time. These qualities can trigger tensions for participants through living with them. Better understanding what specific elements of a slow technology triggers such tensions and how they are grappled with over time by participants is often a key goal of the longitudinal field study. New knowledge in this area will improve our understanding of how slow technologies could be designed in ways that better support end user adoption. Thus, when tensions emerge, critical consideration needs to go into questioning if they are the 'right' tensions. The research team must be prepared to disentangle emergent tensions that may be distractions and complicate achieving the goal of the field study versus tensions that need to unfold over time and be faced by participants to advance new knowledge on their experiences—potentially changing perceptions—of the design artifact over time.

5.2 Maintenance Visits as a Technique to Open Implicit Spaces for Dialog Over Time

This presents a complex balance and nuanced methodological issue to contend with. We found that establishing an occasional, yet consistent routine of maintenance visits to our participants' households offered a technique for productively navigating these difficulties. Conducting maintenance visits gave the research team a practical task to complete as a part of the field study that eased the nature of our engagement with study participants. They did not have to feel the pressure to be prepared to 'report' on their use or experiences with Photobox or Olly. This helped provide the needed space and time for participants to develop their own interpretations of the slow technology that they lived with, while providing a routine opportunity to engage in discussions if desired. This technique was productive in shifting the researcher–participant dynamic by implicitly communicating to participants that the research team was committed to the project (e.g., through the planned manual labor of maintaining the design artifacts), while subtly reinforcing that we wanted participants to engage with the design artifacts on their own terms.

The maintenance visits also provided opportunities to engage with other secondary participants in households that our slow technologies were deployed in. Discussions with secondary participants were highly valuable because they helped us further develop rapport with households over the course of the study, and, importantly, they provided additional perspectives on how each design artifact became unique embedded in the social and environmental ecology of the home. Ultimately, all secondary participants across household in the Photobox and Olly field studies joined our final in-depth interview sessions. This created an opportunity for exploring similarities and differences among perceptions of primary and secondary participants and probing how they collectively may have changed over time. These discussions also often opened up to prospective group reflections on the potential future role and place that slow technologies could have in their lives in the future. Both primary and secondary participants often referenced key experiences they had with our design artifacts and described how they triggered different ways that technology could be designed differently during these speculative, future-oriented discussions. While we did not initially anticipate that the final interviews would include group reflections among primary and secondary participants, they provided valuable insights into the ecological validity of our longitudinal field studies and, importantly, social and environmental factors that may affect the adoption of slow technologies in the future.

6 Conclusion

Longitudinal field studies of research prototypes or research products deployed in the real and situated complexity of people's everyday lives are challenging. In this chapter, we have described tensions that emerged when conducting longitudinal field studies of the Photobox and Olly slow technology design artifacts and reflected on lessons learned to help mitigate emergent tensions. Indeed, field studies of slow technologies come with added constraints as the research team must critically consider (and disentangle) tensions that participants experience over time to guide the investigation to a successful conclusion. This requires providing a space for ongoing discussion with study participants while being mindful to not force these interactions or draw too much attention to the design artifact itself. We found that taking care to offer in-depth demonstrations of the design artifacts when they were installed as well as explanations of the research project's goal and intent helped mitigate initial distractions that can negatively affect a longitudinal field study's progress. Maintenance visits offered a technique to open implicit spaces for dialog with primary and secondary participants. This was highly valuable for the research team to understand the nuances of how our design artifacts were adopted into the social and material ecologies of participating households. This technique was also effective at developing and sustaining rapport with households over time and creating a context for individual and group reflections in our final in-depth interview. Our goal in introducing maintenance visits is to offer a technique for better supporting HCI researchers interested in investigating questions concerning how human technology relations change over time with design artifacts. Importantly, our aim is not to be prescriptive nor conclusive. Rather, the aim is to offer a foundation to help frame future generative work and open up the lessons and techniques discussed here for further development. As the HCI community continues to explore the potential role, pace, and place of technology in people's everyday lives, we hope our work can contribute to a complementary framing for conducting longitudinal research of slow technologies in the HCI community over time and into the future.

Acknowledgements There are many colleagues that I have had the good fortune of working with across the Photobox and Olly projects described in this chapter. For the Photobox project: many thanks to Mark Selby, Abigail Sellen, Richard Banks, David Kirk, and Tim Regan for their essential roles in the Photobox design, implementation, and field study. The Photobox project was supported primarily by Microsoft Research. Additionally, Ron Wakkary, Youn-kyung Lim, and Audrey Desjardins for their collaboration on developing the research product methodology. For the Olly project: many thanks to Jeroen Hol, Bram Naus, and Pepijn Verburg for their essential roles in the Olly design, implementation and field study, as well as Ron Wakkary. The Olly project was funded by the Social Sciences and Humanities Research Council of Canada (SSHRC), Natural Sciences and Engineering Research Council of Canada (NSERC), and 4TU Design United. Finally, many thanks to the research participants themselves that provided considerable time and commitment to participating in these longitudinal studies.

References

1. Elsden C, Selby M, Durrant A, Kirk D (2016) Fitter, happier, more productive: what to ask of a data-driven life. Interactions 23(5):45–45
2. Wallace J, Rogers J, Shorter M, Thomas P, Skelly M, Cook R (2018) The SelfReflector: design, IoT and the high street. In: Proceedings of the 2018 CHI conference on human factors in computing systems (CHI '18). ACM, New York, NY, USA, pp 423:1–423:12
3. Odom W, Sellen AJ, Banks R, Kirk DS, Regan T, Selby M, Forlizzi JL, Zimmerman J (2014) Designing for slowness, anticipation and re-visitation: a long term field study of the photobox. In: Proceedings of the SIGCHI conference on human factors in computing systems (CHI '14). ACM, New York, NY, USA, pp 1961–1970
4. Odom W, Wakkary R (2015) Intersecting with unaware objects. In: Proceedings of the 2015 ACM SIGCHI conference on creativity and cognition (C&C '15). Association for Computing Machinery, New York, NY, USA, pp 33–42
5. Flickr. Retrieved 20 April 2020 from https://www.flickr.com
6. Odom W, Wakkary R, Bertran I, Harkness M, Hertz G, Hol J, Lin H, Naus B, Tan P, Verburg P (2018) Attending to slowness and temporality with olly and slow game: a design inquiry into supporting longer-term relations with everyday computational objects. In: Proceedings of the 2018 CHI conference on human factors in computing systems (CHI '18). ACM, New York, NY, USA, pp 77:1–77:13
7. Odom W, Wakkary R, Hol J, Naus B, Verburg P, Amram T, Chen AYS (2019) Investigating slowness as a frame to design longer-term experiences with personal data: a field study of olly. In: Proceedings of the 2019 CHI conference on human factors in computing systems (CHI '19). Association for Computing Machinery, New York, NY, USA, Paper 34, pp 1–16
8. Hallnäs L, Redström J (Jan 2001) Slow technology—designing for reflection. Personal Ubiquitous Comput 5(3):201–212
9. Odom W, Wakkary R, Lim Y-K, Desjardins A, Hengeveld B, Banks R (2016) From research prototype to research product. In: Proceedings of the 2016 CHI conference on human factors in computing systems (CHI '16). ACM, New York, NY, USA, pp 2549–2561
10. Lim Y-K, Stolterman E, Tenenberg J (2008) The anatomy of prototypes: prototypes as filters, prototypes as manifestations of design ideas. ACM Trans Comput-Hum Interact 15(2):7:1–7:27
11. Houde S, Hill C (1997) What do prototypes prototype?. In: Handbook of human-computer interaction. North-Holland, pp 367–381
12. Odom W, Pierce J, Stolterman E, Blevis E (2009) Understanding why we preserve some things and discard others in the context of interaction design. In: Proceedings of the SIGCHI conference on human factors in computing systems (CHI '09). ACM, New York, NY, USA, pp 1053–1062
13. Odom W, Banks R, Kirk D, Harper R, Lindley S, Sellen A (2012) Technology heirlooms?: Considerations for passing down and inheriting digital materials. In: Proceedings of the SIGCHI conference on human factors in computing systems (CHI '12). ACM, New York, NY, USA, pp 337–346
14. Leong T, Vetere F, Howard S (2008) Abdicating choice: the rewards of letting go. Digital Creativity 19(4):233–243
15. Woodruff A, Augustin S, Foucault B (2007) Sabbath day home automation: "It's like mixing technology and religion". In: Proceedings of the 2007 CHI conference on human factors in computing systems (CHI '07). ACM, New York, NY, USA, pp 527–536
16. Hutchinson H, Mackay W, Westerlund B, Bederson BB, Druin A, Plaisant C, Beaudouin-Lafon M, Conversy S, Evans H, Hansen H, Roussel N, Eiderbäck B (2003) Technology probes: inspiring design for and with families. In Proceedings of the SIGCHI conference on human factors in computing systems (CHI '03). Association for Computing Machinery, New York, NY, USA, pp 17–24
17. Gaver W, Bowers J, Boucher A, Law A, Pennington S, Villar N (2006) The history tablecloth: illuminating domestic activity. In Proceedings of the 6th conference on Designing Interactive systems (DIS '06). Association for Computing Machinery, New York, NY, USA, pp 199–208

18. Gaver W, Sengers P, Kerridge T, Kaye J, Bowers J (2007) Enhancing ubiquitous computing with user interpretation: field testing the home health horoscope. In: Proceedings of the SIGCHI conference on human factors in computing systems (CHI '07). Association for Computing Machinery, New York, NY, USA, pp 537–546
19. Helmes J, Taylor AS, Cao X, Höök K, Schmitt P, Villar N (2010) Rudiments 1, 2 & 3: design speculations on autonomy. In: Proceedings of the fifth international conference on Tangible, embedded, and embodied interaction (TEI '11). Association for Computing Machinery, New York, NY, USA, pp 145–152
20. Van Dijck J (2011) Flick and the culture of connectivity: sharing views, experiences, memories. Mem Stud 4(4):401–415
21. Glaser B, Strauss A (2017) Discover of grounded theory: strategies for qualitative research. Routledge
22. Miles M, Michel Huberman A (1994) Qualitative data analysis: an expanded sourcebook. Sage
23. Last.FM. Last.fm. Retrieved 20 April 2020 from https://www.last.fm/home

Opportunities and Challenges for Long-Term Tracking

Daniel A. Epstein, Parisa Eslambolchilar, Judy Kay, Jochen Meyer, and Sean A. Munson

Abstract As self-tracking has evolved from a niche practice to a mass-market phenomenon, it has become possible to track a broad range of activities and vital parameters over years and decades. This creates both new opportunities for long term research and also illustrates some challenges associated with longitudinal research. We establish characteristics of very long-term tracking, based on previous work from diverse areas of Ubicomp, HCI, and health informatics. We identify differences between long- and short-term tracking, and discuss consequences on the tracking process. A model for long-term tracking integrates the specific characteristics and facilitates identifying viewpoints of tracking. Finally, a research agenda suggests major topics for future work, including respecting gaps in data and incorporating secondary data sources.

Keywords Self-tracking · Long-term · Personal informatics · Physical activity

D. A. Epstein (✉)
University of California Irvine, Irvine, USA
e-mail: epstein@ics.uci.edu

P. Eslambolchilar
Cardiff University, Cardiff, UK
e-mail: EslambolchilarP@cardiff.ac.uk

J. Kay
University of Sydney, Sydney, Australia
e-mail: judy.kay@sydney.edu.au

J. Meyer
OFFIS Institute for Information Technology, Oldenburg, Germany
e-mail: meyer@offis.de

S. A. Munson
University of Washington, Seattle, USA
e-mail: smunson@uw.edu

© Springer Nature Switzerland AG 2021
E. Karapanos et al. (eds.), *Advances in Longitudinal HCI Research*,
Human–Computer Interaction Series, https://doi.org/10.1007/978-3-030-67322-2_9

1   Introduction

New sensors, miniaturization, the ubiquity of smartphones, networking and the Internet of things present designers with a plethora of new applications and systems that promise to provide people with that data to support and improve their personal health, well-being, and fitness, and, for researchers, opportunities to understand health and well-being longitudinally. Many research and commercial systems aim to promote *personal tracking*, or monitoring of one's habits for self-understanding and self-improvement [32]. Substantial work in HCI has demonstrated benefits of *short-term tracking*, where people collect data about their habits and reflect on them for a couple of weeks or months. Short-term tracking interventions have been designed and evaluated for improving physical activity [31, 46], eating habits [59], workplace productivity [27], and other domains. There is also some growing understanding of the ways people can harness long-term tracking data for self-understanding and self-improvement.

Personal tracking tools now support collecting more and more detailed data about ourselves, with varying levels of effort. Wearable devices or smartphones can passively monitor physical activity as total daily steps, as steps per minute, or heart rate based as exertion. Ambient and interaction-free "install-once-and-forget" devices such as Withings Aura or Beddit can monitor sleep as time in bed and time asleep, but may over-promise in other measures they offer [33]. Nutrition can be monitored manually using either lightweight diaries, detailed database approaches, or photo-based tracking, giving insights into general dietary behavior, calorie consumption, or macro- and micro-nutrient intake. Substantial research continues to explore how sensing in wearable devices can passively automate collection of data (e.g., [7]). In spite of these technological advances, we acknowledge that commercial tracking tools often do not meet standards for clinical accuracy, and the resulting data should not be used to support inferences or decisions it cannot [38].

Use of tracking technology has moved from a promising novelty to a long-term phenomenon. For many, tracking happens not just as an exceptional activity for a limited period of a few weeks or a couple of months. Rather, it is a regular part of life, covering years or decades, or even life-long. We are only slowly starting to understand that there are considerable opportunities from such long-term tracking [35, 36]. For example, the availability of long-term tracked personal data can enable identifying and reflecting on long term trends in behavior, early detection of health risks or diseases, monitoring progress against a long term target, giving a lifelong health support, or enabling repeated N-of-1 experiments.

As tracking technology and the practice of long-term tracking become more ubiquitous, opportunities for studying and leveraging long-term tracking in research increase. Studying how tracking tools align with people's lived experiences can lead to recommendations for improving the design of tracking tools, addressing key barriers or challenges. Analyzing the data people collect about themselves can also be used to understand people's practices, such as understanding exercise or nutritional trends [4], following the progression of illnesses, or longitudinal surveillance of health conditions [3].

In this chapter, we first introduce case studies from our personal experiences and prior research which characterize challenges and opportunities for collecting and analyzing long-term tracking data. We then describe conceptual models and theories on people's self-tracking practices. We contrast these models with a model we created to highlight the important feedback loops in long-term tracking and to describe the individuals and entities producing and using data. We then discuss how our model addresses issues identified in the case studies and articulate dimensions that are helpful in teasing apart the ways in which long-term tracking differs from short-term tracking. Finally, we discuss potential future directions for long-term tracking research and considerations when conducting that research.

2 Case Studies in Long-Term Tracking

We present case studies from our prior research and inspired by our personal experiences to characterize challenges in conducting long-term tracking, and therefore in conducting research leveraging long-term tracking. The stories of Jasmin and Joe illustrate difficulties maintaining a long-term record of physical activity. Designing around adherence and the point of lapsing illustrate potential opportunities for designs to make data from long-term tracking more useful for reflection over behavior.

2.1 Jasmin: A Story of Multiple Trackers

Jasmin is a healthy active woman in her forties. Her goal is maintaining a healthy and active lifestyle as her daily job is sedentary and involves sitting for long hours in a confined space. As a result, she invested in an activity tracking watch to monitor her daily activity patterns in 2014. She chose a tracking watch that allowed her to log her sitting time, walking/cycling steps/rides and altitude (for climbing) automatically. Over the course of three months, she collected enough data to build a good picture of her daily/weekly activities via the watch's dashboard. For example, she noticed that some days she was more sedentary than others, and the weather and work deadlines played an important role in her decisions to not cycle or walk to work and not climb. In the following three to six months, Jasmin considered alternatives to increasing activity, e.g., exercising more on weekends and purchased a home trampoline so when the weather was bad, she could exercise at home. Almost one year after buying her first activity tracker, Jasmin felt that she has finally got into a routine that worked for her lifestyle and meant she could maintain her health.

In 2016, while talking to a friend, she learned that it is important to include aerobic exercises in her weekly activities [43]. Her friend recommended buying a watch with heart rate sensor and to start her training in a low heart rate zone and then to include

Fig. 1 Left—Jasmin is following a 5 k running program in 2016. Right—Jasmin is wearing two watches made by two different activity tracking manufacturers

interval training three times a week. Unfortunately, the recommended watch was made by a different manufacturer. For Jasmin, this meant wearing two watches at the same time because she wanted to track with her old tracker while monitoring her heart rate with another (see Fig. 1). The dashboards for both trackers did not talk to each other; she could not close her account down with the old tracker, download her data of 18 months and import it into the new watch's dashboard; she could not find a third-party platform to merge her data either.

Keeping and accessing her old data was important to her for several reasons. Jasmin wanted to track her daily, weekly, monthly and possibly yearly trends and changes to her overall fitness picture, reflect on past activities, and use that data to help her adapt to new situations. Therefore, she had no choice but to wear two watches when she ran. Despite the practical challenges of wearing two watches at the same time, Jasmin found the heart rate training program linked to the watch manufacturer helpful. For example, the watch prompted her if she was running too hard or too slowly or if she had missed a run on a scheduled day. She subsequently participated in a 5 k race in 2016 and completed a 10 k race in 2017 and a half-marathon in 2018. She could not have achieved these without her long-term training program and monitoring her progress on the watch/ dashboard.

Jasmin's old tracker approached the end of its shelf life in 2017, with her battery no longer lasting a full day. The warranty had expired, and the manufacturer was not able to replace the battery or the watch with the same model as tracker had been discontinued. Heartbroken and disappointed with the loss of her first activity companion, she replaced her second tracker with a more advanced model from same manufacturer so she could access her early running training days and benefit from other sensors on the new watch for other activities, e.g., climbing. Jasmin hopes that one day she can download her data from her first tracking device server and combine them with her other data.

For researchers looking to study or design for long-term tracking, Jasmin's story highlights some challenges for long-term tracking: (1) persistent data access over a long period of time on one platform is nearly impossible, (2) frequently changing goals are not necessarily compatible with one device hence multiple devices may be needed, (3) emotional bonds with devices [26] can influence device choice and abandonment, and (4) "old" data can be wished for years later, taking extreme measures to preserve it and seeking out ways to integrate it with new practices or simply to reminisce.

2.2 Joe: 9 Years of Self Tracking

Joe is a healthy man whose interest in self-tracking arose through both an interest in new technologies and curiosity about his personal health. Joe's general goal is to maintain a healthy and active lifestyle, though this is secondary to his curiosity about the technologies. Joe chose a set of consumer-grade, mass-market products to cover a broad range of activities and vital parameters. As his tracking is primarily incidental, without a specific goal, he sought out devices which collected data passively and required as little additional interaction as possible. After trying many options, he ended up using a stable setup of an activity tracker for daily activity, a sports watch for workouts, an interaction-less, ambient sleep monitor, and a networked body scale. Joe also uses a social network to manually "check in" to places he is visiting, including gyms and other sports facilities.

As of this writing, Joe has collected data for a total of 9 years. Joe describes himself as a "power-user," tracking consistently every day when possible. Therefore data about his daily physical activity, workouts, and body composition is mostly complete. The sleep data is susceptible to errors and gaps due to the need for physical re-adjustment of the sensor after a couple of months, which Joe occasionally missed due to the lack of direct feedback about the measurements. On the other hand, the time of stepping on the scale in the morning proved to be a reasonable indicator for wake-up times under routine circumstances.

Joe's tracking behavior influenced the data in several ways. Wearing both the sports watch and the activity tracker during workouts results in duplicate data; this duplication needs to be taken into account when processing and aggregating the data. Joe's very consistent tracking behavior makes deviations from the routine important information. For example, Joe was able to treat not stepping on the scale as a strong indicator of a time that he was not at home. Due to the intentional lack of manual interaction with some devices, technical failures occasionally went unnoticed, resulting in some incomplete or incorrect data (Fig. 2).

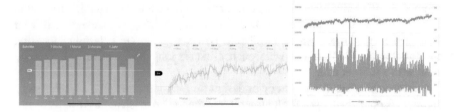

Fig. 2 Trying to make sense of Joe's data: The native apps show the data, steps (left) for one year only, weight (middle) for longer periods. Visualizing both in Excel for the whole period is possible (right), but difficult to comprehend

Joe's experience of tracking points to challenges around maintaining a persistent data record and reflecting on that record amidst so much data from disparate sources. Even as a self-described "power user", Joe's data has gaps, such as not realizing that passively recording devices have stopped syncing [19]. His duplicate data sources may help mitigate this, but require effort to aggregate and analyze. On the other hand, gaps may also tell a story, such as likely absence from home when not stepping on the scale in the morning. Data may well have a secondary, not originally intended use, such as the time of stepping on a scale as a proxy for wake-up time.

For a researcher, Joe's case shows four relevant insights: (1) The choice of devices is very personal, and two different people will probably choose two different set-ups. Even if they chose to use the same devices, their routines for when and how they use them would likely differ. Researchers therefore have to deal with heterogeneous data from disparate sources. (2) Gaps in the data are inevitable; they should not just be considered a normal part of the data, but they may also tell a story on their own. (3) Data will be imprecise or unreliable, but sometimes data may also have some unforeseen value. (4) In spite of all the challenges, the data may provide insights into a person's life that are worth being uncovered and made use of.

2.3   Interpreting Longitudinal Tracker Data in the Real World: Missing Data, Multiple Interpretations, Human-Machine Collaborative Interpretation

This case study is based on IStuckWithIt [55, 56], an interface onto long-term data from a wearable activity tracker. There are three key principles that underpin its design. We now describe these, both as they apply for this interface and in terms of aspects that are relevant to managing longitudinal data of many types in the real world.

First, long-term data from a wearable activity tracker is typically incomplete because people do not wear the tracker all day, every day. This is important for interpreting the data. For example, if a person wore their tracker for 16 h in a day, that is likely to give a quite accurate measure of their total step count. But if they only wore the device for 2 h, the step count recorded may be a gross under-estimate of their true activity level. We introduced the term *adherence* [57] to describe this. Intuitively, 100% adherence means that the person used the device, wearing it, with the device operational and with sufficient power, so that it can track all their steps in the day. We explored several ways to define adherence. Essentially, these are based on the broad idea of defining a *valid day*, one with high enough adherence for the step count to be meaningful. To explore the impact of some of the measures in the published literature, we analyzed 12 datasets from diverse classes of people, including those who chose to volunteer their tracker data for analysis, people who had the trackers as part of medical interventions, and participants in a public health study of university students. These datasets had a total of 753 users and over 77,000 days with any data, as well as 73,000 interspersed days with no data. The choice of adherence definition had different effects on step counts for different datasets. The dataset with the largest difference had a low of 6952 and a high of 9423. This is a clinically significant difference. The core message is that the interpretation of data from long-term sensing based on wearable devices requires careful consideration of adherence.

A second challenge is that the data are not homogeneous over long periods of time, as Jasmin's case study points out. Our evaluations of IStuckWithIt were restricted to data from Fitbit activity trackers. These have been available since 2009, with some early adopters having over 10 years of data, covering several models of the tracker.

One other challenge that we tackled in the IStuckWithIt project was the need to support people in making rich and flexible interpretations of their own data. Once the analysis of long-term data has taken account of the challenges above, it is important to create mechanisms for human-in-the-loop interpretation. To do this IStuckWithIt can be seen as an example of an interface that offers some flexibility in the choices of interpretation available as well as scaffolding to help a person "see" the aspects that are important and that can draw on that individual's own knowledge.

Figure 3 shows an example IStuckWithIt screenshot for a hypothetical user we will call Alice. The label (A) indicates that Alice has selected the steps view of her data that comes from a Fitbit. Other views of the same underlying data can show her activity in terms of the number of moderately active minutes she had each day, very active minutes per day and distance.

The area marked (B) shows her activity in the first part of 2014. The cells are bright blue on days she met her target of 10,000 steps. The light blue cells are for days she was below the target but was above 5000 steps and white indicates days with at least 1 step recorded but less than 5000. In the months of February and March, she has quite a lot of blue cells.

A notable feature of the IStuckWithIt interface is the careful handling of days with no data. Days where there is no data are gray, as can be seen at (C). To help Alice interpret her data, the visualization also communicates adherence. (D) marks the display of the average hours she wore the tracker per day. So, for example, in February, she consistently averaged more than 10 h a day of wear. However, in March she had weeks where she averaged less than 6 h a day of wear. This means that the

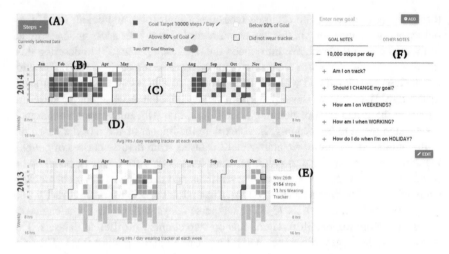

Fig. 3 Example screenshot of IStuckWithIt for a user, Alice

counts visible here are likely to be under-estimates of her actual level of activity. A user can see the precise information for any cell by mousing over it, as shown at (E).

We conducted a study of IStuckWithIt to gain insights about the ways that long-term Fitbit trackers had been using their data and whether they could gain new insights from IStuckWithIt as described above [55]. This study recruited 21 people (7 women), who had an average of 23 months of Fitbit data. Many of these participants were committed to tracking to maintain their level of activity and were in the maintenance phase of the Transtheoretical Model of Behavior Change [45]. This was expected, given we recruited people who had long-term data on the promise of new ways to see it. In terms of broader research on long-term data, these participants have much to offer in terms of their motivations for collecting it, their experiences in doing so, their uses of it, and their insights about the data and how it enabled them to harness it to serve their needs.

The interview asked people about how often they looked at their step count. If needed, this was followed by more detailed probing in terms of the timescales shown in Fig. 4. Despite having long-term data, few of these participants made use of the longer-term data. They indicated that this was too hard to do.

All participants made discoveries about themselves, in terms of their wearing behavior, such as reflecting on what caused them to not have data at certain times, or understanding how many hours a day they tended to wear it. For example, one participant noted from the visual representation: *"That's when I lost it, at end of July, that's why also there is a gap would make sense in that case. I think the gap really affected me, I got out of habit."*. The insights from these dedicated, long-term activity trackers highlight that awareness of their adherence behavior needs to be considered in designing research around such long-term data.

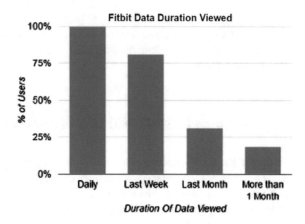

Fig. 4 How frequently participants viewed their data

Most participants made discoveries from their long-term data, such as the influence of their environment on their activity levels (e.g., living in a city vs. a more rural area) or changes in their activity levels because of tracking. Some participants recognized their vacations as the reason for a period with high steps counts. Some consulted their calendars to figure out why step count deviations were notable—this represents a flexible, on-the-fly integration of another long-term data source by the user. Since we did not ask people to provide that data, the control of these separate data stores remained in the hands of the users. In planning studies, researchers should consider what other data sources could triangulate their primary data sources, facilitating answering their research questions, and whether those data can be collected while also balancing participating burden and privacy.

After each participant had explored the main IStuckWithIt interface, the interviewer revealed the scaffolding labeled (F) in Fig. 3. This scaffolding helped them gain new insights [56]. For example, before use of IStuckWithIt, most participants had clearly not considered whether their activity levels changed between weekdays and weekends (even though they stated that they looked at their data each day and we had asked them about this in the earlier interview, potentially priming them to be aware of this). Public health researchers have established that most people are less active on weekends, and consider it important to account for this when measuring activity levels. Even with prompting, 7 participants said they had no idea and could not make an estimate. Of the 6 who thought they were more active on weekdays, three were much more active (by 18%, 49% and 70%), 1 much less so (−90%) and two were about the same (both 2% more). A similarly diverse picture appeared for the 6 people who thought they were less active on weekdays. Once the scaffolding in IStuckWithIt was revealed, 10 participants made new insights about themselves (8 about weekday vs. weekend wear), 2 about workdays versus others, 4 about the impact of holidays and 5 about rethinking the goals). Some of the other participants already had clear goals and intense use of the tracker and did not need this scaffold; they suggested the interface should personalize the scaffolds. For researchers using long-term tracking data to elicit memories and experiences in studies, this highlights that people typically need scaffolding to build self-awareness of key aspects of their data. Our work involved people who were rather dedicated trackers and some had very clear goals; for data from broader user populations, one would expect this is an even stronger factor.

2.4   Designing to Surface Trends at the Point of Lapsing

Lapsing in the act of tracking is a well-known and studied phenomenon, as surfaced in Joe's personal experiences and a history of HCI work [9, 16, 19, 30, 52]. Together with colleagues and published previously [18], we have explored how tracking technology can treat the point of lapsing as an opportunity for self-reflection. As a case study, we explored designs for tracking physical activity, specifically collected by the Fitbit device.

Our technique presented people who had lapsed with visual representations of their data combined with captions. We used *visual cuts*, an approach we had developed previously [17], to surface trends which answer questions people often have about their data, but tools typically do not answer. Cuts typically focus on longer-term trends rather than daily or weekly logs, aligning with people's desire to reflect over their behavior rather than review recent behavior. For example, cuts highlighted when throughout the day people tended to have their activity, or a timeline of people's average activity grouped by month and year that they tracked. Figure 5 shows two cuts we designed.

We paired each visual cut with a *framing technique* derived from taxonomies and strategies for designing persuasive technology and facilitating behavior change [22, 37]. For example, framing techniques drew attention to circumstances where a person was particularly active or an opportunity for improvement, prompting them to consider what prevents them from walking more or comparing their performance to others.

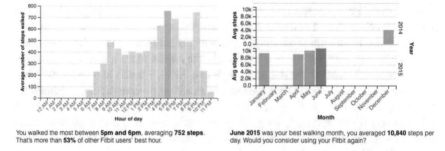

You walked the most between **5pm and 6pm**, averaging **752 steps**. That's more than **53%** of other Fitbit users' best hour.

June 2015 was your best walking month, you averaged **10,840** steps per day. Would you consider using your Fitbit again?

Fig. 5 Two visual cuts and framing captions we created to help people reflect on their data after a lapse in tracking [18]

In an experimental survey, we asked 141 people to rate a series of cuts paired with framing techniques according to how informative and appropriate they found them and describe what they thought of the visualization in a short sentence. We found that cut preference varied by use pattern. Participants who had tracked for a short amount of time (3 months or less) prior to lapsing tended to prefer cuts which aggregated their data by hour or day (e.g., Fig. 5 Left), whereas participants who had tracked for longer preferred aggregations which highlighted their long use (e.g., Fig. 5 Right). Participants with more long-term use described that they had already learned their daily and weekly activity trends from having worn their Fitbit and reflected on their data for a long time. Participant's preference toward framing techniques tended to align with their perspective on whether or not they wanted to return to tracking in the near future. Participants who felt they had learned enough from tracking for the time being preferred framing techniques which surfaced the times they were most active, while those looking to return appreciated framing techniques which nudged them in that direction.

We imagine that in the future, designs can tailor such a presentation to match people's experiences and perspectives. Our study showed that we can leverage properties about people's data to infer what they might find interesting, but designs might benefit from explicitly asking people for their perspective on their tracking experience. For example, the left image in Fig. 6 emphasizes high activity days drawn from a long-term tracking history, while the right highlights the day of the week a tracker averaged the most steps, an approach that can be effective with even a relatively short tracking history.

We anticipate it is relatively easy to detect whether a person has lapsed in tracking. Standalone devices or apps on devices could stop syncing with the cloud servers or local backends where data is stored, or a recent sync will return no data. It is also plausible to detect whether a person has recently reviewed their tracked data by opening the app which collects the data [23] or glancing at the device [24]. Once a

Fig. 6 Designs can surface different information for lapsed trackers who do and do not want to return to tracking

lapse of a reasonable duration is detected, mobile notifications or emails could be used to prompt people to reflect over their data. More difficult, however, is inferring *why* someone has lapsed and sending appropriate messages. For many lapses, frequent prompts or notifications could be overwhelming or annoying. Further study could yield insight into the opportune time to send such a message and further understand how to present it.

This line of research surfaces opportunities for further research on *promoting* long-term self-tracking by identifying and designing interventions for when a person is beginning to stop tracking. We reiterate that lapses in tracking should be expected. There is value in research examining both how designs can encourage people to re-engage in tracking and how designs can provide utility after a person has decided to abandon tracking. It also should be a consideration for studies that seek to use tracking for longitudinal research or public health surveillance. Sustaining engagement in such studies is challenging [29, 44]. While individuals may initially be motivated to participate in these studies to gain personal insights from tracking, they may lose interest or gain the insights they sought, and subsequently chose to lapse even though researchers' goals have not yet been achieved.

3 Theoretical Perspectives on Use of Self-tracking Technology

Aspects of people's experiences collecting long-term data, like Jasmin and Joe, have been characterized in theoretical frameworks. Because these frameworks describe how and why people use tracking technology, building on them is important to studying and supporting long-term tracking. Here, we review key models informing HCI research into tracking.

3.1 Conceptual Models of Personal Tracking Use

Early understanding of how people use tracking technology focused on how collecting data could support linear progress toward a singular goal or decision, such as becoming more physically active or more productive. Inspired by Prochaska & Velicer's Transtheoretical Model of Behavior Change [45] which is very widely used, Li et al. develop a stage-based model describing people's use of tracking technology [32] as an ideally linear progression where people first prepare and collect data, then integrate and reflect on it, and ultimately act on their findings and improve their habits. People often iterate to track new dimensions, and encounter barriers which impact their progress.

Many early adopters of personal tracking systems were professionals in technology-related fields, such as software development, information technology, and data analytics [6, 32]. Participants in the study that informed Li et al.'s model had similar professions. Many were hobbyists in the Quantified Self movement, a group primarily made up of scientists and engineers who sought to build self-knowledge through the collection of numbers about their behaviors [62].

As mobile phones and wearable devices enabled technology with tracking capabilities to further pervade society, who is tracking data and how people collect and engage with data has changed. Though experts and data analysts continue to self-track, today people track for more diverse reasons.

Rooksby et al. characterize people's use of personal tracking tools as "lived informatics", emphasizing that people often do not track with a goal of action, often use multiple tools simultaneously, and are sometimes more socially motivated to track than personally motivated [47]. Epstein et al. draw from this notion to develop the Lived Informatics Model, which characterizes how people use personal tracking tools in their everyday lives [19]. The Lived Informatics Model suggests a more cyclic tracking process where people's varied goals inform the tools they select, collecting and reflecting on data happens simultaneously, and lapses and resuming tracking are frequent occurrences.

The Lived Informatics Model points out that tracking tools often fail to account for the realities of everyday life. People often want or need to migrate between devices or apps as life progresses and as their goals and needs change. In addition to maintaining a continuous record of data to allow people to reflect on long-term trends in their data when possible, tracking tools should account for curiosity-driven goals evolving to self-improvement goals, or from self-improvement to self-maintenance. Tracking over years, compared to weeks or months, particularly highlights a need for designs to account for and address these challenges.

3.2 Modeling Relationships Among Stakeholders and Data in Long-Term Self-Tracking

Long-term tracking introduces complex inter-dependencies between stakeholders, data, users, and applications. We identify five entities: the **primary user** who is collecting data and who has a long-term goal, the **tracking devices and sources** used by the primary user to collect data, the underlying **data** itself coming out of the devices and sources, the **applications** which process and present the data to the user, and finally a **secondary user** who may have reason to access the primary user's data.

Going through the long-term self-tracking loop, we can identify two extreme viewpoints: *purposeful tracking*, going clockwise in the direction of the requirements, and *incidental tracking*, going counter-clockwise following the logical data flow. The purpose of tracking tends to define the tracking behavior the user requires.

Purposeful tracking is the point of view taken in the design of most of today's tracking-based apps. Tracking is often driven by a need for a certain support or service, such as initiating weight loss with a persuasive app or when a person with

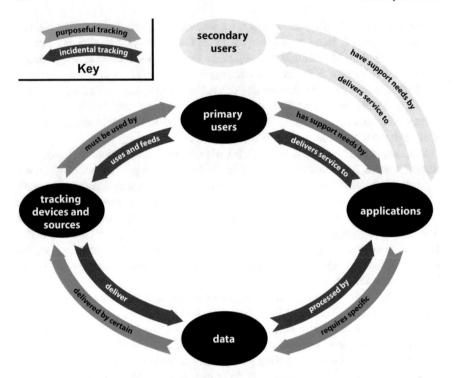

Fig. 7 Long-term self-tracking feedback loops. The outer loop shows purposeful tracking driven needs of the users. The inner loop shows flows in the opposite direction as happens when the user's tracking is an incidental side-effect of their technology use and behaviors

diabetes needs to monitor their blood insulin level. Applications that such purposeful users need demand that the user does a certain amount of work to ensure that there is enough quality data collected for the app to be effective. Therefore the (typically primary) user must use certain tracking devices or dedicated apps to collect that data (e.g., an activity tracker, a scale, a nutrition diary for weight loss case; a glucometer for diabetes).

In contrast, in incidental tracking shown in the inner loop of Fig. 7 and then separately at the right in Fig. 7, the user does not have a specific need. Perhaps they have developed a routine of use [30], tracking for potential later use, or passively collecting data, as happens with mobile phones tracking steps. This incidental tracking determines the type, amount, and quality of data that can be made available for an application, perhaps years after the data was first collected. Such data may have gaps, be imprecise or unreliable.

In practice, researchers should think in terms of both directions of flow. Only then can they really harness long-term data to answer research questions while supporting participants throughout studies and their daily life.

The roles of users Secondary users play an important role, shown at the top of the figure. These people need to make use of the data of the person who needs to ensure their data is collected. They may have many roles and differing relationships with the user collecting the data. For example, they may include advisors, experts, family members, caregivers, clinicians, trainers, or teachers. The particular role of the secondary users may help the user to collect data. More often they will help the user make sense of data. Those in a caregiver role may have more subtle uses such being able to gain peace of mind as they can have assurance that the user is doing well and knowing when to check in with the user [10, 41]. Such roles will typically mean that the relevant data is recent and short-term and the tracking is therefore purposeful. However, this may change if the secondary user discovers a way to make use of long-term data. For example, a caregiver might notice that an elder seems less well and then discover that long-term data can show a steady decline in activity.

In long-term tracking, the user has two roles. On the one hand, by self-tracking the user is the producer of data. The user's tracking behavior determines the availability, amount, and quality of data. Here, a user is likely to want to minimize the burden of tracking, particularly over the long-term, since sustained effort is particularly challenging. This wish for low effort may of course result in less and lower-quality data.

On the other hand, the user is also the consumer of the services delivered by the application such as visualized trends or recommendations for new activities to undertake. Here, the user's priority is to gain the benefits that may only be possible if there is more and higher-quality data.

Balancing the effort of tracking and the quality of data is therefore a key challenge of long-term tracking. There are two general approaches here: improving the data without increasing the effort needed for tracking is one way, e.g., by exploiting secondary sources such as social networks or digital calendars, or by developing better tracking devices that provide more and better data with the same amount of tracking effort. The other way is to motivate the effort needed for tracking, e.g., by providing short-term rewards or long-term benefits. For example, design of applications for long-term monitoring could provide a compelling case in terms of the promise to answer the user's future questions.

3.3 Reflecting on Case Studies

Our refined model of the relationship between different stakeholders and data in long-term tracking processes characterizes some of the dynamics surfaced in our case studies which other models were unable to capture. Jasmin and Joe's experiences demonstrate the relationships between tracking sources, the data they produce, the applications which leverage that data, and the various stakeholders which are involved in long-term tracking processes. IStuckWithIt and designing for lapsing provide example applications for supporting long-term tracking.

Jasmin had primarily purposeful motivations for tracking, trying to maintain a healthy lifestyle. Joe's goals were more incidental, driven to track by curiosity about his health and interest in trying new technologies. Although Jasmin and Joe engaged with secondary stakeholders only minimally, others intersected with their long-term tracking journeys at key points. Joe would occasionally share his activities with others to show his efforts toward maintaining a healthy lifestyle. Jasmin never used an application to share her data with a secondary user, but learned from others what tracking devices supported their needs and adopted them into her own practice.

IStuckWithIt and designing for lapsing are examples of applications which effectively mediate between primary users and their data. For incidental trackers, both applications deliver a service. In the case of IStuckWithIt, helping people make sense of their longitudinal adherence and activity levels. Designing for lapsing points out the opportunity to intervene at a point where users are disengaging. These applications also support the needs of purposeful trackers by helping people understand trends in their data and get value from it. While purposeful trackers might use applications like these to answer specific questions they have about their data (like Joe's use of Excel for his own analysis), they also automatically process the data delivered by tracking devices in ways which incidental trackers might find useful or interesting.

4   Characterizing Long-Term Tracking

To magnify how long-term tracking practices can be used in research, we use our case studies and prior work to explain how people's experiences differ from short-term tracking. Short- and long-term tracking differ in terms of the aspects listed at the left of Fig. 8: the targeted goal, typical duration, method of tracking, and approach to reflection.

As models of personal tracking use have pointed out, tracking can be a cyclic process where people lapse and resume the act of tracking [19]. We see the dichotomy between short-term and long-term tracking similarly. Many people lapse in the goals or methods of tracking we associate with short-term tracking into practices we associate with long-term tracking. Life changes, newfound curiosities, or symptom flare-ups can re-trigger periods of short-term tracking. For example, a person who recently had a child may reflect on their years of passively tracked physical activity data, set a new proximal goal appropriate for their new time demands, and regularly review their activity for a few months. They may then fall into a practice where that data tracking becomes incidental again.

4.1   Targeted Goal

Short-term tracking generally focuses on people's targeted goals, often rooted in their current experiences. Some examples of short-term goals could include, "work

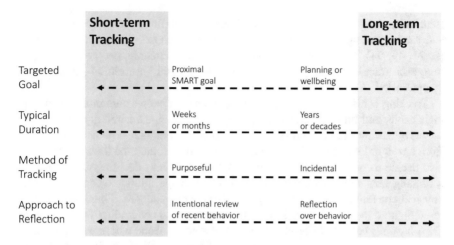

Fig. 8 People's targeted goals, tracking duration, method of tracking, and approach to reflection differ between long-term tracking and short-term tracking

out two times a week," "eat less carbs a day," "or walk three miles every day." For individuals already working out two times a week, for example, increasing the frequency to three times a week could be an manageable short-term goal. Research indicates that people are more likely to succeed if they formulate goals that fit the SMART criteria: Specific and Measurable, Achievable, Relevant, and Time-bound [15]. Alternatively, people's short-term goals may be driven more by curiosity or a desire to build general awareness, such as "understand about how much I walk in a day" [47, 51].

Research and commercial systems have examined a number of packages to support short-term tracking, such as setting a goal based on health standards (e.g., daily step guidelines such as 10,000 [60]) or past activity and recommendations or feedback based on the needs of cohorts [12, 20]. However, tools often provide insufficient guidance about how to identify the right data to collect toward their short-term goal [6] and insufficient support to help people interpret the data they collect [32].

Long-term tracking goals are typically more diverse, exploring broad planning or wellbeing goals versus specific and actionable ones. They sometimes align with more abstract concepts, such as hedonic and eudaimonic wellbeing needs of promoting pleasurable and enjoyable experiences and negative ones [42]. Some people may simply want to collect a long-term record of their activities (e.g., lifelogging) [19]. Other long-term health tracking goals often relate to identifying, enacting, and assessing changes in everyday life that are required to support health outcomes or other goals. These might be broken down into shorter-term goals. For example, losing 10kg in body mass may not be achievable in weeks or even months, and can be broken down into shorter-term tracked goals such as losing a few kilograms at a time. People working to manage chronic conditions may also need to work through an ongoing process of gaining a diagnosis, developing hypotheses about what contributes to symptoms, testing those hypotheses, developing action plans, monitoring, and then repeating and adjusting as circumstances change or symptoms reappear [8, 21, 49, 54]. As contributors to symptoms are understood, people may also use long-term tracking to support predicting—and possibly preventing—more severe symptoms[51, 61].

Tracking goals often change over the long-term as people gain more insight into their habits and limits. For example, people may change desired quantitative outcomes by setting a more aggressive or more realistic weight loss goal, or may switch from a weight loss goal to a maintenance goal. After some time tracking, they may also decide to pursue a different goal altogether, such as deciding to switch from a running goal to a swimming goal to better manage injuries or deal with other physical constraints. For example, some participants using the OmniTrack system re-configured the data they collected after some time to better align with their goals [28]. Jasmin's case study serves as an example of someone whose use of an activity tracker first satisfied a short-term goal of understanding her daily and weekly patterns, extending that to a longer-term goal of maintaining a healthy and active lifestyle.

4.2   Typical Duration

Short-term tracking makes sense for goals that can be achieved in a short time spans (hours, days or weeks). This tracking may have a definitive end, such as when a specific objective has been attained (e.g., a marathon being trained for, a weight loss objective achieved) or when a curiosity has been satisfied [16]. After that point, people may see no benefit on continuing to track [9, 30]. It has frequently been confirmed that many people drop out of self-tracking after short-term goals have been achieved, often within 3 to 6 months (e.g., [52, 53]).

By contrast, the increasing convenience and availability of tracking devices make it ever easier for people to track for years. Long-term tracking may involve multiple short-term goals. It may include multiple phases of changing tracking behavior, including periods of intensive self-tracking followed by months or years where no further data is collected. IStuckWithIt demonstrates how metrics like adherence can effectively represent these phases in designs.

4.3   Method of Tracking

During short-term tracking, data is typically collected purposefully. Depending on the domain and people's preferences, data may be collected manually (e.g., by journaling) or automatically (e.g., by passive sensing). People often find it burdensome to track daily or multiple times per day, though this is often required for domains like diet or weight monitoring. Some self-tracking approaches therefore place explicit time bounds on data collection, such as three-day food diaries [58] and fixed-duration self-experiments [13, 25].

People's long-term tracking methods are often incidental, very low effort or a side effect of using a device like a smartwatch. Joe, for example, intentionally chose tracking tools which would require minimal engagement on his part to best align with his incidental tracking goal. To lower the collection burden, long-term data streams often make use of passively collected data from phones and wearable devices such as location, steps, or heart rate. But people regularly switch what data they are collecting, switch tracking tools, and abandon and resume the same tool [19]. Long-term tracking typically therefore needs to be able to operate with a mix of use of whatever available data streams provide a view into their habits or goals, rather than assuming a single consistent and reliable data source. Jasmin's case study particularly reflects challenges in keeping a single reliable data source.

As a person's goal and purposes and contexts change over time, tracking behavior may change from purposeful to incidental. For example, a person who initially began tracking for weight loss may achieve their goal, but still continue to observe their weight because they developed a habit of logging it. However, they may later pursue another short-term tracking goal with purposeful intent.

4.4 Approach to Reflection

Reflection on short-term data is often an intentional exercise, such as opening an app with the goal of making note of daily physical activity logged by a phone or watch [23] or sitting down with a clinician to review a recent log of diet data [50]. People's review typically focuses on their recent behavior to understand their habits or experiences over the past hours or days.

Reflection over long-term data tends to occur in two ways, aligning with Schön's principles of reflection-in-action and reflection-on-action [48]. The act of collecting data leads some people to learn about their behavior and make changes to their practices (e.g., reflection-in-action) [19]. Jasmin in particular reflects this practice, learning about her practices and improving her ability to manage them over her first months of tracking.

But long-term data also presents opportunities for people to intentionally reflect over their behaviors to understand how they have changed or how their practices have evolved (e.g., reflection-on-action). Joe's efforts to make sense of his data serve as an example of this practice. The approach of presenting visual cuts to people who have lapsed in tracking points out how this specific moment can be leveraged to support reflection-on-action.

Schön also highlighted the importance of reflection-on-reflection, where the user re-assesses how well they have been using reflection. For example, a person who sees takes time each week to reflect on the physical activity progress may realize that this is not enough to recognize long-term drops in activity from one year to the next.

5 Discussion

We highlight a few recommendations when conducting research involving long-term data or developing a new design which collects or represents long-term data.

5.1 Consider Return of Data—and Actionable Insights—To Participants

We notice that researchers sometimes ask how to increase adherence in studies that require purposeful tracking, e.g., through remembering to use a device or answering experience sampling questions, often without returning data to participants [29]. Such studies might be intended to develop or validate new sensing devices or public health surveillance capabilities, or to better understand various aspects of everyday life, and so the return of data may seem like extra work that is not central to the study's goals. If the returned data influences the behaviors being studied (i.e., if it is an intervention), that return of data might be counter to study goals. But in other cases, returning data or insights to participants could be effective for increasing adherence.

However, when study designs collect, but do not return, tracking data, they must align with participant motivations in some other way, such as through participant motivation to support science or through financial or other incentives. Even when these other motivations are present, participants often join long-term tracking studies expecting the study to offer them some insights about themselves or their context, or at least access to and return of their data [29]. We encourage researchers leveraging tracking technology in their studies to consider whether they can support some return of tracking data, and resulting insights, to participants, both as an approach to participant motivation and as a way of making research less exploitative. Doing so also introduces opportunity for further research contributions leveraging long-term data, such as understanding what data and insights participants do and do not find useful for self-understanding or challenge their perceptions of themselves.

5.2 Anticipate and Respect Holes in the Data

Even when returning data or resulting insights effectively motivate participants to engage in long-term tracking and in studies that require it, the, data will have gaps. Holes can be short breaks in use, such as a few hours or days of missing data (e.g., "micro" holes). Or there can be periods where a user decides not to track for weeks, months, or years (e.g., "macro" holes). Most people do not keep complete records and track consistently. The emergent holes can be intentional, such as choosing not to track weight or physical activity over a busy holiday season, or choosing to focus on other priorities at a time when one's tracking goals are not the top concern. They can also be accidental, such as forgetting or losing the device being used to collect data [19].

Having complete and consistent logs may not be necessary or even desirable. A person can often understand their habits after a couple of days, weeks, or months of use. It is perhaps best for tracking tools to fade in and out of people's lives, supporting them in understanding how changes in their lives have impacted their habits and routines. That said, long-term data is essential for continued health in some chronic conditions. For example, a person with type-II diabetes must continually monitor and react to their blood glucose level. Technological advances aim to automate much of this monitoring (e.g., closed-loop insulin delivery systems), but the need to continually monitor still remains for many.

Expecting consistent and reliable long-term data does users a disservice. For "micro" holes, averages summarizing a period of activity can be skewed by including zero-counts or missing data alongside regular activity. For "macro" holes, a risk is that an application assumes that the user has stopped using the tracking device and begins prompting them to re-engage. When in reality, they may consciously decide to pick it up months or years later. Attempting to fill in missing data, in the short or long term, also risks errant conclusions, as events that affect one's goals could also affect one's tracking behavior, confounding results.

By emphasizing adherence in wearing behavior or chastising abandonment, applications and devices imply a "correct" and a "wrong" way of tracking. But the longer someone tracks, the more gaps there are likely to be, whether intentional or not. In general, adherence operates at multiple levels. For estimates of daily step counts and physical activity derived from wearables, it is important to take into account the amount of time the user wore tracker when measuring amount of activity. Similarly, to estimate weekly averages, the adherence matters for both how many days the user wore the tracker and how much of the day they wore it. Studies of large collections of tracker data show that adherence is important for interpreting data [57], but should not be used to tell users how to use their tracker. It is therefore important for an interface to respect and communicate the limitations of the data that a person collects. Likewise, some users may wish for interfaces that keep them engaged in tracking, but designers need to respect when users do not want to be engaged. This often comes into tension with the metrics that commercial products are often judged on, such as retention rate and the daily or weekly time spent in the app. However, we believe that holes in the data should be treated as a normal part of data rather than an exception to be avoided.

Researchers leveraging long-term tracking can use techniques like notifications [2], high financial incentives, or personal follow up when lapses are observed to promote adherence. These are valuable tools when they do not affect the behaviors the researchers are studying. However, they also can introduce confounds: they can interfere with studies to evaluate new tracking technologies. Even when the tracking technology is not the focus, they can affect the behavior or other factors being tracked through the demand effect or just increasing the salience of that behavior or type of data.

Researcher looking to leverage long-term tracking data in their research should not expect study participants to fully adhere to tracker use over a long period, even when strong incentives are offered. Analysis plans should be robust to these gaps, and researchers might consider also falling back to secondary data sources. For example, if collecting step counts, can a researcher supplement with data from a phone when someone does not wear another tracker? Gaps in use might also be relevant to researchers' questions, and so investigating lapses during interviews or by triangulating lapses with other data could offer more insight than tracking alone.

5.3   Leverage Implicit Tracking with Secondary Sources

There are numerous ways to track data. Using a dedicated tracking device such as an activity tracker or a sports watch is one of them; logging data by manually entering information in a diary is another one. In both cases, logging is based on the user's active decision for logging, and on the user being actively involved in the logging process, requiring some additional effort for logging, even if unobtrusiveness and ease of use reduce the effort to a minimum.

However, people also track data as a by-product to our daily digital lives: when posting information to our social networks, when communicating by email or instant message, when using digital calendars, when taking digital photos that store time and location, and when interacting with smart and networked buildings at home and at work. Sometimes people may not be aware the technology they use tracks them (e.g., Google Maps tracking their location, and Apple Health recording their steps). This data provides deep insights into our behaviors and daily lives, and it can be available over very long times without either initiative or ongoing effort from individuals. However, they can also violate people's privacy, or put the person (or others tracked) at risk. Challenges emerge in keeping this data accessible and persistent as people change devices, as there are no requirements for interoperability among different tracking platforms.

As one way to making it easier for people to participate in research that leverages tracking, we encourage researchers to ask "can we answer our research questions using data people are already collecting?" Additionally, similar to how we encourage researchers to consider what data and insights can be returned to participants, we also encourage researchers to ask "how can we help people make sense of the data that is tracked about them and available anyway?" When people may not be aware that this tracking is already occurring, can the research also promote their awareness and help them leverage the data better?

Some research work has already exemplified how such secondary sources may be unlocked. For example, De Choudhury et al. used social media posts in combination with logged food data to understand social support around weight loss [14]. Murnane et al. analyzed use of apps on mobile phones to understand biological rhythms [40], while Mehrota et al. leveraged use and duration of different phone features infer emotional state [34].

Such secondary data may be less precise or accurate than data that is purposefully tracked. This imprecision makes such data difficult to use in studies where small changes in short periods of time are important. However, the fact that no additional effort is required for tracking implies that such data can be made available over a very long time. In spite of the fluctuations, broad trends may well be identified with high reliability. Finally, because the data were generated as a routine part of other behaviors, the tracking may be less likely to influence those behaviors—important for studies intended to observe and understand, but not to intervene. Unlocking secondary sources to facilitate implicit tracking is therefore a strong opportunity for studying or supporting long-term tracking.

5.4   Treat Data as Subjective

Collected sensor data may seem perfectly objective: 5000 steps are 5000 steps, and 6 h of sleep are 6 h of sleep, no matter what. However, there is more to data than just the numbers: data has a meaning and a context, and this severely impacts the objectivity. Somewhat trivially, the devices and measurement methodologies influence the data. Using a dedicated activity tracker that can be worn at all times results in different data than using a smartphone that resides on the table a good part of the day.

However, the fact that a person decided to switch devices may be as or more important than the data itself. Many people change or abandon tools in response to changes in life circumstances, or because they achieved their behavior change goals [16]. In this sense, even the lack of data can help surface important information about technical issues faced, changes in health status, or what life events which triggered the outcome.

The meaning of data also changes over the long term. Walking 1,000 steps on a day can be little for most healthy people, but maybe a huge achievement for someone entering rehab after a severe health incident. Sleeping 4 h in a row during the night is not much for many people, but a lot for young parents. Such fluctuations are inevitable when aiming to make sense of trends in long-term data. Without contextual information it is therefore hard, if not impossible, to actually make sense of the data. Context is important for making use of long-term data in research.

Finally, even the purpose of the data may change over time. A person may originally collect activity data to monitor their personal fitness, but may later use that data to identify periods of depression. Heart rate data collected during sports may initially be used to optimize a workout, but may later provide valuable insights into changing cardiac health. Researchers and designers therefore need to consider how the same data can be used to answer the different questions people have in the long term.

We currently have few tools to make sense of long-term data. It is necessary to understand the story behind the data, which requires much more contextual knowledge than available today. Manual annotations or diaries may be a short-term approach, such as of moments of reduced air quality [39]. But even these measures have a higher cost than most people are able to maintain in the long term. Implicit tracking and secondary sources, whether intended for tracking or not, can help provide these annotations. Calendars, messages, social media posts, photos may provide the contextual knowledge that is necessary to really make sense of the collected data.

5.5   Ethical, Legal, and Social Implications of Long-Term Tracking

As a technology that goes straight into the highly personal life, long-term monitoring raises numerous ethical, legal and social implications. The specifics of these implications vary according to study goals, domain, involved populations, and locale. However, we offer some observations based on our experiences with long-term tracking.

Privacy of data is probably the most salient issue. Collected data are a valuable—often in ways that we may not even fully understand at the time we collect and first analyze them—many stakeholders may be interested in accessing the data or resulting analyses. Depending on the orientation and affiliation of the researcher, people may feel coerced into participating. People who desire tracking tools or the insight they provide, but are financially burdened by the cost of such devices or insights may feel coerced into providing their data, while people with means are free to ignore those incentives. Employers may give their employees a tracking device for free as part of research initiatives, but might want to observe their practices. Life insurance companies may similarly introduce research efforts which reduce customer premiums if their activity trackers record them achieving behavioral goals. This essentially disadvantages those without trackers or who choose not to use them and creates first and second class customers. This can further exacerbate inequities between people who are interested and able to do activities which the tracker does record (e.g., walk around) versus those who cannot or do not want to (e.g., if they live somewhere without sidewalks or good walking paths).

The ability to access one's own data is a topic that is becoming more pressing. Companies happily claim that "your data belongs to you", but at the same time build barriers to access and process the data outside the company's closed ecosystem. For example, many wearable devices only enable fine-grained data export for the past 30 days, making it challenging to provide long-term data exports. Other companies may not offer an API or an easy to process export at all. Policies such as the European GDPR provide a theoretical right to access one's own data. However, processes may be complicated and take a lot of time, and non-technical users may be overwhelmed and unable to understand and process their own data collection.

Data ownership also goes further. Parents may collect their children's data, but at some point need to hand over not just the responsibility, but also the data itself. However, the parents may want to retain some ownership over those data, as they also represent their memories and experiences as well as their children's. And what happens with my digital heritage, my data, after I die? Some of these questions have been discussed in related areas such as data stewardship (e.g., [5]). Self-tracked data introduces new kinds of records to consider preserving, sharing, or archiving, many of which were assumed to remain private.

When conducting research on and with long-term tracking data, we therefore need to be careful in our policies and practices around privacy, ownership, and stewardship. Using commercial self-tracking apps for research purposes can lower the design and deployment burden, but often means participants must consent to share their tracked data with the device manufacturer as well as the researcher. It can be highly ambiguous what about an individual that data might reveal when thoroughly analyzed, such as their habits or demographics. At minimum, it is important to enable research participants to delete or filter any of their data from study inclusion, whether prior to consenting researchers access or long after. Moving forward, it is worth considering how we as researchers can effectively communicate the risks (and benefits) which come from disclosing long-term self-tracked data.

Research studies requiring participants to collect long-term data should further consider what negative feelings or practices that data could evoke. Literature has pointed out how the act of self-tracking can lead to unhealthy changes in behavior, such as eating prepackaged foods because they are easier to journal [11] or trigger negative emotions, such as obsession with data collection to increase the likelihood of becoming pregnant [21]. Long-term tracking exacerbates these risks because the practices get further intertwined with the challenges of everyday life. It is therefore important to enable and support participants in disengaging from tracking, like they might naturally do if long-term tracking outside of a research context.

5.6 Making These Recommendations Work Together

To illustrate how many of these recommendations can work together, we note a study conducted by Propeller Health, the Institute for Healthy Air Water and Soil, and the Department of Civic Innovation at Louisville Metro, Kentucky, USA [1].

This study, AIR Louisville, enrolled 497 people with asthma to use connected rescue inhalers. Every time they used their inhaler, the use and location were automatically logged, and participants were also asked why they used it. This combined incidental data collection (use of the inhalers) with active data collection (asking about why). Data were collected, transmitted, and used consistent with the Health Insurance Portability and Accountability Act (thus following the relevant legal framework), and participants could choose whether to authorize their health provider to view the data (this protecting privacy and also participant ownership of the data). To prevent this study from exacerbating health disparities, researchers provided syncing hubs so that people could participate without a smartphone. These data were then also aligned with environmental data about nitrogen dioxide, particulate matter, ozone, sulfur dioxide, pollen, temperature, humidity, and wind (a secondary data source).

Study participants remained active in the study (defined as continuing to have their data sync) for a mean of 297 days—or about nine months. Results about participant's exposure levels were returned to individuals through Propeller Health's platform. Participants reported that this helped them understand the triggers for asthma in their lives. Collectively, participants achieved 78 percent reduction in rescue inhaler use and a 48 percent improvement in symptom-free days.

The results also informed local policy initiatives, such as where and how to enhance tree cover, recommended truck routes, zoning that creates air pollution buffers, and development of a community warning system for asthma. They also informed federal policy recommendations, lowering the ozone standard for healthy air from 70 to 65ppb.

This study illustrates how researchers can combine purposeful tracking with incidental tracking to answer research questions while providing data—and actionable insights—back to participants. This was achieved with a design that was resilient to lapses in tracking, and within a framework that protected participant privacy and supported their agency in how to share and use the resulting data. Following such a model led to better data, better outcomes for the participants, and societal impact.

6 Conclusion

Long-term tracking presents opportunities for observing people's practices by analyzing years or decades of their data, as well as designing technology to help promote longitudinal reflection over behavior to support planning or self-improvement goals. Compared to short-term tracking, the volume and duration of data generated in long-term tracking result in new considerations in the design of tools. Gaps in data must be expected, passively collected data should be leveraged over more burdensome journals, data must be contextualized in people's lived experience, and the data should be leveraged for personal benefit over surveillance. The use of long-term self-tracking in research is still nascent. There are many open challenges for further design, as well as important considerations when leveraging the practice in research.

Acknowledgements We thank our coauthors on our original research described in the case studies in this chapter: James Fogarty, Jennifer Kang, Laura Pina, and Lie Ming Tang.

References

1. Barrett M, Combs V, Su JG, Henderson K, Tuffli M, Louisville AIR (2018) Collaborative. Air louisville: addressing asthma with technology, crowdsourcing, cross-sector collaboration, and policy. Health Affairs 37(4):525–534
2. Bentley F, Tollmar K (2013) The power of mobile notifications to increase wellbeing logging behavior. In: Proceedings of the SIGCHI conference on human factors in computing systems, pp 1095–1098

3. Bonander J, Gates S (2010) Public health in an era of personal health records: opportunities for innovation and new partnerships. J Med Int Res 12(3):

4. Bot BM, Suver C, Neto EC, Kellen M, Klein A, Bare C, Doerr M, Pratap A, Wilbanks J, Ray Dorsey E et al (2016) The mpower study, Parkinson disease mobile data collected using researchkit. Sci Data 3(1):1–9

5. Brubaker JR, Dombrowski LS, Gilbert AM, Kusumakaulika N, Hayes GR (2014) Stewarding a legacy: responsibilities and relationships in the management of post-mortem data. In: Proceedings of the SIGCHI conference on human factors in computing systems, CHI '14, New York, NY, USA. Association for Computing Machinery, pp 4157–4166

6. Choe EK, Lee NB, Lee B, Pratt W, Kientz JA (2014) Understanding quantified-selfers' practices in collecting and exploring personal data. In: Proceedings of the SIGCHI conference on human factors in computing systems, pp 1143–1152

7. Chun KS, Bhattacharya S, Thomaz E (2018) Detecting eating episodes by tracking jawbone movements with a non-contact wearable sensor. In: Proceedings of the ACM on interactive, mobile, wearable and ubiquitous technologies, vol 2(1)

8. Chung C-F, Dew K, Cole A, Zia J, Fogarty J, Kientz JA, Munson SA (2016) Boundary negotiating artifacts in personal informatics: patient-provider collaboration with patient-generated data. In: Proceedings of the 19th ACM conference on computer-supported cooperative work & social computing, pp 770–786

9. Clawson J, Pater JA, Miller AD, Mynatt ED, Mamykina L (2015) No longer wearing: investigating the abandonment of personal health-tracking technologies on craigslist. In: Proceedings of the 2015 ACM international joint conference on pervasive and ubiquitous computing, UbiComp '15. New York, NY, USA. Association for Computing Machinery, pp 647–658

10. Consolvo S, Roessler P, Shelton BE (2004) The CareNet display: lessons learned from an in home evaluation of an ambient display. UbiComp 2004: Ubiquitous Computing. volume 3205 of Lecture Notes in Computer Science. Springer, Berlin/Heidelberg, pp 1–17

11. Cordeiro F, Epstein DA, Thomaz E, Bales E, Jagannathan AK, Abowd GD, Fogarty J (2015) Barriers and negative nudges: exploring challenges in food journaling. In: Proceedings of the 33rd annual ACM conference on human factors in computing systems, pp 1159–1162

12. Daskalova N, Lee B, Huang J, Ni C, Lundin J (2018) Investigating the effectiveness of cohort-based sleep recommendations. In: Proceedings of the ACM interactive mobile wearable ubiquitous technologies, vol 2(3)

13. Daskalova N, Metaxa-Kakavouli D, Tran A, Nugent N, Boergers J, McGeary J, Huang J (2016) Sleepcoacher: a personalized automated self-experimentation system for sleep recommendations. In: Proceedings of the 29th annual symposium on user interface software and technology, pp 347–358

14. De Choudhury M, Kumar M, Weber I (2017) Computational approaches toward integrating quantified self sensing and social media. In: Proceedings of the 2017 ACM conference on computer supported cooperative work and social computing, pp 1334–1349

15. Doran GT (1981) There'sa smart way to write management's goals and objectives. Manage Rev 70(11):35–36

16. Epstein DA, Caraway M, Johnston C, Ping A, Fogarty J, Munson SA (2016) Beyond abandonment to next steps: understanding and designing for life after personal informatics tool use. In: Proceedings of the 2016 CHI conference on human factors in computing systems, pp 1109–1113

17. Epstein DA, Cordeiro F, Bales E, Fogarty J, Munson SA (2014) Taming data complexity in lifelogs: exploring visual cuts of personal informatics data. In: Proceedings of the 2014 conference on designing interactive systems, pp 667–676

18. Epstein DA, Kang JH, Pina LR, Fogarty J, & Munson SA (2016) Reconsidering the device in the drawer: lapses as a design opportunity in personal informatics. In Proceedings of the 2016 ACM international joint conference on pervasive and ubiquitous computing, pp 829–840

19. Epstein DA, Ping, Fogarty J, Munson SA (2015) A lived informatics model of personal informatics. In: Proceedings of the 2015 ACM international joint conference on pervasive and ubiquitous computing, pp 731–742

20. Feustel C, Aggarwal S, Lee B, Wilcox L (2018) People like me: designing for reflection on aggregate cohort data in personal informatics systems. In: Proceedings of the ACM interactive mobile wearable ubiquitous technologies, vol 2(3)
21. Figueiredo M, Caldeira C, Chen Y, Zheng K (2018) Routine self-tracking of health: reasons, facilitating factors, and the potential impact on health management practices. AMIA ... Annual symposium proceedings. AMIA symposium, pp 706–714
22. Fogg BJ (2002) Persuasive technology: using computers to change what we think and do. Ubiquity 2002(December):2
23. Gouveia R, Karapanos E, Hassenzahl M (2015) How do we engage with activity trackers? A longitudinal study of habito. In: Proceedings of the 2015 ACM international joint conference on pervasive and ubiquitous computing, UbiComp '15, New York, NY, USA. Association for Computing Machinery, pp 1305–1316
24. Gouveia R, Pereira F, Karapanos E, Munson SA, Hassenzahl M (2016) Exploring the design space of glanceable feedback for physical activity trackers. In: Proceedings of the 2016 ACM international joint conference on pervasive and ubiquitous computing, UbiComp '16, New York, NY, USA. Association for Computing Machinery, pp 144–155
25. Karkar R, Schroeder J, Epstein DA, Pina LR, Scofield J, Fogarty J, Kientz JA, Munson SA, Vilardaga R, Zia J (2017) Tummytrials: a feasibility study of using self-experimentation to detect individualized food triggers. In: Proceedings of the 2017 CHI conference on human factors in computing systems, pp 6850–6863
26. Kim D, Lee Y, Rho S, Lim Y (2016) Design opportunities in three stages of relationship development between users and self-tracking devices. In: Proceedings of the 2016 CHI conference on human factors in computing systems, CHI '16, New York, NY, USA. Association for Computing Machinery, pp 699–703
27. Kim Y-H, Jeon JH, Choe EK, Lee B, Kim K, Seo J (2016) Timeaware: leveraging framing effects to enhance personal productivity. In: Proceedings of the 2016 CHI conference on human factors in computing systems, CHI '16, New York, NY, USA. Association for Computing Machinery, pp 272–283
28. Kim Y-H, Jeon JH, Lee B, Choe EK, Seo J (2017) Omnitrack: a flexible self-tracking approach leveraging semi-automated tracking. Proceedings of the ACM on interactive, mobile, wearable and ubiquitous technologies 1(3):1–28
29. Kolovson S, Pratap A, Duffy J, Allred R, Munson SA, Areán PA, Understanding participant needs for engagement and attitudes towards passive sensing in remote digital health studies
30. Lazar A, Koehler C, Tanenbaum J, Nguyen DH (2015) Why we use and abandon smart devices. In: Proceedings of the 2015 ACM international joint conference on pervasive and ubiquitous computing, pp 635–646
31. Lee MK, Kim J, Forlizzi J, Kiesler (2015) Personalization revisited: a reflective approach helps people better personalize health services and motivates them to increase physical activity. In: Proceedings of the 2015 ACM international joint conference on pervasive and ubiquitous computing, UbiComp '15, New York, NY, USA. Association for Computing Machinery, pp 743–754
32. Li I, Dey A, Forlizzi J (2010) A stage-based model of personal informatics systems. In: Proceedings of the SIGCHI conference on human factors in computing systems, CHI '10, New York, NY, USA. Association for Computing Machinery, pp 557–566
33. Mantua J, Gravel N, Spencer R (2016) Reliability of sleep measures from four personal health monitoring devices compared to research-based actigraphy and polysomnography. Sensors 16(5):646
34. Mehrotra A, Tsapeli F, Hendley R, Musolesi M (2017) Mytraces: investigating correlation and causation between users' emotional states and mobile phone interaction. In: Proceedings of the ACM interactive mobile wearable ubiquitous technologies, vol 1(3)
35. Meyer J, Beck E, Wasmann M, Boll S (2017) Making sense in the long run: long-term health monitoring in real lives. 2017 IEEE international conference on healthcare informatics (ICHI). IEEE, New York, pp 285–294

36. Meyer J, Kay J, Epstein DA, Eslambolchilar P, Tang LM (2020) A life of data: characteristics and challenges of very long term self-tracking for health and wellness. ACM Trans Comput Healthcare 1(2):1–4
37. Michie S, Ashford S, Sniehotta FF, Dombrowski SU, Bishop A, French DP (2011) A refined taxonomy of behaviour change techniques to help people change their physical activity and healthy eating behaviours: the calo-re taxonomy. Psychol health 26(11):1479–1498
38. Montgomery-Downs HE, Insana SP, Bond JA (2012) Movement toward a novel activity monitoring device. Sleep Breath 16(3):913–917
39. Moore J, Goffin P, Meyer M, Lundrigan P, Patwari N, Sward K, Wiese J (2018) Managing in-home environments through sensing, annotating, and visualizing air quality data. Proceedings of the ACM on interactive, mobile, wearable and ubiquitous technologies 2(3):1–28
40. Murnane EL, Abdullah S, Matthews M, Kay M, Kientz JA, Choudhury T, Gay G, Cosley D (2016) Mobile manifestations of alertness: connecting biological rhythms with patterns of smartphone app use. In: Proceedings of the 18th international conference on human-computer interaction with mobile devices and services, MobileHCI '16, New York, NY, USA. Association for Computing Machinery, pp 465–477
41. Mynatt ED, Rowan J, Craighill S, Jacobs A (2001) Digital family portraits: supporting peace of mind for extended family members. In: Proceedings of the SIGCHI conference on Human factors in computing systems, pp 333–340
42. Niess J, Woźniak PW (2018) Supporting meaningful personal fitness: the tracker goal evolution model. In: Proceedings of the 2018 CHI conference on human factors in computing systems, pp 1–12
43. Piercy KL, Troiano RP, Ballard RM, Carlson SA, Fulton JE, Galuska George SM, Olson RD (2018) The physical activity guidelines for americans. JAMA 320(19):2020–2028
44. Pratap A, Neto EC, Snyder P, Stepnowsky C, Elhadad N, Grant D, Mohebbi MH, Mooney S, Suver C, Wilbanks J et al (2020) Indicators of retention in remote digital health studies: a cross-study evaluation of 100,000 participants. NPJ Digital Med 3(1):1–10
45. Prochaska JO, Velicer WF (1997) The transtheoretical model of health behavior change. Am J Health Promot 12(1):38–48
46. Richardson CR, Buis LR, Janney, Goodrich DE, Sen A, Hess ML, Mehari KS, Fortlage LA, Resnick PJ, Zikmund-Fisher BJ et al (2010) An online community improves adherence in an internet-mediated walking program. Part 1: results of a randomized controlled trial. J Med Int Res 12(4):e71
47. Rooksby J, Rost M, Morrison A, Chalmers M (2014) Personal tracking as lived informatics. In: Proceedings of the SIGCHI conference on human factors in computing systems, pp 1163–1172
48. Schon DA (1984) The reflective practitioner: how professionals think in action, vo 5126. Basic Books
49. Schroeder J, Chung C-F, Epstein DA, Karkar R, Parsons A, Murinova N, Fogarty J, Munson SA (2018) Examining self-tracking by people with migraine: goals, needs, and opportunities in a chronic health condition. In: Proceedings of the 2018 ACM conference on designing interactive systems conference, pp 135–148
50. Schroeder J, Hoffswell J, Chung C-F, Fogarty J, Munson S, Zia J (2017) Supporting patient-provider collaboration to identify individual triggers using food and symptom journals. In: Proceedings of the 2017 ACM conference on computer supported cooperative work and social computing, pp 1726–1739
51. Schroeder J, Karkar R, Murinova N, Fogarty J, Munson SA (2019) Examining opportunities for goal-directed self-tracking to support chronic condition management. In: Proceedings of the ACM interactive mobile wearable ubiquitous technologies, vol 3(4)
52. Shih PC, Han K, Poole ES, Rosson MB, Carroll JM (2015) Use and adoption challenges of wearable activity trackers. In: Conference 2015 proceedings
53. Shin G, Feng Y, Jarrahi MH, Gafinowitz N (2018) Beyond novelty effect: a mixed-methods exploration into the motivation for long-term activity tracker use. JAMIA Open 2(1):62–72
54. Sun S, Belkin NJ (2016) Managing personal information over the long-term, or not? experiences by type 1 diabetes patients. In: Proceedings of the 79th ASIS&T annual meeting: creating

knowledge, enhancing lives through information & technology, ASIST '16, USA. American Society for Information Science

55. Tang LM, Kay J (2017) Harnessing long term physical activity data-how long-term trackers use data and how an adherence-based interface supports new insights. Proceedings of the ACM on interactive, mobile, wearable and ubiquitous technologies 1(2):1–28

56. Tang LM, Kay J (2018) Scaffolding for an olm for long-term physical activity goals. In: Proceedings of the 26th conference on user modeling, adaptation and personalization, pp 147–156

57. Tang LM, Meyer J, Epstein DA, Bragg K, Engelen L, Bauman A, Kay J (2018) Defining adherence: making sense of physical activity tracker data. Proceedings of the ACM on interactive, mobile, wearable and ubiquitous technologies 2(1):1–22

58. Tremblay A, Sevigny J, Leblanc C, Bouchard C (1983) The reproducibility of a three-day dietary record. Nutrit Res 3(6):819–830

59. Tsai CC, Lee G, Raab F, Norman GJ, Sohn T, Griswold WG, Patrick K (2007) Usability and feasibility of PMEB: a mobile phone application for monitoring real time caloric balance. Mob Networks Appl 12(2–3):173–184

60. Tudor-Locke C, Hatano Y, Pangrazi RP, Kang M (2008) Revisiting how many steps are enough? Med Sci Sports Exercise 40(7):S537–S543

61. Woldaregay AZ, Årsand E, Walderhaug S, Albers D, Mamykina L, Botsis T, Hartvigsen G (2019) Data-driven modeling and prediction of blood glucose dynamics: machine learning applications in type 1 diabetes. Artif Intell Med

62. Wolf G (2009) Know thyself: tracking every facet of life, from sleep to mood to pain, 24/7/365

Augmenting Gestural Interactions with Mid-Air Haptic Feedback: A Case Study of Mixed-Method Longitudinal UX-Testing in the Lab

Lawrence Van den Bogaert, Isa Rutten, and David Geerts

Abstract Ultrasound mid-air haptic feedback is a novel output technology that allows users to experience a sense of touch in mid-air on the unadorned palm and fingers of the hand. Even though a growing body of research has studied various aspects of the UX of mid-air haptics, little is known about what happens to the users' perception and experience after repeated use. The main reason for this is that today, mid-air haptic technology is not easily integrated in everyday devices (e.g. smartphones) nor widespread, making it difficult for it to be tested outside of a lab environment. This chapter describes the set-up of a longitudinal in-lab study, in which a mixed-method design was used to understand how the hedonic, pragmatic and emotional aspects of the UX of mid-air haptics changed over time. In eight sessions, spread over a five-week period, 31 participants interacted with a gesture-controlled home automation system augmented with mid-air haptic feedback. We report in this chapter on our participant recruitment and retention approach, the mixed-method set-up that was used, and (an excerpt of) the main results. Subsequently, we summarize best practices and propose suggestions for researchers who in the future intend to conduct a multimethod longitudinal study.

1 Introduction

As novel technologies emerge at a fast-paced rate and researchers' resources are generally limited, studying user experience or design aspects over a longer period of time is often a challenge in human–computer interaction (HCI). Especially when

L. Van den Bogaert (✉) · I. Rutten · D. Geerts
Meaningful Interactions Lab (mintlab), Parkstraat 45, 3000 Leuven, Belgium
e-mail: lawrence.vandenbogaert@kuleuven.be

I. Rutten
e-mail: isa.rutten@kuleuven.be

D. Geerts
e-mail: david.geerts@kuleuven.be

© Springer Nature Switzerland AG 2021
E. Karapanos et al. (eds.), *Advances in Longitudinal HCI Research*,
Human–Computer Interaction Series, https://doi.org/10.1007/978-3-030-67322-2_10

the technology or interface of interest cannot be taken home or incorporated in participants' everyday lives (e.g. installed as an app), longitudinal testing becomes cumbersome and impractical, both for the researcher as well as for the participant. Nevertheless, long-term user tests can indeed yield valuable or even unexpected insights, making them worthwhile.

This chapter reports on a case study that was part of a research project on mid-air haptics, where we undertook such a longitudinal user study. With the sense of touch becoming of increased interest in the HCI field, researchers have been seeking ways to convey touchless haptic feedback to users as an alternative for vibrotactile feedback. Ultrasound mid-air haptic feedback, often referred to as mid-air haptic feedback or simply mid-air haptics, does so by generating ultrasound pressure fields that actuate the sense of touch in the palm and fingers [1]. In addition to a relatively accurate localization error of less than 1 cm [2], mid-air haptics can provide multipoint feedback as well as different modulation frequencies, allowing for idiosyncratic touch sensations [3]. Particularly promising is the combination of this technology with gestural interfaces, which intrinsically lack any form of haptic feedback.

Today, mid-air haptic technology is not commonly integrated in everyday devices (e.g. smartphones) nor widespread, making it difficult for it to be tested outside of a lab environment. As a consequence, insights on the effects of its prolonged repeated use are scarce. Even though research shows that mid-air haptics augment the user experience when added to, e.g. movie experiences [4], VR [5] and car simulations [6], it is unclear whether these beneficial effects stand the test of time.

We conducted a longitudinal study with 31 participants who each engaged with mid-air haptics on 8 separate occasions over a 5-week period in order for us to gain a better understanding of the effects of repeated interaction with this novel technology. Because we only disposed of one mid-air haptic device—they are not commonly available and still expensive—and because this device can not simply be connected to other hardware, each session of the study was conducted in-lab, requiring a considerable engagement from participants. In this chapter, we focus on the methodological challenges we encountered during this study. We will share our findings in terms of recruitment, participant retention and overall study design. In summary, this chapter aims to report best practices and study set-up suggestions for HCI researchers who in the future intend to conduct in-lab longitudinal studies.

2   Related Work

2.1   Assessing the UX of Mid-Air Haptics

To evaluate a product's UX and design aspects, a variety of methods, assessment tools, frameworks and theories has been proposed and discussed in the HCI field. Hassenzahl's [7] framework on hedonic and pragmatic aspects of user experience is one of the most prevalent and distinguishes, on the one hand, between product attributes that are connected to the user's need to achieve behavioural goals (pragmatic), such as performing a task effectively or understanding the functionalities of a product easily, and on the other hand, product attributes that are connected to the user's self (hedonic) such as the human need to express oneself through objects (identification). In line with Hassenzahl, Mahlke and Thüring's [8] holistic model of UX also identifies instrumental (or pragmatic) and non-instrumental (or hedonic) components of the UX, but adds a third component: the users' emotional reactions.

In their pursuit to 'measure the added value' of specifically mid-air haptics, Maggioni et al. [9] built on this three-part model. Maggioni et al. [9] too consider the dualistic pragmatic/hedonic nature of UX (mainly drawing on Hassenzahl's work and the related AttrakDiff questionnaire as an assessment tool for these two components) and add to that the assessment of the user's valence and arousal as indications of emotional reactions, in line with Mahlke and Thüring [8]. In addition, as a fourth component, they incorporate the potential effect of the user's pre-exposure expectations, as these have been shown to influence users' experiences [10].

Next to Maggioni et al. [9], other authors also gauged the effects and outcomes of adding mid-air haptics to an interface. Whereas Ablart et al. [4] found an increase in arousal and valence (i.e. emotional response) when mid-air haptics augmented a one-minute video viewing experience, Hwang et al. [5] showed an increase in enjoyment when playing a VR piano that was augmented with mid-air haptic feedback. Limerick et al. [11], in turn, used the User Engagement Scale (UES) to demonstrate that users were more engaged with a digital poster when their interaction was augmented by mid-air haptic feedback. In contrast to these predominantly hedonic added values, less consensus exists on whether mid-air haptics also adds to pragmatic aspects of the UX, such as perceived workload. Freeman et al. [12] did find that tactile feedback can enhance above-device gesture interactions with a smartphone (i.e. a more utilitarian task) but detected no preference for mid-air haptic feedback over vibrotactile feedback in this regard. Harrington et al. [6] reported a significant increase in accuracy for slider-bar tasks in a driving simulator when mid-air haptics was added, but Sand et al. [13] in turn did not find a similar effect for gesture-based button selection in VR.

Even though all these studies have provided new and enriching insights into the different aspects of the UX of mid-air haptics, none of them have considered the effects of prolonged use. By assessing the UX over a longer period of time, it becomes possible to investigate whether and how the UX of mid-air haptics would change over time.

2.2 Temporal Aspects of UX

The studies mentioned above demonstrate that in particular with regard to mid-air haptics, little attention has been paid to studying prolonged use of this new technology. However, a growing body of UX research on other product categories or technologies considers temporal aspects and their influence on how users' experience of products or services changes over time. McCarthy and Wright [14] conceptualize experience with technology as consisting of four threads: the sensual, emotional, compositional and spatio-temporal (p. 80). The latter refers to a sense of space and time while using technology, showing the importance of time as an integral aspect of our experience with technology. Further on, McCarthy and Wright propose a tool for analysing how people make sense of technology introducing six processes of sense-making, which can occur at various moments in the use of technology and that can be analysed from the perspective of each of the threads. The six processes include anticipating use, connecting with a product or service, interpreting an unfolding experience, reflecting on the experience, appropriating an experience and recounting it to others. While not per se linear or in the order as presented here, the authors highlight how the various processes might differ between initial use or prolonged use.

While research on most of these processes is a more recent phenomenon, a lot of earlier scholars had already focused on users' initial intention to use. The original Technology Acceptance Model (TAM) considers perceived usefulness as the main predictor of intention to use, along with perceived ease of use [15]. Some later theoretical developments, which were based on the TAM, focused on technology acceptance in the consumer context, as opposed to the workplace, and added non-pragmatic UX components as well. An example is the Unified Theory of Technology Acceptance and Use 2 (UTAUT 2), where hedonic motivation or perceived enjoyment, defined as 'the fun or pleasure derived from using a technology' was added next to the pragmatic UX components [16]. In line with these theoretical models, Köse, Morschheuser, Hamari [17] found that if a product is perceived as mostly utilitarian, pragmatic aspects of the UX are dominant in predicting intention to use and continued use. However, when a product has a mostly hedonic nature, perceived usefulness loses its predictive power in favour of perceived enjoyment, which then becomes the main predictor of intention to use and prolonged use [17, 18].

In the meantime, some researchers have tried to capture various aspects of long-term use. Von Wilamowitz Moellendorff et al. [19] argue that our perception of the qualities of a product are dynamic and changeable over time. Their research on mobile phone use showed that as we get accustomed to a product, we develop and attach different weights to different qualities: whereas the initial focus might be on usability, this could shift to, e.g. novel functionality or communication of a favourable identity. Continuing the same line of thought, and based on two longitudinal user studies, Karapanos presents a framework of UX over time [20]. He shows how users initially evaluate a product based on its use, and that pragmatic quality, i.e. usefulness and ease-of-use, is of most importance in the beginning. However, after prolonged use, they evaluate the product based on their ownership of it and the importance of how well they identify with the product, i.e. what the product expressed about their self-identity in social contexts, increases. Furthermore, they found that the extent to which a product is found 'stimulating' (i.e. original, creative, new, innovative) has an effect on how beautiful it is considered to be, but this effect of 'stimulation' seems to diminish and makes place for 'identification' as the most important predictor of how beautiful a product is perceived.

2.3 Novelty Effect of Mid-Air Haptics

Related to the 'stimulation' mentioned above, scholars have identified an additional phenomenon to consider when assessing a product's UX; the so-called novelty effect, which often occurs at the first interaction(s) with a new technology (cf. 'connecting' in terms of McCarthy and Wright [14]). Novelty effect is defined by Koch et al. as 'an increased motivation to use something, or an increase in the perceived usability of something, on account of its newness' [21]). Koch also showed, however, that the usage patterns and/or perceived usability changes when novelty eventually fades [21].

As for mid-air haptic technology, most studies on its UX are cross-sectional and do not address the potential impact of a novelty effect [5, 6, 9, 12, 13]. In one study, a familiarization phase was included before starting with the experimental task, with the aim of mitigating a novelty effect. However, no assessment of perceived novelty was included to verify whether it actually decreased after the familiarization phase [11]. In a recent study [22], the impact of a novelty effect on the user experience of mid-air haptic feedback was tested by statistically controlling for perceived novelty. In this study, mid-air haptic feedback showed to provide added value on top of visual feedback in a gesture-based interface when considering attractiveness and pleasure during the interaction. However, these effects disappeared after statistically controlling for perceived novelty. This could imply that a decrease in novelty might go hand in hand with a decrease in attractiveness and pleasure. Longitudinal research is needed to investigate how the user experience of mid-air haptics evolves over time, and what happens when the novelty effect fades.

We are aware of only one study testing the repeated experience of mid-air haptics sensations: Ablart et al. [4] investigated the added value of mid-air haptics while watching one-minute movies at two points in time, with a time lapse of two weeks. They observed that mid-air haptic sensations increased the arousal ratings at both points in time, but that the skin conductance response (SCR) dropped at the second assessment, which reflects a drop in implicit arousal. This discrepancy between mid-air haptics' impact on self-rated arousal and implicit arousal over time is interesting from the perspective of the novelty effect. The results might be understood in terms of a fading novelty effect, reflected in the lower SCR. If this would be indeed the case, the unchanged self-rated arousal at both sessions could mean that subjective arousal is not particularly sensitive to a novelty effect.

3 The Study: 'Mixed-Method', 'Longitudinal' and 'in the Lab'

The present study evaluated the user experience of mid-air haptics over an extended period of time. In the following section, we will go over (a) the device and interface that were used for our participants to experience mid-air haptics; (b) participants and recruitment procedure; (c) the study set-up and procedure; (d) the UX assessment;

and (e) an excerpt of the main results. In the discussion section, we will further reflect, where relevant, on the decisions that were made against the light of our research purpose, as well as the implications and discerned best practices.

3.1 Apparatus

One company that began commercializing mid-air haptic technology is UltraLeap. Known before as UltraHaptics (before merging with LeapMotion), this company started as a spinoff from the university of Bristol (UK) and has developed a range of ultrasound mid-air haptic devices. As mentioned, the newness, cost and complexity of this technology make it not something that can be taken home or easily integrated in everyday devices and, as such, in the everyday life of participants. For our study, we used a Stratos Development kit by UltraLeap and linked it to a gesture-controlled home automation interface. It showed a groundplan of a house on which one could select and deselect rooms to then adjust the lighting, temperature, blinds and air conditioning through a set of four simple gestures (as shown in Figs. 1 and 2).

3.2 Participants

Participants were recruited on-site at the campus where the study took place. In total, 126 people signed up of which 31 were selected. We were very strict in the requirements for study participation in terms of availability and commitment: via an anonymized doodle, participants had to select eight time slots spread over a period of five weeks. For the first week, one long session (45 min) had to be selected. Over the second, third and fourth weeks six short sessions (15 min) had to be selected, and for the fifth week a final long session (45 min) again. Only when eight sessions were selected and distributed evenly over the five-week span, participants were considered

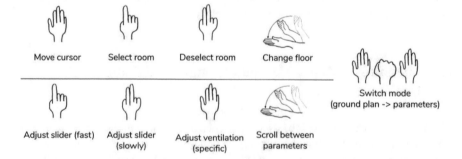

Fig. 1 Gestures to interact with the home automation interface

Fig. 2 Study set-up: participants used their right hand for gestural control above the UltraLeap kit and their left hand to draw and read scenario cards (cfr. 3.3 Procedure)

eligible. By having each participant define, in advance, their own dedicated five-week participation schedule, we hoped to decrease the chances of study dropout. Our strategy was successful as only one participant dropped out during the course of the study. One other participant encountered technical errors during the first session, resulting in valid data only in the final/closing session. Finally, we had to exclude one participant from the study because of an insufficient knowledge of Dutch, which was the language in which the experimental tasks, questionnaires and interviews were set up. As such, the initial number of 31 reduced to 28 final participants, which we considered as an acceptable number given the required engagement. Of the 28 remaining participants, the mean age was 20.79 (SD = 2.44), with an age range between 18 and 26. Six participants were male, and 22 were female. This study was approved by the local social and societal ethics committee: G- 2019 10 1780.

3.3   Procedure

Each participant came to our lab on campus at eight separate times. In each session, they were given a set of eight tasks to complete in the home automation system's interface described above by using the appropriate gestures. Gestures were either complemented by mid-air haptic feedback (first condition) or unadorned (second condition). These two conditions were presented in counterbalanced order over all sessions. As such, within each condition, participants each time completed four different tasks. These tasks were part of a narrative in which participants were members of an imaginary household and would encounter home-specific scenarios that required them to perform small tasks. An example of a scenario would be 'You have visitors tonight. Set the temperature of the living and dining room to a comfortable degree (21 °C). Then deselect the rooms again'. Scenarios were presented on cards randomly drawn from a face-down deck. There were four separate decks, each one corresponding to a different household functionality. The first deck contained tasks to adjust the lighting, the second deck had tasks to change the temperature (thermostat), the third one was related to the air conditioning and the last one to the window blinds. Two experimenters were allocated randomly to all sessions and each time followed the same experimental script. This means that participants were tested by two different experimenters across the eight sessions, based on random allocation.

3.3.1   Introductory Session

Upon arriving at our lab, participants first received extensive information about the five-week study schedule and procedure and were given the time to carefully read and sign the informed consent. After signing, participants were introduced to the mid-air haptic device and could familiarize with it through a range of sensations and patterns. Next, the home automation system was introduced. Participants were given time to get acquainted with the different gestures (Fig. 1). When they indicated feeling comfortable using the gestures, we asked what they expected from the combination of mid-air haptic feedback with this gestural home automation interface. The answers to this question were audio recorded and visited again during the last session. At this point, the actual experimental tasks started. Participants started interacting with the home automation system either with or without mid-air haptic feedback, depending on the order they were assigned to (counterbalanced). In each condition, they picked one scenario card from each of the four decks and completed the tasks one by one. We emphasized that they had to perform the tasks as accurately as possible but not as fast as possible. It was important that they did not feel stressed or hurried while interacting with the home automation system, but rather calm in order to be able to experience the interaction to the fullest. After completing four scenarios in the first condition (either with or without mid-air haptic feedback), they received a questionnaire to assess their experience with the home automation system (cfr. UX Assessment, Questionnaire section). They then repeated this with four new scenario cards (with or without mid-air haptics, depending on the previous condition) and filled out the same questionnaire for a second time. When both conditions were completed, a qualitative segment followed in which participants answered a set of open-ended questions (cfr. UX Assessment, Interview). At the end of the session, which took about 45 min, participants received a €10 bol.com voucher.

3.3.2   Repeated Sessions

After the more extensive introductory session, participants returned for six short repeated sessions. In these sessions, participants again completed four tasks in each condition (with/without mid-air haptic sensations) in counterbalanced order. These sessions took about 15 min to complete. Again, in each condition, one scenario card was picked from each of the four decks, totalling four different tasks in each condition, and eight different tasks in total. To enable participants to quickly drop by and perform the sessions right before, after, or in between classes, no questionnaire or interview was included in these short sessions.

3.3.3   Closing Session

The last session was again a long one and took about 40 to 45 min to finish. After completing the scenarios (picked from the four different card decks), participants received the same questionnaire as in the introductory session for each condition. When both conditions were completed, we revisited the expectations they expressed in session 1 and asked them whether they were met or not. This question was used to instigate the conversation on their overall experience. In addition, it gave participants the chance to nuance their questionnaire answers further. As such, we again elaborated on the same variables as those from the first session, to broadly understand why certain experiences changed or did not change over the five-week period (see also Sects. 3.4 and 3.5). At the end of this session, participants received the €40 bol.com voucher, as a reward for participating in all eight sessions.

3.4   UX Assessment

To (a) evaluate the changes in user experience over time quantitatively; and (b) gain deeper insights in participants' perception of the experience using a qualitative approach, we applied a mixed-method design that offered a broad understanding of our participants' attitude towards mid-air haptics. Here, we describe both the questionnaires that were used, as well as how this data was enriched with insights captured by the open-ended interviews. We then briefly discuss some of the main results.

3.4.1 Questionnaires

In line with the models introduced in the Related Work section, our questionnaire assessed both pragmatic and hedonic aspects of the UX, as well as the valence and arousal of the user's emotional reactions.

The questionnaire started with some general questions on age, gender and handedness. Subsequently, participants had to indicate the condition they had just completed tasks in: with or without mid-air haptic feedback. This was intended as an exclusion criterion item: it enabled us to filter out participants who had not paid any attention to the presence or absence of mid-air haptic feedback. Subsequently, a combination of existing standardized questionnaires was included in randomized order: the Affective Slider (AS) [23], User Experience Questionnaire (UEQ) [24], User Engagement Scale Short-Form (UES-SF) [25], perceived usefulness and perceived ease of use of the TAM [15, 18], enjoyment, continued use and user conception based on Köse et al. [17] and Van der Heijden [18]. We thus obtained four completed questionnaires from each participant: two on their experience with the interface with mid-air haptic sensations (one from the first session and a second one from the last session) and two about their experience without mid-air haptic sensations, again from both the first and the last session.

3.5   Interview

In addition to the more standardized quantitative assessments described above, both our first and last sessions ended with a set of open-ended questions which were audio recorded and transcribed for thematic analysis. The purpose of this set of wrap-up questions was to allow participants to elaborate further on their quantitative responses, stimulating them to reflect and add nuance and supplementary information that was not recorded in the questionnaire. The interview questions were therefore mapped to segments from the quantitative questionnaire: we asked about 'efficiency' (i.e. 'did you find the home automation interface more efficient with or without the mid-air haptic feedback?'), 'ease of use' (i.e. 'did you find the home automation interface easier to use with or without the mid-air haptic feedback?') and in the same fashion 'enjoyment' and 'continued use' (i.e. 'would the addition of mid-air haptic to the interface have an influence on whether you continue using it?'). In addition, we also asked about their overall preference (with or without mid-air haptic feedback).

3.6   Results Excerpt

To illustrate how the questionnaire data were analysed, we report in this section the statistical analyses used to obtain the results of three variables of main interest: enjoyment (hedonic UX), ease of use (pragmatic UX) and the valence of the emotional reaction. 'Enjoyment' was assessed as the mean score on four 7-point Likert items [17, 18]. Similarly, 'ease of use' was also assessed as the mean score on four 7-point Likert items [15, 18]. The valence of the emotional reaction was assessed using the affective slider, with a scale from 0 to 100 [23]. We used repeated measures (RM) ANOVA (R package ez [26]), with two within-participant factors: condition (with/without mid-air haptics) and session (session 1/session 8). A separate RM ANOVA was performed for the three dependent variables: enjoyment, ease of use and valence. We tested for both the main effects of condition and time and the interaction between both. All analyses were performed on complete data of 28 participants.

With enjoyment as dependent variable, we observed a main effect of condition, $F(1, 27) = 8.97$, $p < 0.01$, $\eta_G^2 = 0.02$, with the condition including mid-air haptics leading to significantly higher enjoyment than the condition without mid-air haptics. This can be understood as an added value of mid-air haptics in terms of enjoyment. A main effect of session was observed as well, $F(1, 27) = 15.10$, $p < 0.001$, $\eta_G^2 = 0.08$, with significantly lower enjoyment during the last session compared to the first session. Although there appears to be a decrease in the added value of mid-air haptics regarding enjoyment, when comparing session 1 with session 8 (see Fig. 3), this interaction effect was not statistically significant, $F(1, 27) = 1.18$, $p = 0.29$, $\eta_G^2 = 0.00$, which means that the added value of mid-air haptics in terms of enjoyment was similar during the first and last session.

Regarding ease of use, only a significant main effect of session was observed, $F(1, 27) = 7.32$, $p = 0.01$, $\eta_G^2 = 0.06$, with overall significantly higher ease of use during the last, compared to the first session. Condition showed no main effect, $F(1, 27) = 0.04$, $p = 0.85$, $\eta_G^2 = 0.00$, which means that there was no added value

Fig. 3 A main effect of condition and session, but no interaction effect, when considering enjoyment

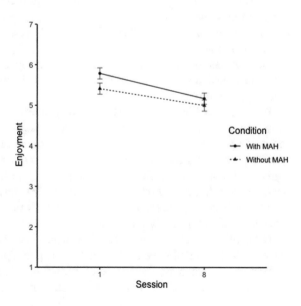

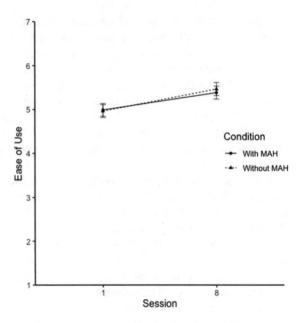

Fig. 4 A main effect of session, but no main effect of condition and no interaction effect, when considering ease of use

of mid-air haptics in terms of ease of use. Finally, no interaction effect between condition and session was present either, $F(1, 27) = 0.28$, $p = 0.60$, $\eta_G^2 = 0.00$ (see Fig. 4).

Concerning the valence of participants' emotional reaction: there was a main effect of condition, $F(1, 27) = 8.11$, $p < 0.01$, $\eta_G^2 = 0.05$, a main effect of session, $F(1, 27) = 7.61$, $p = 0.01$, $\eta_G^2 = 0.04$, and a significant interaction effect between condition and session, $F(1, 27) = 4.82$, $p < 0.05$, $\eta_G^2 = 0.02$. Therefore, we only interpreted this interaction effect (see Fig. 5). At session 1, the home automation system with mid-air haptics led to more experienced pleasure than without mid-air haptics, but this added value of mid-air haptics disappeared at session 8. This means that after repeated use, the added value of mid-air haptics in terms of experienced pleasure disappeared.

This is a clear illustration of what could be considered a novelty effect: initially, there was a significant increase in experienced pleasure due to the newness of the mid-air haptic sensations, but this effect disappeared after repeated use, when the novelty possibly faded away. When considering enjoyment, there appears to be a similar trend towards a fading added value of mid-air haptics at session 8 (Fig. 3), however this interaction effect was not statistically significant. Concerning ease use, we observed no evidence for a novelty effect, as the presence of mid-air haptic sensations did not have any impact at all on ease of use (Fig. 4).

The qualitative segment uncovered how nuanced and ambiguous preferences and UX experiences actually were. Only half of the participants maintained their initial preference (pro, contra or indifferent of mid-air haptics). Participants who after all eight sessions retained their preference for actuation of the home automation interface

Fig. 5 A main effect of condition and session, and a significant interaction effect between both, when considering valence of the emotional reaction

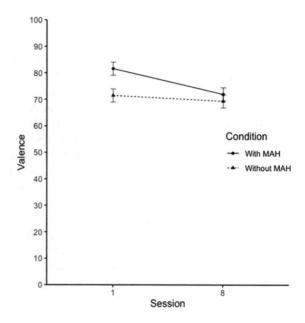

with mid-air haptics often mentioned how the mid-air haptics made the interaction more pleasant but not necessarily more practical. Some of them mentioned this was due to the guidance and confirmation they received through the mid-air haptic sensations, while others associated it with a heightened sense of agency over the system. In contrast, participants who preferred the interface without mid-air haptics very often mentioned a sense of being startled by the sudden sensations, making the experience unpredictable and thereby uneasy and unpleasant. Additionally, an interesting temporal component that was shown by the interviews was how mid-air haptics were either preferred in the beginning sessions versus only later on. Some participants described how the mid-air haptics helped them to get acquainted with the home automation system and the gestures used to control it, while others experienced the mid-air haptics as distracting at first, but grew fond of them once they got used to them.

4 Reflections and Implications for Longitudinal Research

As longitudinal research in HCI is rather scarce, especially in an in-lab setting, we now share the main methodological and practical take-outs of the present study, as well as reflect on the decisions (and their implications) that were made.

4.1   Planning

For in-lab studies, participants will engage in dedicated, stand-alone interaction sessions for which they need to visit the research lab on a regular basis. Especially when the amount of participants as well as the amount of sessions is high (as was the case in our study), it is paramount to plan well in advance. This facilitates the process both for participants as well as the researcher. That is why we had the people who showed interest to participate ($n = 126$) fill out time slots on an anonymized Doodle calendar with the chosen time slots disappearing as options for new participants. Everyone was instructed to spread their sessions evenly over the five-week period. The main reason for this was that we wanted participants to have a well divided interaction interval with the interface (rather than, e.g. seven interactions during the first week and only five weeks later an eight time). In addition, this not only made the effort for participants themselves more dispersed, but also allowed us as researchers to maintain a balanced data collection schedule. Unfortunately, having a predefined schedule is no guarantee for each session to take place exactly as planned. Technical issues, session cancellations or requests for rescheduling unavoidably take place when having over a hundred test moments. As such, it is important to build in buffer time as well as flexibility. In our case, we wanted catch-up sessions to take place as close as possible to the original test moment, for an even spread of sessions over time to be maintained for each participant. Participants were made aware that they would only receive the last part of their remuneration (cfr. infra) after attending all eight sessions.

In conclusion, having participants select their own time slots not only allows researchers to keep a structured overview, but also, and maybe even more importantly, implies to the participants that they have committed to a schedule of their liking. As such, there is less excuse to not show up or to drop out. Nonetheless, rescheduling will happen, and it is of importance to be both prepared as well as agile in this regard. Even though these measures might seem self-evident, we want to emphasize that this could make a difference in terms of retention and study dropout.

4.2   Trade-Off on Session Duration

Next to the session frequency, the session duration is of importance too when it comes to participant attrition. By keeping sessions short, as we did for the largest part of our study, participants will tend to remain more motivated and come back for each session. With relatively long sessions at the start and the end of the study, we thus deliberately decided to keep the intermediate sessions short and not collect data in them. This decision came at a cost, however. Having only two points of data collection for each participant causes restraint on the conclusions that can be drawn from a longitudinal perspective. The current data allows us to report on the changes in enjoyment, ease of use and valence between the start and finish of the study, but not on possible shifts in between. One might wonder, for example, whether valence might have increased in session 2 and 3, to only then make the reported drop. The 'shape of change' for our variables is in that sense unknown, and asks for further research. When mid-air haptic technology becomes more easily integrable in daily devices and thereby more widely available, the possibilities to have more data collection points will obviously increase too. Capturing data at several points in time over a prolonged period feasibility of collecting data entries at multiple points in time would enrich our understanding of longterm UX of mid-air haptics by shedding light on this currently occluded period between the first and last session. As such, it might provide answers to questions such as when the decline in enjoyment and valence exactly set in, and whether variables first show trends in other directions.

4.3   Recruitment

It is self-explanatory that a big, heterogeneous and representative participant pool is desirable in order to be able to generalize results as much as possible. However, there are always practical limitations to consider, especially in the case of a longitudinal study. As a participant, committing to a longitudinal in-lab study not only requires a considerable amount of time but also demands repeated logistic efforts. If participants are required to come to the lab often and frequently, it is sensible to take into account geographical factors. For our study, we therefore deliberately recruited at the campus of our lab, to reach potential participants who were there regularly and (hopefully) lived nearby. In addition to practical reasons, this approach had, for our study in particular, the additional advantage of reaching the target group that is known to be most perceptible to mid-air haptics. Research has shown that the sensitivity to, and ability of perceiving mid-air haptic sensations, declines with age [27].

4.4   Fun Factor

Data collection can be a tedious process. For the participant, there is often not much variation and tasks tend to get monotone and boring. Especially for multiple sessions with repeated tasks, you might consider gamifying the process or add a narrative to it. We included a simple story of participants being household members who, in their homes, encountered everyday 'scenarios'. These scenarios were presented through the card decks described previously. What was actually a very plain on/off exposure to mid-air haptic feedback now became a set of micro narratives that gave purpose to the interactions. When conducting a longitudinal study with repeated contact moments, we suggest knitting these stand-alone sessions into a bigger whole, possibly with a conclusion to be reached at the end.

4.5 Remuneration

If the study's budget allows remuneration for participants, this is of course an obvious benefit in terms of recruitment and retention. However, there are multiple ways to approach its distribution and spread. First of all, in some studies there is only one or a few 'rewards' or 'prizes' distributed among participants. Especially when asking for a long-term commitment, this might feel insufficient and unfair towards participants who miss out, which is why we would recommend distributing the budget evenly and compensating each participant with at least a small, even, remuneration. In addition, instead of foreseeing this compensation at the end of the study, one might consider spreading it. By doing so, retention and loyalty can be encouraged implicitly. The budget of our study allowed us to thank our participants with a €50 gift voucher each. This in itself is of course a significant amount and will facilitate retention. However, we did decide to give €10 already after the first session, and the remaining €40 at the end of the last session. This metaphorically 'reeled in' participants for the initial session, to then have them 'bought in" sufficiently to last until the final one.

5 Conclusion and Future Research

This chapter describes the set-up of a longitudinal in-lab study of which the goal was to assess the UX of a novel technology—ultrasound mid-air haptic feedback— over a prolonged period of time. We wanted to investigate how the hedonic and pragmatic UX of mid-air haptics would evolve over time and how participants' emotional reactions to this type of feedback would change. Building on a set of existing models and questionnaires, we applied a mixed-method design to generate a broad understanding of our participants' attitude towards mid-air haptics. During eight sessions (spread over a five-week period) participants interacted with a gesture-controlled home automation system, augmented with mid-air haptic feedback half of the time. This approach provided unprecedented insights and understandings of how people experience mid-air haptic technology, in particular after repeated use. Results showed that the pleasure and enjoyment participants experienced after their first interactions with mid-air haptics, significantly decreased over time. Regarding experienced pleasure, the added value of mid-air haptics at session 1 even disappeared at session 8, indicating that after repeated use, the presence of mid-air haptics no longer led to higher experienced pleasure compared to when absent. Although a similar trend for the hedonic UX of mid-air haptics (enjoyment) appeared to be present, this was not statistically significant. This means that the added value of mid-air haptics regarding enjoyment was relatively stable across both sessions, with a general decrease in enjoyment (whether or not mid-air haptics were present) from session 1 to session 8. Interestingly, participants reported no added value of mid-air haptics with regard to ease of use (an aspect of the pragmatic UX). Overall (whether or not mid-air haptics were present), the ease of use significantly increased from session 1 to session 8, as can be expected when interacting regularly with a new device. The findings from the interviews confirmed these results for the largest part, but at the same time revealed much nuance and ambiguity in participants' preferences. Hedonic and pragmatic preferences were regularly in conflict with each other and for some participants the added value of the mid-air haptic feedback increased instead of decreased. They, for example, mentioned that it took some time getting used to the sensations, but that the 'startling effect' over time faded, accustoming them to the mid-air haptics. Based on the participant pool we had, we could not discern interpersonal traits that provided a salient account or explanation for this. Future work to assess the relation between such personal traits and a negative vs. positive aptitude for mid-air haptic feedback will be interesting and necessary in that regard. Another remark to be made here is that measuring the UX of mid-air haptics typically happens with the mid-air haptic sensations being part of a larger interface, in our case: a home automation system. Earlier research (e.g. [6, 11]) similarly assessed the mid-air haptics as part of a larger whole, seeing that mid-air haptics as a stand-alone output typically makes less sense and lacks applicability and relevance (for exceptions, see Van den Bogart et al., 2019). Although the interface in casu (and its either pragmatic or hedonic character) unavoidably influences the user experience in its entirety to some extent, we mitigated this as much as possible by calculating the difference score between participant's evaluation of the home automation system with versus without mid-air haptics.

As mentioned, given the novelty and uncommonness of mid-air haptic technology, it was not possible for participants to interact with it on an individual day-to-day basis in their own home. A lab-setting was needed for our study. In addition to the traditional challenges of longitudinal research, this confinement to the lab brought about extra challenges, mainly in terms of participant engagement and retention. We therefore deliberately stuck to two data collection points in order not to overburden participants. The trade-off for this decision, however, was that we can only report on these measures and not on what happened to our variables in between. This leaves other questions (e.g. 'is the decline of valence and enjoyment linear?') unanswered and up to future research.

Regardless, we have applied and discussed additional techniques (other than financial remuneration) to foster participant retention and avoid study dropout. By gamifying or adding a narrative to required study tasks, their obligatory character can be dissolved, making continued participation more pleasant and casual. A well-planned schedule and time table, created by the participants themselves, not only keeps things clear and structured, but also increases the participants' sense of commitment. In addition, we recommend considering pragmatic elements when recruiting participants in order for the process and logistics to remain feasible for both them and the researchers.

References

1. Carter T, Seah SA, Long B, Drinkwater B, Subramanian S (2013) UltraHaptics: multi-point mid-air haptic feedback for touch surfaces. In: Proceedings of the 26th Annual ACM symposium on user interface software and technology, pp 505–514. UIST '13, ACM, New York, NY, USA. https://doi.org/10.1145/2501988.2502018
2. Wilson G, Carter T, Subramanian S, Brewster SA (2014) Perception of ultrasonic haptic feedback on the hand: localisation and apparent motion. In: Proceedings of the SIGCHI conference on human factors in computing systems, pp 1133–1142. CHI '14, ACM, New York, NY, USA. https://doi.org/10.1145/2556288.2557033
3. Obrist M, Seah SA, Subramanian S (2013) Talking about tactile experiences. In: Proceedings of the SIGCHI conference on human factors in computing systems, pp 1659–1668. CHI '13, ACM, New York, NY, USA. https://doi.org/10.1145/2470654.2466220
4. Ablart D, Velasco C, Obrist M (2017) Integrating mid-air haptics into movie experiences. In: Proceedings of the 2017 ACM international conference on interactive experiences for TV and online video. pp 77–84. TVX '17, Association for Computing Machinery, Hilversum, The Netherlands. https://doi.org/10.1145/3077548.3077551
5. Hwang I, Son H, Kim JR (2017) AirPiano: enhancing music playing experience in virtual reality with mid-air haptic feedback. In: 2017 IEEE world haptics conference (WHC), pp 213–218. https://doi.org/10.1109/WHC.2017.7989903
6. Harrington K, Large DR, Burnett G, Georgiou O (2018) Exploring the use of mid-air ultrasonic feedback to enhance automotive user interfaces. In: Proceedings of the 10th international conference on automotive user interfaces and interactive vehicular applications, pp 11–20. AutomotiveUI '18, Association for Computing Machinery, Toronto, ON, Canada. https://doi.org/10.1145/3239060.3239089
7. Hassenzahl M (2004) The interplay of beauty, goodness, and usability in interactive products. Hum-Comput Interact 19(4):319–349. https://doi.org/10.1207/s15327051hci1904_2
8. Mahlke S, Thüring M 2007) Studying antecedents of emotional experiences in interactive contexts. In: Proceedings of the SIGCHI conference on human factors in computing systems, pp 915–918. CHI '07, Association for Computing Machinery, San Jose, California, USA. https://doi.org/10.1145/1240624.1240762
9. Maggioni E, Agostinelli E, Obrist M (2017) Measuring the added value of haptic feedback. In: 2017 ninth international conference on quality of multimedia experience (QoMEX), pp 1–6. https://doi.org/10.1109/QoMEX.2017.7965670, ISSN: 2472-7814
10. Kujala S, Mugge R, Miron-Shatz T (Feb 2017) The role of expectations in service evaluation: a longitudinal study of a proximity mobile payment service. Int J Hum-Comput Stud 98:51–61. https://doi.org/10.1016/j.ijhcs.2016.09.011, http://www.sciencedirect.com/science/article/pii/S1071581916301239
11. Limerick H, Hayden R, Beattie D, Georgiou O, Müller J (2019) User engagement for mid-air haptic interactions with digital signage. In: Proceedings of the 8th ACM international symposium on pervasive displays, pp 1–7. PerDis '19, Association for Computing Machinery, Palermo, Italy. https://doi.org/10.1145/3321335.3324944
12. Freeman E, Brewster S, Lantz V (2014) Tactile feedback for above-device gesture interfaces: adding touch to touchless interactions. In: Proceedings of the 16th international conference on multimodal interaction—ICMI '14. ACM Press, Istanbul, pp 419–426. https://doi.org/10.1145/2663204.2663280
13. Sand A, Rakkolainen I, Isokoski P, Kangas J, Raisamo R, Palovuori K (2015) Head-mounted display with mid-air tactile feedback. In: Proceedings of the 21st ACM symposium on virtual reality software and technology, pp 51–58. VRST '15, ACM, New York, NY, USA. https://doi.org/10.1145/2821592.2821593
14. McCarthy J, Wright P (2004) Technology as experience. https://doi.org/10.1145/1015530.1015549
15. Davis FD (1989) Perceived usefulness, perceived ease of use, and user acceptance of information technology. MIS Q 13(3):319–340 (1989). https://doi.org/10.2307/249008

16. Venkatesh V, Thong JYL, Xu X (2012) Consumer acceptance and use of information technology: extending the unified theory of acceptance and use of technology. MIS Q 36(1):157–178. https://doi.org/10.2307/41410412
17. Köse DB, Morschheuser B, Hamari J (2019) Is it a tool or a toy? How user's conception of a system's purpose affects their experience and use. Int J Inform Manage 49:461–474. https://doi.org/10.1016/j.ijinfomgt.2019.07.016, http://www.sciencedirect.com/science/article/pii/S0268401219301550
18. van der Heijden H (2004) User acceptance of hedonic information systems. MIS Q 28(4):695–704. https://doi.org/10.2307/25148660
19. Wilamowitz Moellendorff M, Hassenzahl M, Platz A (2006) Dynamics of user experience: How the perceived quality of mobile phones changes over time. In: User experience—towards a unified view, workshop at the 4th Nordic conference on human-computer interaction
20. Karapanos E (2013) User experience over time. In: Karapanos E (ed) Modeling users' experiences with interactive systems. Studies in Computational Intelligence, Springer, Berlin, Heidelberg, pp 57–83. https://doi.org/10.1007/978-3-642-31000-3_4
21. Koch M, von Luck K, Schwarzer J, Draheim S (2018) The novelty effect in large display deployments—experiences and lessons-learned for evaluating prototypes. https://doi.org/10.18420/ecscw2018_3, https://dl.eusset.eu/handle/20.500.12015/3115. (Accepted 2018-04-30T19:58:18Z)
22. Rutten I, Geerts D (2020) Better because it's new: the impact of perceived novelty on the added value of mid-air haptic feedback, p 13
23. Betella A, Verschure PFMJ (2016) The affective slider: a digital self-assessment scale for the measurement of human emotions. PLOS ONE 11(2)
24. Laugwitz B, Held T, Schrepp M (2008) Construction and evaluation of a user experience questionnaire. In: Holzinger A (ed) HCI and usability for education and work. Lecture Notes in Computer Science, Springer, Berlin, Heidelberg, pp 63–76. https://doi.org/10.1007/978-3-540-89350-9_6
25. O'Brien HL, Toms EG (2013) Examining the generalizability of the User Engagement Scale (UES) in exploratory search. Inform Process Manage 49(5):1092–1107. https://doi.org/10.1016/j.ipm.2012.08.005, https://linkinghub.elsevier.com/retrieve/pii/S0306457312001124
26. Lawrence MA (2016) ez: Easy analysis and visualization of factorial experiments. https://CRAN.R-project.org/package=ez
27. Rutten I, Frier W, Van den Bogaert L, Geerts D (2019) Invisible touch: how identifiable are mid-air haptic shapes? In: Extended abstracts of the 2019 CHI conference on human factors in computing systems—CHI EA '19. ACM Press, Glasgow, pp 1–6. https://doi.org/10.1145/3290607.3313004

A Six-Month, Multi-platform Investigation of Creative Crowdsourcing

Vassilis-Javed Khan, Ioanna Lykourentzou, and Georgios Metaxas

Abstract Crowdsourcing platforms can be roughly divided into two kinds: the ones that offer simple, short, and unskilled work (microtasking) and those that offer complex, longer tasks, which are difficult to break down and usually involve creativity (macrotasking). Past research has mapped the landscape of microtask crowdsourcing. Little, however, is known about where commercial platforms stand when it comes to creative crowdsourcing. Which types of creative tasks are offered? How are these remunerated? Do all platforms facilitate the same type of creative work? Given the increasing importance that creative crowdsourcing is expected to play in the near future, in this chapter we partially map the current state of this type of online work over time. During a six-month period, and on a daily basis, we collected public data from seven creative crowdsourcing platforms. Our data, covering more than thirteen thousand tasks, show that there are plenty of graphic design tasks but better financial rewards for other types of creative tasks, as well as a trend for creative crowd work platforms to offer longer tasks. Judging from the total rewards in those six months, we can also conclude that creative crowdsourcing will benefit from a shift to dynamic rather than fixed rewards, but also that this type of crowd work is still at an embryonic stage and has growth potential. Finally, our results highlight the need for a platform data watchdog, as well as the need for a more nuanced perspective of creative crowdsourcing, distinguishing between the types of platforms within this genre of online work.

Keywords Crowdsourcing · Longitudinal data analysis · Multi-platform data analysis

V.-J. Khan (✉)
Eindhoven University of Technology, Eindhoven, The Netherlands
e-mail: v.j.khan@tue.nl

I. Lykourentzou
Utrecht University, Utrecht, The Netherlands
e-mail: i.lykourentzou@uu.nl

G. Metaxas
Fontys University of Applied Sciences, Eindhoven, The Netherlands
e-mail: g.metaxas@fontys.nl

© Springer Nature Switzerland AG 2021
E. Karapanos et al. (eds.), *Advances in Longitudinal HCI Research*,
Human–Computer Interaction Series, https://doi.org/10.1007/978-3-030-67322-2_11

1 Introduction

Crowdsourcing is a socio-technical phenomenon in which large numbers of people complete on-demand, work-related tasks on Web sites. These Web sites are more commonly known as *crowdsourcing platforms*. Initial milestones of this phenomenon are a 2006 article on Wired magazine that is credited with coining the term *crowdsourcing* [11], and the launch of Amazon's Mechanical Turk platform[1] in that same year, in which all sorts of digital tasks (e.g., annotating images), known as Human Intelligent Tasks (HITs), can be completed.

As this phenomenon became more popular and grew, crowdsourcing platforms became more mature, and their classification is becoming more nuanced. A 2015 World Bank report [15] recognizes two major segments in crowdsourcing: *"microwork"* and *"online freelancing"*. This report defines microwork as work that can be *"broken down into microtasks that can be completed in seconds or minutes"* and defines online freelancing as work that is *"performed over longer durations of time—hours, days, or months"*. This report also identifies that microwork typically pays a small amount to workers per completed task. It also breaks down online freelancing into *"open services platforms"* and *"managed services platforms"*, in which the former act as a marketplace in which direct communication between requesters and workers takes place, whereas in the latter the relationship between the two are managed. In terms of revenue, online freelancing was estimated to have grossed almost $2 billion in 2013 and projected to grow to more than $4 billion in 2016 and at least $15 billion by 2020 [15]. It is important to highlight that these figures are estimates and that the report recognizes a limitation in empirical data.

In the academic sphere, there is relatively plenty of research that has focused on mapping the landscape of microwork (or microtasking, as it is known) and the demand side of crowdsourcing and more specifically Amazon's platform: Mechanical Turk [9, 12]. However, when it comes to the other type of crowd work, research is scarce. Furthermore, the academic focus on microtask crowdsourcing also implies cross-sectional research studies, which leave out the temporal aspect in their investigations. The crowdsourcing studies that do focus on temporal aspects have focused on a single platform and most of those focus on Amazon's Mechanical Turk.

With this chapter, we would like to contribute to the existing body of literature by investigating several crowdsourcing platforms over a long period of time. Furthermore, we investigate platforms other than MTurk, which would be characterized as creative, in that they offer tasks other than microtasks, i.e., tasks that require expertise are complex and time, also known in literature as macrotasks [17]. Based on our six-month investigation of seven crowdsourcing platforms, we draw design lessons for future crowdsourcing platforms. Additionally, we believe that our investigation will also appeal to other scientists and more specifically ones in the social sciences. Given the current COVID-19 virus crisis, we believe that this type of work might become

---

[1] https://www.mturk.com/.

more important due to social distancing and due to the large numbers of people who have suddenly become unemployed. We, therefore, believe that our study is timely to map the current landscape of creative crowdsourcing and sketch its future.

2 Background

Initially, crowdsourcing was, and perhaps to some extent till now is, primarily associated with microtasks, i.e., the completion of short, typically simple tasks that are currently difficult for machines to complete whereas are easy for humans [21]. However, more recently, there is a research focus on macrotask crowdsourcing, i.e., tasks that generally are more complex, might require collaboration and certainly take time to complete [17]. More specifically, prior research work on the overlap between longitudinal studies and crowdsourcing has looked into the:

(1) Adaptations and extensions that are necessary to leverage crowdsourcing platforms for conducting longitudinal research studies [5, 18, 19];
(2) Workers-side context (i.e., the supply side) [6, 9], and
(3) Requesters-side context (i.e., the demand side), but only within a single platform [2, 3, 25].

With regard to leveraging crowdsourcing platforms to conduct longitudinal research studies, the primary focus of research has been Amazon's crowdsourcing platform: Mechanical Turk (MTurk). MTurk was primarily developed to conduct short, one-off tasks, such as for example annotating a photo and therefore lacks several salient features for conducting long-term research studies. However, the fact that it has a large and stable number of people working on the platform [6], has attracted researchers to both investigate the extent to which MTurk can be used for longitudinal research studies and the design extensions needed to better support these types of studies.

An important finding in relation to conducting longitudinal studies is that MTurk has *"the same advantages as student samples and commercial research panels without their significant disadvantages"* [5]. More specifically in three studies, [5] examined salient longitudinal variables such as non-response biases, the stability and consistency of demographic and self-report measures. They conducted their studies across time periods of two, four, eight, and thirteen months. However, to conduct their studies, they had to develop custom software to bulk message their participants in MTurk. The realization that many common research tasks are difficult and time-consuming to implement on MTurk has led researchers to develop systems such as TurkServer [18] and TurkPrime [19]. For example, TurkServer monitors workers' activity during an experiment, to check whether they are actually participating and was designed as a research platform that integrates with MTurk and supports tasks that are common to the social and behavioral sciences. TurkPrime has more extensive features such as being able to exclude workers based on tasks' past participation, and in that way support between subject's designs; edit a task after actually launching it; support flexible payment mechanisms. When it comes to longitudinal studies, TurkPrime supports launching a task that is open only to workers that have participated in previous studies; matching a worker's ID across data files; notifying a worker to inform them that a task is available for them.

With regard to the supply side, i.e., what to expect when it comes to people participating as workers in crowdsourcing platforms, the primary focus of research has also been focused on Amazon's MTurk. For example, we know that there are approximately 100 K workers active in MTurk and even more importantly, *"at any given time there are more than 2K active workers"* and that a Turker's (this is how people working on MTurk are known) half-life is approximately a year, with the rate of new Turkers balancing the departures rate [6]. These findings were based on a survey conducted over 28 months, from forty thousand unique workers [6]. When it comes to Turkers' hourly earnings, Hara et al. [9] report a median of approximately only $2 with only 4% of them earning more than the average US minimum hourly wage of $7.25. Sources of unpaid effort that negatively impacts the hourly wage are spending time and effort in searching and dealing with rejected and returned tasks on MTurk. These findings were based on tasks logs collected from September 2014 to January 2017, accounting a total of more than three million tasks by more than 2.5 K unique workers. Furthermore, we know that workers utilize tools to find honest requesters to ensure fair rewards. Two well-known tools are Turkopticon [13], initially developed by HCI researchers and the online community Turker Nation, which was initially a forum and has now moved to Reddit [20].

With regard to the demand side, i.e., what to expect when it comes to the tasks posted by requesters of work, the primary focus of research has been investigating a single platform. More specifically, in the context of creative crowdsourcing, Araujo [2] surveyed 99designs.com, a popular creative crowdsourcing platform for graphic design contests and collected more than 38 thousand logo design contests between 2010 and early 2012, from more than 63 thousand unique designers. In terms of contest rewards, he found that most rewards, for the USA, were $299, $499, or $699—the three default rewards of the platform at the time in the USA. This research focused primarily on what are the effects of the reward to attract designers and not what the platform offers in terms of the number of tasks available, their duration, and overall rewards. More specifically in terms of effects, he found that higher financial incentives do not translate to designers' increased effort; however, they do have an impact on contests' quality because they attract more designers. Another salient finding is that most contests were dominated by few designers, the most active, and effective ones.

In an earlier study, Zheng et al. [25] surveyed 283 designers in the Chinese Taskcn platform. Additionally, they gathered a sample of 7162 contests in a period of 14 months, from August 2008 to October 2009. The top contest types were graphic design (logos and ads, $N > 3$ K) followed by name and slogan design ($N = 676$), followed by Web site design ($N = 502$). Their findings suggest an *"inseparable and balanced view of extrinsic and intrinsic motivation"* to encourage participation in crowdsourcing. Thus, if extrinsic motivation is as important as intrinsic, in creative crowdsourcing, the question which arises is: What rewards are actually available for creative crowd workers? In other words, what can creative crowd workers expect in terms of the supply side from the broader range of existing platforms? Both the aforementioned studies contribute significantly in addressing this question but for a single platform, 99designs and Taskcn, respectively.

In this paper, we contribute to the literature by focusing on the second segment of crowdsourcing, which we dub "creative crowdsourcing". For a period of six months, we daily collected public data from seven creative crowdsourcing platforms. Our analysis wishes to describe the current state of creative crowdsourcing. Our analysis is important because one of the main drivers for crowd workers, in both microtasking [4, 15] and macrotasking are their financial rewards [25]. More specifically, we contribute by presenting data on the supply side of creative crowdsourcing across seven platforms.

Our study is the first, to the extent of our knowledge that investigates over a period of six months seven platforms in the creative crowdsourcing space. Therefore, our research focus is both longitudinal and multi-platform. More specifically, our main research questions are as follows:

RQ1. How do number of tasks and rewards fluctuate over time, across different platforms?

RQ2. What are some critical limitations of crowdsourcing platforms to further develop the field over time?

3   Method

We collected data from seven platforms (Table 1). The data collection took place daily at 14:00 GMT from the August 1, 2017, to the January 31, 2018, i.e., for six months. To choose the platforms, we assigned five industrial design students to go through a list of 100+ crowdsourcing platforms and shortlist ones that they would prefer to work on. The rationale behind asking students to shortlist such platforms was based on the aforementioned World Bank report that states millennials being the main population in crowdsourcing and *"are expected to make up 75 percent of the global workforce by 2025"* [15].

More specifically, we collected the task's title; financial reward; task ID—that was issued by the platform; URL; expiry date; and the posted date (i.e., the date we collected). We also collected a screenshot of the task's webpage. Based on the posted and expiry date, we calculated a task's duration in days.

We then manually corrected a few cases where the collected data were incorrect. We corrected this data by visiting the webpage in which the task was posted and directly changed the data in our file. These cases were actually restricted only to platform seven (P7) ($N = 31$ cases). We identified these cases by using scripts to identify outliers or data types other than the ones we expected.

Table 1 Short description of the platforms we surveyed in this study

Platform	Description
P1	A graphic design online marketplace. It is essentially a freelancer platform for connecting graphic designers and potential clients
P2	Brainstorm at scale and solving design and innovation challenges by more than 120K creative professionals and innovation experts
P3	Ideas for creative contests. It focuses on fueling innovation, improving brand communication and customers' experience
P4	Design and technology online marketplace. Began with coding competitions but has now grown into a diverse technology community spanning the entire software development life cycle with more than one million members
P5	Thinking of innovative solutions to challenging problems for Dutch-based companies and organizations
P6	Open innovation for design contests. It essentially connects companies through design contests, with a worldwide community of creative talents
P7	Focuses on R&D challenges. It essentially enables organizations to publish their unsolved problems, framed as 'Challenges', out to the crowd to solve. The crowd can either be the employees of the organization (i.e., internal crowd) or external to the organization

The description is based on the platforms' "About" page and homepage. The main reasons for anonymizing the platforms are that we are interested in mapping the broader landscape of creative crowdsourcing and to ensure their privacy

Furthermore, we removed cases in which the tasks had already expired ($N =$ 22). Before importing the data into SPSS for analysis, we converted all the financial rewards into Euros, based on the exchange rates retrieved on xe.com on the February 11, 2018. Finally, we randomly checked 100 tasks to inspect and ensure that there were no differences between the collected data and the data in the respective platforms' webpages.

4 Results

In the period of six months, we collected a total of 13,421 tasks (Figs. 1 and 2).

The distribution of the number of tasks posted is extremely skewed (Table 2). One platform (P1) posted the vast majority of tasks (93.24%). P1 primarily hosts graphic design type of tasks. P1 was followed by P4, which posted 5.79% of the total tasks. That means that these two platforms posted cumulatively 99% of the tasks. One can imagine that the results are influenced by P1, given its dominance. However, this dominance in the number of tasks has adverse effects, for example, in the average reward per task (Fig. 5). Given this dominance, we also make sure to conduct analysis that excludes P1 (e.g., see Fig. 3).

In the surveyed period of six months, the platforms posted an average of approximately 74 tasks per day ($M = 74.56$; SD $= 10.43$) with a maximum of 119

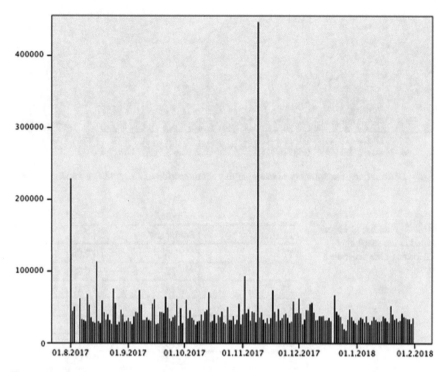

Fig. 1 Distribution of the sum of financial rewards per day across platforms. The Y-axis displays the financial reward in € and X-axis the date. We observe that there is a rather stable amount of financial rewards on any given day with a few exceptions

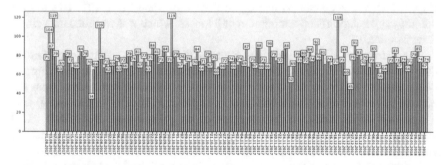

Fig. 2 Distribution of the number of tasks per day for the period of six months. As it was the case in Fig. 1, here we also observe that there is a rather stable number of tasks on any given day with few exceptions

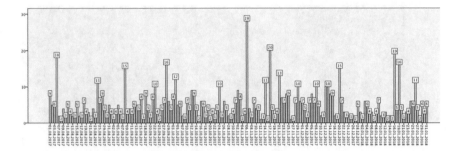

Fig. 3 Distribution of the number of tasks per day for the period of six months, excluding tasks of P1

Platform	Frequency	%
P6	6	0.04
P5	12	0.08
P2	14	0.10
P7	31	0.23
P3	66	0.49
P4	778	5.79
P1	12,514	93.24
Total	13,421	100

Table 2 Number of tasks posted in the respective platforms in the six-month period

tasks, which was recorded on two dates: 06/08/2017 and 02/10/2017 (we use the dd/mm/yyyy notation) and a minimum of 34 tasks, which was recorded on a single date: 24/08/2017.

The distribution of tasks per day is quite even (Fig. 2); however, when removing the dominant platform P1, the shape of the distribution changes dramatically (Fig. 3). Descriptive statistics for the number of tasks, when excluding the ones from P1, include an average of approximately five tasks per day ($M = 5.03$; $SD = 4.16$) with a maximum of 28 tasks, which was recorded on a single date: 06/11/2017 and a minimum of zero tasks which we recorded in 15 dates, throughout the sampling period.

In regard to the financial reward that the tasks paid off, which we converted when necessary to Euro (€) revealed a total turnaround of more than €7.5 M (€7,538,453_. If we calculate the average task reward, that was more than €550 per task ($M =$ €561.69 per task, $SD =$ €4032.35). The maximum reward that a platform paid off for a day was €410 K, which we recorded on 09/11/17 and was offered by P7. The minimum was €0, and we recorded 101 such cases on P4. Typically, those tasks, in that platform, would either offer non-monetary rewards such as T-shirts, or they would not specify the monetary reward, in the task description.

The distribution of the sum of rewards resembles an exponential distribution (Fig. 4, Table 3) with P1 again topping the list. Nevertheless, we find that the ranking of platforms is different compared to the distribution of the number of tasks (see Table 2); namely P7 ranks second in the sum of financial rewards (Table 3) but ranks fourth in the number of tasks (Table 2). It is noteworthy that when we calculate the average financial reward per task per platform the ranking of the platforms drastically changes (Fig. 5), with P7 topping the list and P1 being last. More specifically, a task on P7 will pay off on average a whopping €37,508 while on P1 €394. Therefore, although, less frequent tasks on P7 are very lucrative.

Looking at the financial rewards per day, these include an average of M = €41,880 (SD = €35,860) with a maximum topping €446,563, which was recorded on 09/11/2017 and a minimum of €17,668, which was recorded on 26/12/2017. Figure 1 presents the distribution of financial rewards per day across the platforms.

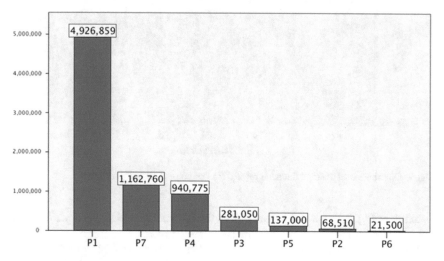

Fig. 4 Distribution of the sum of financial rewards per platform. Amounts in Euros—converted in case of other currencies

Table 3 Distribution of total financial rewards converted in €, ranked in ascending order of their sum of financial reward

Platform	Sum of Financial Reward (in €)
P6	21,500
P2	68,510
P5	137,000
P3	281,050
P4	940,774
P7	1,162,760
P1	4,926,859
Total	7,538,453

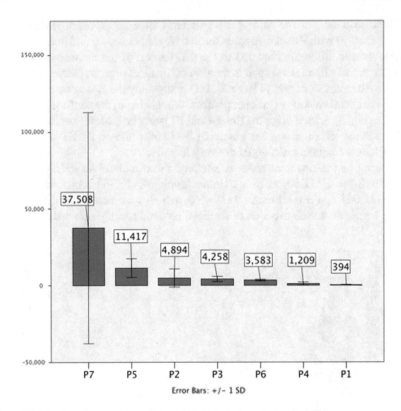

Fig. 5 Distribution of average financial reward (in Euros) per task per platform

Looking at Fig. 1, it becomes evident that the total amount of monetary rewards is rather stable throughout the six-month sampling period.

When it comes to the currencies used for the tasks (Table 4), USD tops the list with EUR being the second most used currency. It is noteworthy that the list includes 12 different currencies with the Mexican Peso being representative of Latin America's currencies, the Japanese Yen, Hong Kong Dollar, and Singapore Dollar being representative of Asia's currencies and the British Pound, Swiss Franc, Norwegian, and Danish Corona, in addition to the Euro, being representative of Europe's currencies.

Finally, in regard to task duration, this is an average of slightly more than four days ($M = 4.26$ days; SD $= 5.11$ days), with the maximum duration of a task being 366 days, which we recorded on P7 and the minimum duration being a day (Min $=$ 1 day), which we recorded on P1. We note that in 33 cases (20 for P1, 7 for P3 and 6 for P4), the task duration was 0 (zero), and we excluded these ones from this specific analysis (i.e., had total $N = 13,388$ cases). The reasons were either valid, for example in the case of P4 the "task" was essentially registration for some participants of a local challenge, or the expiry date was not properly recorded by our software (e.g., for the 20 cases of P1) due to technical reasons.

Table 4 Currency distribution of the tasks

Currency	Frequency	%
MXN	46	0.3
DKK	61	0.5
HK$	64	0.5
SGD	70	0.5
NOK	70	0.5
JPY	94	0.7
CHF	325	2.4
CAD	546	4.1
GBP	610	4.5
AUD	1238	9.2
EUR	1872	13.9
USD	8425	62.8
Total	13,421	100.0

Table 5 Holiday effect? When zooming in on Christmas dates, which we would expect to be celebrated in large parts of the world, we find a reduced number of tasks when compared to other dates

Date	Number of tasks	Sum of rewards
24/12/17	60	€27,069
25/12/17	48	€19,650
26/12/17	45	€17,668

It is also noteworthy that there might be a "holiday effect," namely around Christmas. We observe during the December 24, 25, and 26, 2017, the number of tasks and the sum of rewards dropping (Table 5). Although in the case of the number of tasks, the minimum was on the August 24, 2017, and during Christmas the number of tasks is well below the average of approximately 75 tasks. That is also the case with the total rewards per day; the rewards on Christmas days drop well below the average ($M = $ €41,880). This is an interesting inverse parallel as in the actual workplace employees typically receive a bonus during the end of the year, which coincides with Christmas (at least that is the case in most European countries), whereas people working on crowd work platforms might have even trouble finding tasks to work on. An ethical treatment of such type of work would necessitate that crowdsourcing platforms and task providers rethink their financial rewards, particularly on popular holidays such as Christmas.

5 Discussion

In this section, we draw the key points that can be supported from our study and which can help future researchers work on, with particular emphasis in longitudinal aspects.

1. **From fixed to dynamic financial rewards**.
    In their highly cited paper, *"The future of crowd work"* [14] highlights *"the dynamic nature of motivation and its dependence on context"*, among many other points. By *"dynamic"*, they meant that crowdsourcing platforms need to go beyond financial rewards and consider other motivators, of intrinsic nature. With our work, we extend the notion of *"dynamic"* rewards, addressing a well-known strong motivator of workers in such platforms, namely that of **dynamic financial rewards** [25]. For example, in Table 5 we observe that there are some days that fewer tasks are posted online. We also observe the same in Fig. 3 and to some extent in Fig. 2. Difallah et al. [6] have shown that on MTurk, the worker population remains *"relatively stable"*. Although we do not have data about the stability of the worker population in other platforms, but based on Difallah et al. (2013) work and assuming that the population would be stable, we can draw a salient point about the future development of crowdsourcing systems. We know from microeconomics if the demand of work (i.e., the number of tasks) drops when the supply of work remains stable, we would expect the financial reward of that set of tasks to drop [24], because there are plenty of people to complete those tasks. Note that we would also expect the opposite, i.e., when there is an increase in the number of available tasks, while the worker population remains stable, we would expect the financial reward of those set of tasks to increase. However, nowadays, this is not what is occurring. To the extent of our knowledge, there is no crowdsourcing platform that implements dynamic financial rewards. To some extent, this dynamic rewarding can be done within the boundaries of a certain platform, since the platform itself can log both the number of tasks as well as the number of available workers and could therefore recommend an appropriate reward to the task's requester. However, given that the threshold of a worker subscribing to another platform is relatively low, essentially one has to only create a new account, dynamic financial rewards could be very attractive to increase competition between platforms. **This is a first takeaway from our study, and something that future researchers could focus on, namely enabling dynamic rewards in crowdsourcing platforms.**

2. **Data transparency and the need for a platform data watchdog.**
    Nevertheless, we would argue to enable dynamic rewards, there is a need of computational analytical tools that current crowdsourcing platforms need to implement to support **transparency of their basic data**, such as number of tasks, rewards, and task duration. Currently, it seems that platforms shy away from implementing such tools. We can only speculate on why is this case. We imagine that it is a combination of lack of resources and fear of exposing too much to competitors. By *lack of resources,* we mean a combination of allocating

financial resources to develop, for example, an API and perhaps lack of know-how. Nevertheless, we would argue that this exposure of data is a crucial aspect for the further development of the field as a whole.

A first step toward opening up crucial data of crowdsourcing platforms could be an independent indexing platform that logs and presents platform data over time, an open "data watchdog" in a sense. To use an analogy, we imagine that indexing platform being a Skyscanner[2] of crowd work. Another analogy, closer to online marketplaces, is L2, a firm developed by Scott Galloway, a NYU professor. L2[3] gathers data from more than two thousand consumer brands, over time, and benchmarks their social, search, mobile, and site performance [7]. Such an indexing platform will drive the development of the field further and will lead to several advancements, such as dynamic financial rewards, as well as dynamic placement of tasks. **This is a second takeaway from our work for future researchers, namely to design and develop an independent, indexing platform for providing an overview of the supply of published online tasks**.

3. **Creative crowd work gradually shifts to longer tasks.**

Another design-related takeaway point can be drawn when examining Fig. 3 in combination with Fig. 5. This examination suggests the need for a cross-platform notification software for both requesters and workers alike. On the one hand, workers might be interested in a notification when there are lots of tasks available on a certain date, or when there are high rewards, despite the number of active tasks. On the other hand, requesters might be interested in increasing or decreasing their task reward based on the current active number of tasks and rewards that would be available online. Likewise, requesters might decide to postpone or even advance the publication of their task based on that figure. For example, when in a certain week, there are few tasks with a low average reward that week might be an opportunity to attract the best workers.

Another discussion point of longitudinal nature regards the question of growth of crowdsourcing. According to a 2015 World Bank report, their prediction for the year 2020 was that the overall revenue in crowdsourcing platforms would at least triple from roughly $5 billion to $15 billion, suggesting a linear growth of the sector [15]. However, their prediction was not based on empirical data from several platforms. Although limited, our study is the first, to the extent of our knowledge, longer-term cross-platform study, to gather empirical data to evaluate that prediction. Nevertheless, our data do not support such a prediction. More specifically, the distributions we present in Figs. 1 and 2 neither support projections of growth nor of shrinking. Our data show a rather stable landscape for creative crowdsourcing both in terms of number of tasks and monetary rewards. Nevertheless, the corona pandemic might change this, since more people stay at home and therefore spend more time online [23]. Combining this

---

[2] Skyscanner.com is essentially a website that crawls airline websites to index information about flights. In that way travelers looking for a flight to a certain destination can easily compare between flights.

[3] L2 was acquired and is currently owned by Gartner.

trend with rising unemployment might lead to more people turning to crowd-sourcing platforms for having an alternative income. **This is a third takeaway from our work for future researchers, namely we provide empirical data that show a rather steady development of creative crowdsourcing platforms in terms of number of tasks and rewards on the longer term**.

When we compare the platform with the most tasks on average (P1) to the platform with the highest reward on average (P7), we can presume that there are two types of creative crowdsourcing platforms. Up and until now, the land-scape of this type of work might have been perceived as monolithic, namely thought of as being represented by platforms that offered creative types of tasks. With our investigation, we show that **there are at least two types of creative crowdsourcing platforms**. On the one hand, platforms have a constant, rela-tively large, and rather stable number of tasks posted daily, which have short durations and pay in hundreds of Euros. On the other hand, platforms have infrequent posting of tasks, which have much longer duration and pay in thou-sands of Euros. Prior work has classified crowdsourcing platforms in terms of their input and output [8], type of remuneration and initiating actor [10], how well they adhere to community heuristics [1], worker role [22], among other classifications. With our work, **we introduce a classification that is based on longitudinal data**. For example, platforms can be classified in the frequency of tasks that they post. **This is the fourth takeaway point from our work, namely a new classification of crowdsourcing platforms**.

4. **Creative crowdsourcing is expected to grow a long way.**

Finally, one might rush to think that more than €7.5 million Euros distributed in six months is an impressive figure. However, when compared to revenues in the actual marketplace, it feels like a needle in a haystack. According to a 2014 report, in 2012, in Europe alone the revenues of the "creative industries" was €535.9 billion [16]. The term "creative industries" arguably includes aspects of the marketplace such as "performing arts" that might be impossible to crowd-source, nevertheless, in the same report, "visual arts" had a revenue of €127.6 billion. Of course in our study, we only included seven platforms but we believe those figures show that creative crowdsourcing is only at an embryonic phase and still has a long way to grow; if there was only 1% of only the visual arts to be crowdsourced the revenue of that would be more than €1 billion. **This is the fifth and final takeaway point from our work, namely we expect creative crowd work to grow and invite future researchers to investigate how to support existing creative work with crowd wisdom**.

6 Limitations

Our data collection approach might have introduced some limitations. In our analysis, we took into account the date that the task was posted. However, the date that task would actually start might have been different. Although we did sample and manually checked 100 tasks in the pool of more than 13K tasks, we cannot exclude that there might be slight deviations between the date the task was posted in the platform and the date it actually starts.

Furthermore, we sampled seven platforms. While our study, to the extent of our knowledge, is the first to attempt a multi-platform investigation, those seven platforms are obviously not exhaustive of the entire marketplace. Having said that, there is no official index of platforms that we are aware of to estimate what kind of percentage do those seven platforms represent. Therefore, another design-related opportunity for future work would be to create such an index of the different platforms that currently exist.

7 Conclusion

Although broadly speaking, there are two types of crowdsourcing platforms, research on the supply side of platforms primarily focuses on one, which is microtasking. In this work, we present a longitudinal study of creative crowdsourcing platforms, which are platforms that offer work that is difficult to decompose and requires expertise and time to complete. For a six-month period, we daily surveyed seven creative crowd-sourcing platforms gathering more than 13K creative tasks. Our analysis revealed that in this type of platforms, there is plenty of work for graphic designers, but also plenty of financial rewards for other types of creative crowd workers. Judging from the total rewards that we recorded, we can also conclude that creative crowdsourcing is at an embryonic stage and still has a long way to grow. Finally, although prior estimations have predicted a steady growth over time, our data do not support that. We conclude this study with key takeaways points for future research, namely the need for dynamic rather than fixed rewards, the need for a platform data watchdog, the fact that creative crowd work gradually shifts to longer tasks, and the forecast that creative crowdsourcing is expected to grow further in the future.

References

1. à Campo S, Khan VJ, Papangelis K, Markopoulos P (2019) Community heuristics for user interface evaluation of crowdsourcing platforms. Future Gener Comput Syst 95:775–789
2. Araujo RM (2013) 99designs: an analysis of creative competition in crowdsourced design. In First AAAI conference on human computation and crowdsourcing
3. Bayus BL (2013) Crowdsourcing new product ideas over time: an analysis of the Dell IdeaStorm community. Manage Sci 59(1):226–244
4. Berg J (2016) Income security in the on-demand economy: findings and policy lessons from a survey of crowdworkers. International Labour Office, Inclusive Labour Markets, Labour Relations and Working Conditions Branch. - Geneva: ILO, 2016 (Conditions of work and employment series ; No. 74)
5. Daly TM, Nataraajan R (2015) Swapping bricks for clicks: crowdsourcing longitudinal data on Amazon Turk. J Bus Res 68(12):2603–2609

6. Difallah D, Filatova E, Ipeirotis PG (2018) Demographics and dynamics of mechanical Turk workers. In: Proceedings of the eleventh ACM international conference on web search and data mining (WSDM '18). ACM, New York, pp 135–143. https://doi.org/10.1145/3159652.3159661

7. Galloway S (2017) The four: the hidden DNA of Amazon, Apple. Random House, Facebook and Google

8. Geiger D, Rosemann M, Fielt E, Schader M, Huang M-H (2012) Crowdsourcing information systems—definition typology, and design. In: ICIS 2012 : proceedings of the 33rd international conference on information systems (ICIS 2012). Atlanta, Ga.: AISeL: Paper 53

9. Hara K, Adams A, Milland K, Savage S, Callison-Burch C, Bigham JP (2018) A data-driven analysis of workers' earnings on Amazon Mechanical Turk. In: Proceedings of the 2018 CHI conference on human factors in computing systems, pp 1–14

10. Howcroft D, Bergvall-Kåreborn B (2019) A typology of crowdwork platforms. Work Employ Soc 33(1):21–38

11. Howe J (2006) The rise of crowdsourcing. Wired Maga 14(6):1–4

12. Ipeirotis PG (2010) Demographics of mechanical Turk (March 2010). NYU Working Paper No.; CEDER-10-01. Available at SSRN: https://ssrn.com/abstract=1585030

13. Irani LC, Silberman MS (2013) Turkopticon: interrupting worker invisibility in Amazon mechanical Turk. In: Proceedings of the SIGCHI conference on human factors in computing systems (CHI '13), pp 611–620. https://doi.org/10.1145/2470654.2470742

14. Kittur A, Nickerson JV, Bernstein M, Gerber E, Shaw A, Zimmerman J, Horton J (2013) The future of crowd work. In: Proceedings of the 2013 conference on computer supported cooperative work, pp 1301–1318

15. Kuek SC, Paradi-Guilford C, Fayomi T, Imaizumi S, Ipeirotis P, Pina P, Singh M (2015) The global opportunity in online outsourcing

16. Lhermitte M, Perrin B, Melbouci L (2014) Creating growth; measuring cultural and creative markets in the EU. Ernest & Young

17. Lykourentzou I, Khan VJ, Papangelis K, Markopoulos P (2019) Macrotask crowdsourcing: an integrated definition. In: Macrotask crowdsourcing. Springer, Cham, pp 1–13

18. Mao A, Chen Y, Gajos KZ, Parkes DC, Procaccia AD, Zhang H (2012) Turkserver: enabling synchronous and longitudinal online experiments. In: Workshops at the twenty-sixth AAAI conference on artificial intelligence

19. Litman L, Robinson J, Abberbock T (2017) TurkPrime.com: a versatile crowdsourcing data acquisition platform for the behavioral sciences. Behav Res Methods 49(2):433–442

20. Turker Nation. Retrieved April 27, 2020 from https://www.reddit.com/r/TurkerNation/

21. Von Ahn L (2008) Human computation. In: 2008 IEEE 24th international conference on data engineering. IEEE, New York, pp 1–2

22. Wang Y, Papangelis K, Saker M, Lykourentzou I, Chamberlain A, Khan VJ (2020) Crowd-sourcing in China: exploring the work experiences of solo crowdworkers and crowdfarm workers. In: Proceedings of the 2020 CHI conference on human factors in computing systems, pp 1–13

23. Wiederhold BK (2020) Social media use during social distancing

24. Wikipedia contributors (2020) Supply and demand. In: Wikipedia, the free Encyclopedia. Retrieved 07:34, August 27, 2020, from https://en.wikipedia.org/w/index.php?title=Supply_and_demand&oldid=974813303

25. Zheng H, Li D, Hou W (2011) Task design, motivation, and participation in crowdsourcing contests. Int J Electron Commer 15(4):57–88

Printed in the United States
by Baker & Taylor Publisher Services